THE
FORGOTTEN
IRISH

THE
FORGOTTEN
IRISH EMIGRANT
EXPERIENCES IN AMERICA
IRISH

DAMIAN SHIELS

For Sophie, Isabella and Freya, modern-day Irish emigrants.

Front cover illustration: The Farrell family in America. (National Library of Ireland)
Back cover illustration: Unidentified soldier in Union uniform. (Library of Congress)

First published 2016

The History Press Ireland
50 City Quay
Dublin 2
Ireland
www.thehistorypress.ie

The History Press Ireland is a member of Publishing Ireland,
the Irish book publishers' association.

British Library Cataloguing in Publication Data.
A catalogue record for this book is available from the British Library.

ISBN 978 1 84588 333 1

Typesetting and origination by The History Press
Printed and bound by TJ International Ltd.

Contents

Acknowledgements

As with my previous book, *The Irish in the American Civil War*, this work has its origins in research I began for my website, www.irishamericancivilwar.com. In the more than six years the site has been active, it has afforded me an opportunity to write extensively on the Irish experience of the civil war and nineteenth-century America, and has also put me in touch with multitudes of people – many of whom are now good friends – who share my interest in the impact of this conflict on Irish emigrants. Without the readers of the site and the community I engage with surrounding it this book would not have been possible.

A number of individuals have directly contributed to some of the family stories that appear here, adding both to the information I was able to provide and in pointing me towards additional or supplementary sources. In that regard particular thanks are due to Jane Gastineau, Lincoln Librarian at the Lincoln Financial Foundation Collection, Allen County Public Library, Fort Wayne, Indiana. Jane answered an appeal I had placed seeking details on a set of papers known to have existed relating to the Garvin family, the first story to appear in this book, and by doing so greatly enhanced what was already an intriguing and heartbreaking chapter. Among the many others to assist directly with specific elements of the stories that follow are Chris Barr of the National Park Service, Barbara Harvey Freeburn, Jim McGrath, Carol Mitchell and Peter Patten.

The majority of the research undertaken for this book was conducted from Ireland. This is something that would not have been possible prior to the increased accessibility of online records that has been a hallmark of recent years. Though nothing can truly replace direct archival research, the accessibility of millions of scanned primary documents online has provided a unique opportunity for scholars, particularly those located outside the country in which they have an interest, to engage with (and hopefully contribute towards) their chosen subject. To that end, I owe a particular debt of gratitude to the National Archives in Washington DC and Fold3 for making the decision to digitize many of the pension files which form the heart of this book. Had that decision not been taken, this book would not exist.

I had the great privilege of meeting some of the NARA team whose hard work in digitizing the pension files allowed me to explore these Irish stories. They include Archives Specialist Jackie Budell, who coordinates the project. Over the years Jackie has been a constant source of encouragement, advice, support and friendship, for which I am extremely grateful. More than any other she deserves a special note of thanks for helping this book come to fruition.

Despite having to endure an almost endless stream of discussion about the information held in American Civil War pension files over recent years, Angela Gallagher, Dr Louise Nugent and Sara Nylund nonetheless gave willingly of their time to read through drafts of the book, and make helpful suggestions both in terms of readability and layout, which have improved the final version. Thanks also to my publishers The History Press Ireland, particularly Ronan Colgan and Beth Amphlett, for their fine work in the production and formatting of the finished product.

The lot of an independent researcher can be a challenging one, both in terms of time and expense. It is something that necessarily impacts on other elements of one's life, and as a result the lives of those around you. Angela Gallagher has been instrumental in supporting my efforts. I owe a particular debt to my long-suffering partner Sara, who (with Ben and Ivra) has been a constant companion through this process. I have been fortunate to enjoy her support and encouragement, as well as her remarkable acceptance of the fact that free-time and weekends have been consumed by writing, while holidays have become dedicated to wandering far-flung American battlefields. I am fortunate indeed.

Preface

On 28 August 1874 Catherine McCabe sat down to tell the story of her life. The woman, who was illiterate, began with her marriage, recalling the ceremony that had taken place a quarter of a century earlier in the Chapel of Cortown, County Meath. Catherine told how she and her new husband Michael had set out for America only two months after their wedding, hoping to make a future for themselves in Manhattan. She related how, as new immigrants, they spent their first two weeks in Brannon's lodging house on Washington Street, before renting a room at 20 Pearl Street, close to where they had first stepped off the boat at Castle Garden. They had eventually settled into two rooms at 31½ 'White Hall', where they went on to spend the next four years. Their son James was born there on 5 May 1852, and baptised in nearby St Peter's church. To support his family, Michael worked his trade as a mason in the city. Catherine remembered how her husband preferred to wear 'small whiskers' rather than a beard or moustache. Though short, he was nonetheless of 'stout make', with red hair and blue eyes.[1]

By the time Catherine came to tell her story, she was once again living in Ireland. She had made the short journey from her home in Maperath to the town of Kells that August day in order to have it set down on paper. The reason she did so could be traced to events of a decade previous. On 24 May 1864, her husband Michael had been present at the North Anna River, Virginia, as a private in the 170th New York Infantry. There he was struck by a 'minnie ball fired by the enemy' which passed 'through the brain', killing him instantly. Catherine was telling her tale in order to secure a United States pension based on her dead husband's service. Today it is kept with the rest of her file in the record stacks of the National Archives in Washington DC. There it is surrounded by 1.28 million others. Each one contains the successful application of a widow, parent, sister or child of a soldier who died as a result of service in the United States military between 1861 and 1910, the vast majority during the American Civil War. Thousands of them relate specifically to Irish-American emigrants. The rich detail they contain provides an insight into the soldiers, their families and their loved ones. As well as charting their experiences between 1861 and 1865, these records frequently tell their story across decades, often allowing the reader to follow them on their journey from Ireland to new lives in America. Through their pages they give voice to many illiterate working-class Irish whose personal history would otherwise remain silent.[2]

On the eve of the American Civil War, 1.6 million Irish-born people were living in the United States. The majority had emigrated to the major industrialised cities of the north; New York alone was home to more than 200,000 Irish, one in four of the total population. The Great Famine had affected many of those who left Ireland in the late 1840s and '50s, and for some the conflict that erupted in 1861 would represent a second great trauma in their lives. By the time of the war's conclusion in 1865, somewhere in the region of 200,000 Irishmen had served, the vast majority of them – perhaps as many as 180,000 – in Union blue. Such figures do not include those thousands of soldiers and sailors who were born in the United States, Canada and Britain to Irish emigrant parents, who often considered themselves as much a part of the Irish-American community as their Irish-born brethren. No figures exist as to how many of these Irishmen lost their lives as a result of their service, but it undoubtedly ran into tens of thousands. Many of them left behind widows, parents and children, who would later seek pensions based on their service, in the process revealing something of the story of their lives.[3]

The pension files on which the stories in this book are based owe their origins to an act signed into law by President Abraham Lincoln on 14 July 1862. It provided for monthly pensions for both widows and men totally disabled by the American Civil War. As well as seeking to recognise the sacrifice made by volunteers up to that point, it was also part of a drive that summer to increase mobilisation into Union forces. In the decades that followed, a series of additional pension acts expanded and refined the entitlement criteria, until by 1893 the government was spending $165.3 million a year on military pensions. This figure included payments to both veterans and the widows and dependents of deceased servicemen, and represented some 40 per cent of the entire federal budget.[4]

Initially the act provided the widows of private soldiers with a monthly pension of $8, with an additional $2 monthly supplement for each child under the age of sixteen. In addition to widows, the dependent mothers, dependent sisters and the minor children of deceased soldiers could also claim the pension. From 1866 dependent fathers and orphaned minor brothers were also entitled to benefit. The basic rate of $8 per month was increased to $12 from 1886, and by the standards of the day this was a significant sum. In 1890 it equated to ⅓ of the average American annual wage and was being given out to huge numbers of dependents – 145,359 widows of Union soldiers and sailors were recorded in that year alone. The changes to the entitlement criteria through the course of the century had a major influence both on who could claim these pensions and also on the type of information those claimants had to provide. For example, prior to 1873, dependent parents were required to prove they had been financially dependent on their dead son, whereas after that date it was sufficient to demonstrate only that he had either aided them financially or contributed to their support 'in any other way'. By far the most influential alteration to the pension system occurred in 1890. Where previously veterans had to demonstrate that their disabilities were a direct result of service, after this date they became eligible regardless of the cause, which could include old age. Similarly, the entitlement for widows was expanded. Prior to 1890 they had to prove that their husbands had died as a result of war service, but now they became eligible regardless of cause of death, provided they had been married prior to 27 June 1890. These changes effectively created and old-age-pension system for Union army veterans and their dependents.[5]

The richness of the widows and dependents files lies in the material submitted to demonstrate pension eligibility. Proving a relationship and/or dependency on a deceased soldier was a difficult task, and was significantly more onerous than that required of surviving soldiers seeking a veteran's pension. As a result, the pension files of widows and dependents invariably contain significantly more detail on the lives of their subjects and families than those of men who survived the fighting. The greatest abundance of information on the social lives of the applicants is contained within the affidavits they supplied, which on occasion can take a first-person narrative form. In addition to the claimant's affidavit, myriad others are commonplace in the files, from family members, friends, acquaintances, employers, landlords, shopkeepers, physicians or servicemen. Where widows were unable to provide Church certification of their marriage, affidavits of witnesses to the ceremony or of those who knew the couple as man and wife were required. Here the strong bonds that many Irish kept with immigrants from their local area came to the fore, as old neighbours from Ireland often became new neighbours in the United States. Dependent parents needed affidavits to show that their son had financially supported them, and so these contain detail on where they had worked, what they had earned and on what they spent their money. In cases where the soldier's father was still alive, affidavits had to be produced to illustrate that he was incapable of earning a living through manual labour. No matter who provided it, every affidavit was designed to add another layer of supporting evidence to a claim, and it is these documents more than any other that provide the building blocks for reconstructing some of the life experiences of these Irish emigrants.

Among the many other forms of evidence in the pension files are baptismal records, military records and medical appraisals. But by far the most poignant documents that can be found come in the form of original letters. As with the affidavits, these were included to provide proof of both relationships and financial support. Thousands of letters written by Irish emigrant soldiers survive in the files as a result of this practice. Often multiple letters were included in a single application, sometimes together with the correspondence that informed wives and parents of their loved one's death. These letters are clearly a significant source for the Irish experience of the American Civil War, but they also offer a much wider insight into Irish emigrant life. Many of them provide the only surviving written record left behind by otherwise illiterate families. Although many Irish emigrants could neither read nor write, the letters show that this did not stop them corresponding with one another. Soldiers at the front would dictate their letters to literate comrades, and upon their arrival these letters would be read aloud to the recipient by a literate friend or relation, often in a communal setting. In many cases the letters included with the applications must have been treasured possessions, submitted only out of dire economic need. Once they had been sent to the pension bureau, they would not be returned.

The vast bulk of Irish-American widows' and dependents' pension files relate to families who made their home in the United States, but that was not always the case. In 1883 a list of all veterans and widows/dependents then claiming a military pension was compiled, and included a total of 219 people then receiving payments in Ireland. Though concentrated in the major towns and cities, these pensioners were spread throughout the island. They included the parents and widows of emigrant servicemen who had themselves never been outside of the country, and also emigrants – like Catherine McCabe from County Meath – who had returned home following their husbands' death. Those seeking pensions from Ireland had an even more arduous process to endure than those in the United States, largely due to the vast distances involved. There are numerous cases of ageing dependent parents electing to journey to America in order to expedite their applications. Among those who chose to stay in Ireland, many relied heavily on the assistance of US consuls based in the country to help them navigate the pension system. It is of note that despite the scale of Irish service in the American Civil War, the number of pension recipients in Ireland itself never seems to have been higher than a few hundred at any one time. This in itself is testament to just how rare it was for Irish emigrants to return home on a permanent basis once they had chosen to make a new life elsewhere.[6]

From a potential cast of thousands, the chapters in this book examine the personal stories of just thirty-five Irish families. In each case a widow's or dependent's pension file has been used as the basis on which to build the narrative, supplemented in every instance by additional research from sources such as census returns, passenger lists, contemporary newspaper reports and military records. What follows is not a book about the American Civil War, but rather one made possible as a result of it. Many of the stories do not have the conflict as their focus, but use the available material to explore aspects of the Irish emigrant experience.

The family narratives are divided into four broad themes, each providing a slightly different focus. The first two sections, 'Wives and Parents' and 'Community and Society', emphasise the lives of soldiers' families, where experiences are often described in the applicant's own words. These sections seek to illustrate how the pension files can be used to examine topics such as family emigration, chain migration, financial dependence and the maintenance of transatlantic connections, as well as social issues such as indigence, alcoholism, domestic violence and bigamy. The final two sections, 'A Life in Letters' and 'A Death in Letters', are aimed at providing a direct insight into the lives and emotions of some of these emigrant soldiers, using their own correspondence, and also at investigating how their loved ones received news of, and coped with, their deaths.

Before proceeding, it is appropriate to sound a note of caution for the reader. The treasure trove of material made available by the widows' and dependents' files comes with a cost. In every instance, the file only exists due to the death of a soldier or sailor. What follows are not the experiences of families who did not have a loved one in military service, nor of those whose loved ones returned home and lived long lives. An inherent sadness permeates the majority of these stories, which in itself can take an emotional toll. It is important to remember that though these files afford us unparalleled insights into many aspects of Irish emigrant life, they are but one set of experiences – many are the stories of success that Irish immigrants in America enjoyed following their departure. Given their purpose, the pension files accentuate hardship and struggle over happiness and prosperity. Indeed, as we shall see, some claimants were not above committing fraud in order to secure them. These stories are only one version of the historical truth for these families. Although they offer us extraordinary insights into their experiences, all we can gain are glimpses – we can never hope to gain a truly complete picture of their lives.

A Note on Conventions

Large portions of the book consist of quotes and letters taken directly from the pension files. Where possible the original spelling and punctuation has been retained in order to maintain the integrity of the historical voice, though in some instances, minor addition has been unavoidable in order to aid legibility for the reader. Where necessary, additions or clarifications were added in brackets [ ]. In general text, modern place names have been preferred. Therefore, Offaly is favoured over the nineteenth-century King's County, and similarly Laois is used in place of Queen's County. In the case of Derry/Londonderry, the term deemed most appropriate to the specific pension file has been chosen. Identifying the location in Ireland where emigrants originated is a process fraught with difficulty. Where their place of origin has been precisely located, the Irish county is provided at the head of each chapter. Where it has not been identified, but the place of birth is confirmed, only 'Ireland' is specified in the chapter heading.

ONE
Wives and Parents

The death of a spouse or child as a result of military service has a profound impact on all those left behind. For some Irish emigrant families, the loss was an event that irretrievably altered their futures, casting a long and dominant shadow over them in the years to come. For others, it represented another hardship in what was already a struggle for survival. 'Wives and Parents' examines the stories of both. Here we learn of one mother who spent her life searching for her mentally disabled boy, stolen away into the army, and of another who despaired of her fate should her son fall in battle. We hear one Irish woman describe the harsh realities of her life on the prairies of the Midwest and of another who made her home on one of Ireland's remote offshore islands. Here too are the stories of those who, though they never left Ireland, still had cause to recall with sadness far-off locations in both the United States and Nicaragua.

THE GARVINS: LIMERICK AND NEW YORK

 'My poor Con; I must go and find him!'[1]

In late 1863, details of a sensational case began to emerge in the newspapers of the Union. It was a story that would be told and retold for decades to come, and was ever-after remembered by all who had come into contact with the particulars. At its centre was an intellectually disabled boy from County Limerick, who had been stolen from a New York almshouse and sold into the Federal army. For months his frantic mother would haunt the Union forces like a spectre, searching relentlessly for her son. The case would eventually involve such figures as the Mayor of Troy, the Governor of New York, the secretary of war and the head of the secret service. But the most notable individual to take a personal interest was none other than President Abraham Lincoln. The events are so remarkable as to seem the stuff of fiction; in reality they are some of the most compelling and heartrending of the Irish emigrants' experiences in the United States.

Virtually all the contemporary documentation regarding Cornelius Garvin called him an 'idiot'. This was a term used in the nineteenth century to refer to someone with an intellectual disability. The precise nature of Cornelius' (or Con's) disorder is not known, but whatever it was, one of the ways in which it impacted him was that he was easily led, and was quick to do what others told him. Con was born in the townland of Grange Hill, Grange, County Limerick in 1845, the son of Matthew and Catharine Garvin. His parents had married in Grange around 1838, where Matthew farmed a 'large and productive' piece of land. All that changed with the Famine, which brought a reduction in fortunes that forced the Garvins to seek the emigrant boat. They left for America via Liverpool in 1849, sailing aboard the *JZ* captained by John Zerega. After a voyage of eight weeks, the family of Matthew (35), Catharine (32), Mary (8), Con (4) and Matthew Junior (8 months) landed in New York on 10 January 1850. They initially settled in Troy, New York, but soon headed west for Chicago where they spent five years before returning to Troy around 1855. It was here that Matthew passed away, dying in 1860. Young Con received some schooling with the Christian Brothers, but financial constraints meant he had to give up his education. Instead he embarked on a series of jobs associated with the wood and paper industry, including a stint at Orrs Papermill on Troy's River Street, a position with wood dealer Patrick Brandon, and finally occasional labouring piling lumber and working on the city docks, for which he earned between $1 and $2 per day. He used to give this money to his mother, who would use it every Saturday to buy provisions for the family at John Warr's 'Choice Wines, Teas and Family Store' on 278 River Street. Although Con was able to function in the community, all was not well with the young man. From about 1861 it became readily apparent to everyone that Con was struggling, and his ability to undertake work diminished rapidly.[2]

As Con's condition grew worse, his mother Catharine did her best to support the family by working as a cleaner in Troy's banks on First Street. But Con was becoming more and more of a handful. Her son had taken to wandering away from their Fourth Street home late at night, often being taken into the station house by the police for safekeeping. This became such a regular pattern that when Con went missing, Catharine would go to the station house in the early hours of the morning and wait for him to be brought in. Wartime brought with it new dangers for Catharine. During one of his wanderings, Con encountered a recruiting officer, who for $2 induced him to enlist. He was swiftly taken off to the military barracks in Albany to become a soldier. A distraught Catharine, not knowing where Con had gone, placed a missing-persons advertisement in the newspapers. Thankfully, Con's condition was such that he was soon deemed unfit for service and released. The officer who took the decision had seen the advertisement and made sure that the boy got home. Unfortunately, the episode would prove a harbinger of future woes.[3]

Catharine was unable to both work and to provide her son with the care he needed. Having no option but to seek help, she sent Con for medical examination in the hope he might be cured, as he had 'lost the use of his mental faculties'. Con went to Troy's Marshall Infirmary, an institution that specialised in patients with mental illnesses. Con spent six months as a patient, after which the infirmary determined that he was 'incurable and partly idiotic' and discharged him to the care of the Rensselaer County Almshouse (also sometimes referred to as the Rensselaer House of Industry).

Catharine took every opportunity she could to visit her son. Then, one day in September 1863, Catharine arrived at the almshouse to be greeted with shocking and extremely upsetting news – her boy had disappeared.[4]

The disappearance of 'idiot boy' Con Garvin would soon become a media sensation, as would Catharine's desperate efforts to find him. First, fearing he may have drowned, she spent a number of days combing the banks of the Hudson River looking for his body. When nothing turned up, Catharine decided to check the barracks in Albany to see if he had once again been taken into the army. Upon arriving there she met an officer who recognised her description of Con; he informed Catharine that he had indeed been enlisted, and had passed through on his way to Riker's Island, New York, bound for service in the 52nd New York Volunteers. It was quickly becoming apparent that the young man had fallen foul of unscrupulous substitute brokers, who had effectively 'sold' Con into the federal army in order to receive the financial bounty then available for recruits. Catharine wasted no time and set off immediately after her son.[5]

Catharine knew she would have to get a high-level military authority to order Con's release from the army. They didn't come any higher than Abraham Lincoln. In October 1863 the Limerick woman travelled to Washington with the intention of taking her case to retrieve Con directly to the President. Securing a letter of recommendation from Judge Abram B. Olin, a former New York congressman, she headed for the White House. Soon afterwards she recounted what had occurred to journalists, who in the style of the period attempted to capture her Irish accent in their transcriptions:

Judge Olin, God bless him, gave me a fine letther, an' with it I wint to see ould Lincoln. Whin I called at the front door, a man who tould me that he was the President's Secretary, asked me what I wanted. I told him me sthory, and he said that justice must be done you, Mrs. Garvin. Here's a note to the War Office. I thanked him, and then inquired for the War Office, which I soon found. I gave the man there me note, and told him me business, but he only humbugged me. I again wint to see Lincoln, but couldn't get a peek at him – och, it's very hard to see the ould fellow! The Secretary gave me another note to the War Office, which made the fellow there trate me decent. Whin I told me story – how my poor crazy Con had been sold from me – he said: 'When you get home, take a pistol and blow the man's brains out, that sold him!' – an' faith, I'll do it yet! He telegraphed to Alexandria to know if poor Con was in the Fifty-second regiment, an' got an answer saying that he was not. I thin got a pass to go to Alexandria meself, to see after me lad. I wint there, and found the Colonel of the Fifty-second regiment, who treated me kindly. An' I ses, 'It's I that's glad to meet you, Colonel; do you know anything about a poor crazy boy of mine, named Con Garvin, who was sould for a sojer?' He examined his books for a while, and then he told me that Con was in his regiment as a substitute, but that on the road from Riker's Island to Washington, one hundred of his men got strayed, and among them was my poor Con! … Sure I had nothing more to do, so I spent three days and three nights in the hospitals and camps of Alexandria, thinking that I could find some one who saw Con. I happened to come across a member of his regiment, who knew him well, an' sure 'twas I that was to talk wid him. Con told him on the Island that he had been sold for $400 from the County House, at Troy, by a man … connected with the House! Do you see! He was taken out of the coal shed in the night time, without a coat on him, and taken to New York. An' that's the way they made $400 on my poor boy Con! Oh, the rascals! As sure as there's a God in Heaven, I'll shoot that fellow … who sould him.[6]

By November articles seeking Con's whereabouts were being placed in newspapers across the north. On 19 November, the *Washington DC National Republican*, describing Con as about 18-years-old, with dark hair and dark eyes, reported he had been 'decoyed from the House of Industry' in Troy and enlisted in the 52nd New York. The article repeated the theory that Con had strayed away from the group of recruits on their way from Riker's Island to Washington, and stated that he could not be found by either the officers or his mother, who had 'twice traversed the route to find him'. The paper felt that he was 'doubtless in some institution for idiots or insane persons in Washington, Baltimore, or Philadelphia'. They were wrong.[7]

The months passed, and Catharine became increasingly desperate at the lack of news. Then she received a report that Con had been seen at Mitchell's Station, Virginia in United States uniform, which suggested he was still in the army. Her time was thereafter spent searching the faces of the army of the Potomac for her boy; her efforts were broken only by brief returns to Troy or Washington DC, in order to earn sufficient money to continue her search or to appeal for the administration's support. It was said that as she made her way around the troops, she 'carried always in her apron a large number of letters, and other memoranda, from prominent officers and others, given to aid her ...' Apparently, although she was illiterate, she was always able to place her hand on the correct document as she required it, and having finished her story would often leave for the next regiment saying, 'My poor Con; I must go and find him!' Meanwhile, word of the outrage continued to spread countrywide, and it was increasingly suggested that it was those who had been entrusted with Con's care who betrayed him. In March 1864 the following 'information wanted' advertisement was published:

> INFORMATION WANTED of the whereabouts of Cornelius Garvin, a lunatic, and late an inmate of the County House at Troy, New York, from which he was taken in September last, and sold for a substitute by John Ar[i]s, the keeper of said place. He is five feet seven inches high, black eyes, black hair and dark complexion. Supposed to be a member of the 52d New York State Volunteers. Any information sent to Mrs. Garvin, at Troy, New York, will be thankfully received by his distressed mother.[8]

Some other states in the Union were quick to capitalise on the story, which was particularly damaging to New York, as it suggested that underhand techniques were being employed in order to fill the state's manpower quota for the army. From 1863 onwards each state was periodically required to fill a quota of enlistments into the military; failure to do so brought the threat of draft. As a result, competition for recruits could be high. On 16 March 1864 the *Cleveland Morning Leader* in Ohio ran the story under the headline 'How New York Fills Her Quota', stating that Con's fate was an 'illustration of the manner in which the State of New York is filling her quota. It ought to attract the attention of the War Department'. By April 1864 the mayors of Troy and New York, no doubt influenced by both the pleas of Catharine Garvin and the terrible publicity surrounding the incident, joined the hunt for Con. They offered a $100 reward for any information on him. It was now an accepted fact that he had been 'taken from the county house in Troy and sold in New York City for a substitute in the 52d New York Volunteers'.[9]

On 4 April, Mayor of Troy James Thorn wrote about the case to New York's Governor Horatio Seymour detailing Catharine's efforts:

> *To discover and retrieve him* [Con] *is the sole purpose to which this devoted mother has consecrated her time, her energies, her life. She has made two journeys to the Army of the Potomac – has visited every regiment in which her son Cornelius has been likely to be found – has met with kind treatment and sympathy from all – even the President of the United States consenting to grant her an interview and hear her story. Undaunted by the fruitless result of her search thus far, Mrs. Garvin has determined to continue it … Mrs. Garvin is well-known to myself and other citizens of Troy as a woman of unblemished character; and the great blow which she suffered in the loss of her son at the hands of bounty brokers or traffickers in human flesh has developed traits of heroism in this humble woman which will long remain as living proofs of a mother's love …*[10]

Time was fast running out for Catharine to locate Con before the start of the much-anticipated 1864 Union offensive. After the Overland Campaign finally commenced on 4 May, Catharine found herself wandering through federal hospitals in search of news. On 16 May, while searching Queens Street Hospital in Alexandria, Catharine encountered Corporal Townsell J. Chapman (recorded in the rosters as Townsend) of the 52nd New York Volunteers. He had been wounded at Spotsylvania on 10 May, and gave the following statement:

Queens Street Hostal [sic]
Virginia May 16th 1864

I certify that I have seen Cornelius Garvin in the 52d N.Y.V.
ten days ago in Company I. Capt George Digen [Degener]
gave him a different name so that his mother could not get him
when she was at the Regt last Winter I being at the same Regt
in Company H. Signed
*   Townsell J Chapman*

Finally, this appeared to represent some solid information. Con was still in the 52nd New York, but was under an assumed name. Chapman was also suggesting that there was complicity on the part of Con's captain, who had intentionally concealed the young man from his mother when she came looking for him. Catharine must have hoped that her boy would be more fortunate than Corporal Chapman; the 24-year-old died of his wounds in Alexandria on 29 July.[11]

It was around this time that Catharine's plight once again crossed the desk of the most powerful man in America. This was likely prompted by a direct appeal to the president from famed New York Democrat Fernando Wood, who penned the following lines from the House of Representatives on 26 April 1864:

Dear Sir,
The bearer Mrs Garvin is a poor woman in search of her son,
who is deranged and attached to the army – any aid you can
give will be truly charitable.

*   Very truly yours*
*   Fernando Wood.*[12]

This prompted Lincoln to compose a note for the attention of Secretary of War Edwin Stanton, which was eventually passed to Catharine:

There is reason to believe this Cornelius Garvin is an idiot, and that he is kept in the 52nd N.Y. concealed & denied to avoid any exposure of guilty parties. Will the Sec. of War please have the thing probed?

A. Lincoln
May 21, 1864[13]

On the same day that Lincoln wrote this, yet another member of the 52nd New York reported seeing Con. The first lieutenant of Company I, William Von Richenstein, stated that he had seen 'the son of Catharine Garevan [*sic*] at the camp of 52 Regt some fourteen days ago'. This statement, coming from an officer, placed Con in the ranks at the start of the Overland Campaign.[14]

Catharine continued her search of the army, scouring prisons, hospitals and the regiments themselves. The intense scrutiny that was focused on the case was apparent to everyone involved. In a letter given by J. Rutherford Worster to Catharine for the attention of the Provost Marshal of Fredericksburg on 23 May, it was made clear that the President and secretary of war had taken a personal interest in events. The Fredericksburg military authorities were informed that:

> ... she [Catharine] will depend on you for facilities to search the Regt. in which her son is doing menial duty. As her case is one which has attained great notoriety every act of any officer or citizen will be duly scanned by Press and people ...[15]

The ultimate result of Lincoln's directive to Secretary of War Edwin Stanton was the formal appointment to the case of Lafayette C. Baker, commander of the Union's Intelligence Service. Baker first dispatched a detective officer to Troy to investigate the almshouse and the circumstances of Con's disappearance in order to establish some leads. But as May turned to June, Catharine was still wandering the Union camps. Following the Battle of Cold Harbor she managed to meet with the surgeon of the 52nd New York. He told her what was undoubtedly the last thing she wanted to hear – Con had been killed in action at the Battle of Spotsylvania. However, how was she to know if this information was accurate?[16]

Catharine, shaken by what the surgeon had told her, decided to return home. She had become such a familiar sight to the soldiers during those long months that some mentioned her in their letters home. Many of them even knew her name:

> As Hancock's corps was filing past Grant's Headquarters – a magnificent sight, calculated to stir the blood – I espied near the Commanding General a sight not very common here, – the form of a woman. The face seemed familiar, and on looking closely I discovered that it was Mrs. Garvin, in search of her son.[17]

Back in New York, State Governor Horatio Seymour continued to take an active part in the case. On 13 June he wrote to District Attorney Colby in Rensselaer County instructing him to 'make a thorough investigation of the case of Cornelius Garvin, sold as a substitute into the Fifty-Second New York Volunteers; and, if possible, bring the guilty parties to justice'. A few days later news that Con might have been killed reached home. The *Troy Daily Times* ran the headline 'Con Garvin Dead' on 20 June. Catharine had reached Troy that morning carrying an 'autograph letter from the President of the United States'. The newspaper related how the efforts of Governor Seymour, British Consul Archibald and Mayor Thorn had all been invoked in the search, but in vain:

> Mrs. Garvin, the devoted mother, will no longer search camp and regiment for her idiot boy. Con is dead … Poor Con will no longer excite the solicitude of his mother; but she now announces her purpose of living for vengeance. So that although the hero of the strange story is dead, it is probable that his name will still be kept before the public by his untiring mother. True it is: O, woman, in our hours of ease. Uncertain, coy, and hard to please: When pain and anguish cloud the brow; A ministering angel, thou![18]

Despite the prospect that Con was dead, investigations ploughed ahead. Colonel Ludlow of General Dix's staff was in Troy in July 1864 investigating the matter, and consulted 'with persons who have heretofore been cognisant of the case'. By now the story had crossed the Atlantic, and it was being reported by newspapers such as the *Dublin Evening Mail*. Whatever occurred over the summer months, there appears to have been a revival of some hope through the end of 1864 and into 1865 that Con might be alive. On 3 June 1865 Lafayette Baker wrote to Mayor Thorn in Troy saying that he believed the boy may yet be found. He determined to 'spare neither time or means in prosecuting my investigations, with a view to bring to speedy justice all those engaged in this inhuman and diabolical outrage'. In July 1865 the *New York Irish American* was still running 'information wanted' pieces, supposedly at the behest of Catharine, hoping to reveal new information on Con. On 29 July it reported that the 52nd New York had now been mustered out of service, 'the idiot not being present'. The paper appealed to former members of the regiment for details on the Irish boy, who had apparently been given the nickname of 'Watches' or 'Watchless' in the army.[19]

The lack of a definitive answer regarding Con's fate allowed hope to linger long after the war's conclusion. In April 1866 Catharine visited the New York State Soldier's Home in Albany to see if Con might have ended up there. A disabled veteran called Joseph Kerwin, overhearing her tale, told Catharine he had seen a Garvin matching Con's description at the US General Hospital on David's Island in New York. Catharine showed Kerwin a photograph of her son, and he felt sure it was the boy. On hearing this news, Catharine 'was so overjoyed that she could scarcely refrain from expressing her feelings in tears'. An inquiry was immediately sent to David's Island by Mr Hays of the Albany Home:

Mrs. Garvin is a poor woman but men whose names stand as high in our nation's history as is possible for names to reach have befriended and assisted her in her maternal search ... should the missing man and the Garvin at your hospital be one and the same it would be quite impossible for pen to portray the joy which will gladden the mother's heart at the discovery of her son whom she had about given up for dead as in fact she had heard that such was the case on several occasions. She will call at my office again one week from today to hear the result of my communication.

When Catharine did return, her hopes were again dashed. There was no soldier by the name of Cornelius Garvin at David's Island.[20]

Catharine's 1866 disappointment seems to have been the one that finally confirmed for her that Con was dead. In the end it was a piece of evidence that had emerged in March 1865 that she eventually accepted as the truth. On 14 March, in the US General Hospital in Albany, New York, Private Frederick Rolf of Con's company provided the following statement:

> I, Frederick Rolf, private of Co. I, 52d Regiment, N.Y.V., do hereby certify that I was acquainted with Cornelius Garvin, a private of Co. I, 52d Regiment N.Y.V., and that I saw him engaged with the enemy in the fight of 18th day of May, 1864, at the battle of Spotsylvania, Va.; also that I saw him when he was struck with a ball which took effect in the head, that I saw him carried to the rear, and that I know the wound to have been mortal.[21]

It was alleged that Con had been hidden from both the authorities and his mother through the use of an alias on the company rosters. The entry for 'Charles Becker', the supposed alias under which Con had been enlisted, states that he was captured in action at Spotsylvania on 18 May and subsequently died of disease at Andersonville on 1 August 1864. Both versions of Con's fate were included in his mother's subsequent pension application, but Catharine (and indeed the balance of evidence) suggests that the disabled Limerick man died on the field at Spotsylvania, even as his mother searched the camps and hospitals for him.[22]

The story of Cornelius Garvin would remain famed for many years. *The New York Times* recalled the events fifty years later in an 1894 article, as did the *Troy Record* in 1965. They were still fresh in American Civil War veteran Thomas Livermore's mind decades after the war. In his *Days and Events 1860–1866* published in 1920, he remembered the 'singular case' which he investigated and 'which became one of the traditions in the War Department'. Livermore had been told to investigate the case by Winfield Scott Hancock when Catharine had first arrived at Second Corp Headquarters looking for Con. He remembered how Catharine had twice gone to Washington to obtain letters and endorsements before returning to the corps to search for her son, and that by the end her papers 'bore nearly seventy endorsements of officers, from the President down, all of whom forwarded her mission'. Livermore's account of Catharine's search appears to be inaccurate and unkind – if anything adding further pathos to the story. He recalled it as follows:

> I took the picture of her son which she had and went down to the regiment [the 52nd New York]. The commander said that he never had seen the boy, and that probably he had been drowned on the way out; that his mother had not been satisfied with his assurance that her son was not in the regiment in 1863, but had haunted his camp, and often paced up and down his line peering into the faces of the men until she became intolerable; and asked what could any one suppose he wanted an idiot in his regiment for. I made sufficient search to find that the boy was not there, and reported the fact, and also that the woman's conduct indicated her mind was unsettled, and recommended that she be sent back to Washington, which was done. In 1865 I began telling this story in General Breck's presence, when he said 'Cornelius Garvin'. That was the boy's name, and as I have said his story was well known in the War Department, as this shows.[23]

What actually happened to Con? Lafayette Baker gave his thoughts in his book *A History of the Secret Service*, published in 1867. In a section devoted to the incident, he expressed little doubt as to the true course of events. By the time of his writing, Baker was sure the boy had died in the army. His investigation had ascertained that following his taking from the almshouse, Con had been enlisted, sent to Riker's Island and then to the 52nd New York. He had been identified at Mitchell's Station and again at Mine Run, but Captain Degener, who commanded Con's company, 'attempted to intimidate, by threats of punishment, those privates of his company who were disposed to assist Mrs. Garvin and others engaged in the investigation'. Baker's investigator in Troy reached the conclusion that the superintendent of Rensselaer Almshouse had been complicit in Con's abduction, though the evidence was not sufficient to prove it beyond doubt. Baker also felt Captain Degener was complicit, as when the 52nd New York Volunteers returned home he had him arrested for questioning. Although the guilt of the two men seems likely, it does not appear that any charges were ever brought against them.[24]

As for Catharine, she spent many years living in Troy, returning occasionally to Limerick before seemingly settling back in Ireland permanently in 1890. She lived variously in Ballygrennan and Balline in the east of the county, with the post office address for her pension given as Bruff. She died in County Limerick in 1896, probably never fully recovered from her harrowing wartime experiences. An interesting postscript to the tragic story appeared in the *Troy Record* of 1965, when it was reported that a D.J. Ryan of the *Cork Examiner* newspaper had written to Mayor Ahern of Troy in the 1940s, saying he was a relative of Catharine Garvin. Ryan had in his possession many of Catharine's Civil War papers, including a handwritten letter to her from Abraham Lincoln, which he was trying to sell. The fate of this material remained unknown until 2015. It became apparent that the letters were sold to a Lincoln collector in the United States, from whom they were in turn acquired by the Lincoln Financial Foundation Collection based at Allen County Public Library in Fort Wayne, Indiana. They survive in that institution to this day. Named the Catharine Garvin Collection, these fifty-five documents are not only preserved but now available to view online. Among the many letters in the collection is the note from Abraham Lincoln, as well as numerous military passes and statements from soldiers. The papers are unquestionably those that Catharine 'carried always in her apron' as remembered by Civil War soldiers. The fact that she kept them even after her return to Ireland is testament in itself to her devotion to her son, and the long, heartbreaking and ultimately fruitless search she undertook to find him.[25]

THE MURPHYS: MONAGHAN AND ILLINOIS

 'Debilitated by having borne 13 children.'[26]

In May of 1871 a 57-year-old Monaghan woman, described as 'infirm and broken in body,' made the journey into Chicago from her 'Irish Shanty' on the open prairie a few miles outside of the city. Jane Murphy, who possessed little more than a 'scanty wardrobe', had come to see her lawyer about a pension. It was not her first visit. Earlier that year, she had dictated her entire immigrant story for the pension bureau – part of a process she hoped would secure the finances she desperately needed for her survival. That May, with her husband lying on his deathbed, and with no response forthcoming from the pension bureau, she could take no more. At her wits' end, she sat in her lawyer's office and broke down in tears.[27]

Jane was seeking a pension based on the service of her son, Michael. On 7 October 1862, at the age of 19, he had enlisted in the 90th Illinois Infantry, known as 'Chicago's Irish Legion'. Michael became a private in Company G, which had been raised in Chicago. He was described as a 'large, stout, industrious young man, the prop of their [the Murphys] declining years'.[28]

One of the letters Michael wrote home from the Western Theater of war survives:

Head Quarters 90th Reg. Ill. Inf.
Camp Sherman Sept 15th 1863

Dear Mother,
I received your letter on the 7th inst and I am sorry to hear that you are not well. I am also sorry that I cannot send you any money as there is no signs of us been paid for some time – Dear Mother I am surprised at you not mentioning my Father or Brother James in your letters and I wish you to let me know in your answer to this how they are – I am glad to hear of your receiving the money I sent you last March – I was very sorry to hear of John & Charles Hudsons death, also of Mrs Floods death. Let me know what Regiment Jas O'Donnell is in and what place and if Mr Kenney gets any word from John – Enclosed find my likeness and I would like to have yours and Annes likeness by Leut Duffy or Sargt Mc Namara that is going to Chicago – Let my Father know that I will send him money by next Christmas anyhow. Patrick

Smith sends his best respects to you all and he enjoys as well as me good health,

I remain your loving son,
Michael Murphy.[29]

As the letter suggests, Michael was upset that his mother had failed to provide news on his father, who suffered from ill health, or his brother James, who was an invalid. It is likely that he felt responsibility towards their upkeep, as prior to enlisting he had been the family's main support. The Murphys made their living from the wild prairie grass that surrounded their shanty to the west of Chicago. Michael had brought the grass to market in the city where he sold it as hay, making a few dollars for every ton he transported. This was an income the family supplemented with a cow and the growing of vegetables. Even after he joined the army, Michael made sure to look after those at home. He gave $25 of his bounty money to his mother and forwarded her $90 from his pay in the year following his enlistment. All that ended a little over two months after he wrote this letter. On 25 November 1863 Michael and the 90th Illinois were part of the Union assault on Missionary Ridge, Tennessee. At that battle the young Monaghan man was killed in action, one of the 117 casualties sustained by the 'Irish Legion' during the attack.[30]

Michael's premature death during the American Civil War was only part of the reason for his mother Jane's distress in 1871, as she sat crying in the office of her lawyer, J. W. Boyden. The letter he wrote to the pension bureau as a result of that visit highlights the unimaginable hardships she was then enduring:

Chicago, May 18, 1871
Dr. Trevitt,

Dear Sir,
For special reasons, I ask that Jane Murphy's claim, No. 194,826, as dependent mother of Michael Murphy, deceased Private, Co. G, 90th Illinois Vol. may be taken up out of its regular order and disposed of.

She is in my office today; debilitated by having borne 13 children, by prolapsus uteri, and by a 6 inch tumor on back of her neck; and in tears, having walked four miles, from her shanty home on the open prairie, to see about her pension.

She reports that her husband has been, for about two months, unable to leave his shanty, by reason of ill health from induration of the liver and chronic inflammation of the stomach, and is in a dying condition.

Their invalid son James is confined at home with white swelling of the knee, and helpless.

The additional evidence that I have today forwarded to the Pension Office by the mail that takes this letter, makes a strong, meritorious, urgent claim, and discloses a special emergency and need of her pension.

Very Respectfully,
On behalf of Mrs Jane Murphy
J.W. Boyden, Her Atty.[31]

Jane had travelled to Boyden's office on 18 May because she had been asked by the pension bureau to prove that her 65-year-old husband Patrick was physically incapable of financially supporting himself and his family. With her husband still alive, this was a necessary step in securing a dependent mother's pension based on her son's service. In order to prove this incapacity, Patrick had to either travel to an official pension surgeon in Chicago, or pay for one to come and examine him. The family doctor noted that this was an impossibility, as Patrick 'has not been out of his shanty, two months past, is in a dying condition, and cannot be brought safely 4 miles to be examined by a Pension Surgeon in Chicago, and has no money to pay the Board or any member of it to go out and examine him'.[32]

The Murphys' physician clearly felt deep sympathy for the family's terrible plight. In support of Jane's application, it was noted how the couple were 'poor, worthy old people'. They had 'long lived out on the open prairie, on a small patch of ground, west of the settled portion of the city'. Michael's enlistment in the army had inevitably placed a heavier physical burden on Jane, and by 1872, aside from her other ailments, her doctor described her as 'an invalid and disabled from supporting herself by manual labor'.[33]

As part of her pension application, Jane Murphy gave an affidavit outlining her circumstances. Unusually for such documents, it was written in the first person. It is an extraordinary record of her life from her marriage in County Monaghan in 1830 through to Illinois in 1872. Jane was illiterate, so her statement was dictated – so vivid is her account that one can almost imagine her relating the story in her Chicago lawyer's office:

… I was married, December 25, 1830, in Ireland, to my husband Patrick Murphy, I have never owned any property, except my wearing apparel, and have had no other means of support than my own labor when in health; my husband's labor when he was able to work, and the labor of our two sons, James and Michael Murphy.

I have given birth to thirteen children: John, the oldest, in 1851, left me in Ireland and emigrated to America, probably to some Southern state, and I have never, since 1851, seen, or heard from him. James, the second, emigrated with me in 1853, has always lived with me, unmarried, has done nothing, by reason of pulmonary consumption, during ten years past, more than enough to pay for his board at home and clothes.

Mary came, in 1851, with John to America; worked as house servant till her marriage, about 1858, to Thomas Hudson; has had 7 children and neither she, nor her husband have contributed to my support, nor can they, having all they can do to support their family. Ann, my 4th, is unmarried, consumptive, works out as house servant; does and can do nothing towards my support;

nor can Catherine, my 5th, nor her husband, John Whalen, who live in Texas, at Houston, nor are they able to contribute to my support. Michael, my 7th, was the soldier, born in October, 1842, and was killed, when 21 years and 1 month old. Peter, my 8th, was born and died in Ireland in 1846. Patrick, my 9th, died in 1864, at 16 years of age. Another Peter, born in 1850, died Feby 14, 1868, and was my 10th, Jane, my 11th, born in 1853, has lived in Texas with Catherine since she was 14 years old [where the sisters worked as dressmakers]. Francis, my 12th, born in 1858, and Robert, my 13th and last, both live at home, but are both too young to contribute towards my support. My husband and James and Michael helped support me by keeping a cow and raising a few vegetables, but chiefly by cutting and hauling prairie grass, or hay to Chicago hay market, when they were well.

Michael Murphy was always large and stout for his years. He left off going to school, in 1855, when almost 13 years old. During the seven years thereafter, till his enlistment in October 1862, Michael lived at home, worked in the garden, took care of the cow, but earned his money by sales of prairie hay in Chicago market, hauled, and cut or mowed by himself, assisted by his father and brother James; at from 50 to 60 loads annually, for $2 to $4 per load. All his earnings were applied to the support of the family, including myself; as well as $25 Bounty he gave to me at enlistment and $90 sent home to me of his pay; and $200 Bounty received after his death by his father; who has no property except a prairie lot, shanty, cow house, old furniture & clothing, all worth not over five hundred dollars.[34]

The couple's marriage may be that recorded as taking place in Monaghan, County Monaghan in 1830 between Patrick Murphy of Kilmore Parish and Jane Scott of Monaghan Parish. Jane's submission is a remarkable window into the life of nineteenth-century Irish emigrants, particularly with regard to familial relationships between parents and children. Thankfully, her pension application was approved, and Jane received $8 per month to an address at 975 West Madison Street, Chicago. Her husband Patrick did not benefit from it for long. He passed away on 12 July 1871, his death ultimately recorded as resulting from stomach cancer.[35]

THE DONOHOES: GALWAY AND MASSACHUSETTS

 'Widow Donohoe of the South Island of Arran.'[36]

In early 1861 John Donohoe lived in one of the remotest parts of Europe. He made his home on the island of Inisheer (Inis Oírr) – only 2 miles long and 1½ miles wide, this is the smallest of the Aran Islands off the Atlantic coast of County Galway. Along with many of the island's other native Irish-speaking inhabitants, John was a farmer, eking out a living with his brothers and parents on a small farm. Just a year later, John's life had changed utterly. Early 1862 found the Aran islander on the other side of the Atlantic, preparing to go into action as a Union soldier on the Virginia Peninsula. His fate would reverberate all the way back to his island home on Inisheer.[37]

The 1850s Griffith's Valuation for Inisheer confirms the presence of the Donohoe family. John's father Peter Donohoe was listed as renting 4 acres valued at £4 and buildings valued at 15 shillings from Miss Elizabeth F. Digby. The Digby family of Kildare had been the major landowners on the Aran Islands since the middle of the eighteenth century. Although Peter's name was on the lease, he was burdened by ill health. What was variously described as 'consumption', 'asthma', 'heart disease' and 'dropsy' prevented him from undertaking manual labour. As a result both he and his wife Bridget became reliant on their sons, John, Thomas, Peter junior and Morgan, to manage the farm and crops for them. The results of their efforts were valued at around £10 per year. John grew to adulthood working the smallholding, having left school at the age of 13 to dedicate himself to the farm full time.[38]

The family's 4 acres on Inisheer were not enough to support the young men of the Donohoe household. Either through choice or necessity (perhaps both), the future for at least three of the boys lay away from the island. John, Thomas and Peter junior all decided that future lay in America. John Donohoe was just over 18 years old when he left Inisheer for the last time, in June 1861. A few weeks later he arrived in Boston, Massachusetts. Suddenly immersed in the sights and sounds of a strange, bustling city, the young islander must have experienced a profound culture shock. Whatever his impressions, John didn't tarry long. On 19 September 1861 he presented himself at an army recruiting station. There he was recorded as standing 5 feet 8¾ inches tall, with grey eyes, light hair and a sallow complexion. From that point forward he was Private John Donohoe, of Battery H, 1st United States Artillery.[39]

By 5 May 1862 John had been in the United States for a little over ten months. That morning he and his comrades of Battery H found themselves travelling along a road with their guns and limbers, just outside the city of Williamsburg. They were part of a force of some 41,000 Federals who were about to engage 31,000 Confederates in what would become the first major battle of the Peninsula Campaign. It was an engagement in which John found himself to the fore. As he had never seen serious action before, nervous energy must have been coursing through his body when he realised he would soon face battle. Perhaps he took a moment to think of his tiny island home, a setting that could not be further removed from the sea of organised military chaos that now surrounded him.[40]

It was early in the fight when John's guns were ordered forward to take position and engage the enemy. Two of Battery H's pieces unlimbered in the middle of the road, while four more drew up in an adjacent field. They came under immediate fire from Confederate infantry and artillery, which included shells that screamed in from the nearby Rebel Fort Magruder. Only seconds into the action, two officers and two privates went down in the hail of fire, and the other men of Battery H, panicking, scampered to find cover. Only eighteen of them could be persuaded to return, and volunteers had to be sought to help fire the pieces. Amid torrential rain the artillerists worked the guns, exchanging salvoes with the Confederates only 700 yards away. For seven hours the sporadic struggle continued. In the end it was events on the left flank that sealed the gunners' fate. There the Union infantry was forced back; when they retreated they exposed the cannoneers to attack from that direction. As the buoyant southerners poured forward they reached the artillery, capturing four of Battery H's guns. The survivors had to endure fire from Confederate sharpshooters concealed in fallen timber for the remainder of the day. When sunset ended the fighting, the unit had lost two men, while eight had been wounded in what would become known as the Battle of Williamsburg. One of those who had lost their life was John Donohoe of Inisheer.[41]

It may be that the Donohoe boys had thoughts of joining the federal military even before they left the Aran Islands, seeing in the conflict an opportunity for steady employment, as John was reportedly not the only member of the Donohoe family to serve in the army. His mother Bridget would later claim that Thomas also donned Union blue, only to contract a disease which she said led to his discharge and ultimately his death. Back on Inisheer, as the 1860s progressed, the Donohoe family fortunes continued in a downward spiral. In the immediate aftermath of John's death the 1st US Artillery sent his outstanding backpay to his father Peter, but this provided only temporary respite. Peter Donohoe's debilitating illness, which had incapacitated him for ten years, eventually claimed his life. After a final two-month personal battle, he died on 23 May 1868. Bridget could now no longer rely on the assistance of either her husband or her sons. She was forced to give up the farm in May 1870, and became reliant on the charity of her fellow islanders. Now 60 years of age, she approached the United States Government in search of a pension based on John's military service.[42]

The application procedure for a dependent mother's pension could be onerous even in ideal circumstances, but it was made all the harder when the applicant was based on the Aran Islands. Bridget sought and received the assistance of the US consul in Galway, but even so it proved a difficult process. Her problems were exacerbated by the fact that the physician who had treated her husband, Dr James Johnston Stoney, had himself since died on 25 June 1869, as a result of an 'overdraught of laudanum'. Without another medical man on Inisheer who had known her husband, Bridget struggled to prove that Peter had been physically incapable. She eventually employed the services of attorney James Shannon of Ballingaddy, Ennistymon, County Clare to assist her in gathering together the evidence she needed. This included securing death certificates for both her husband and Dr Stoney, before seeking affidavits from friends and neighbours to vouch for her story. These included Simon Maher, who had taken over her farm in 1870, Inisheer farmers Coleman Conneely, Pat Griffin, Martin Griffin and Martin O'Donnell, and Martin Hernon of the 'North Island' (Inis Mór).

In her application Bridget outlined her precarious position, stating that she would 'have to go to a workhouse to end her days unless a pension be granted to her'.[43]

It was clear from Bridget Donohoe's pension statements that she never knew exactly where her son had died. She knew only that he had been 'shot in the American War' while serving in the Union army. The pension application of the 'Widow Donohoe of the South Island of Arran' was eventually accepted. She gave her post office address as 'South Island of Arran, County Galway, Ireland', from where she claimed her monthly payment of $8 for the remainder of her life.[44]

THE COYLES: DONEGAL AND PENNSYLVANIA

 '… alas he is gone and we have no support for I am doubtfull the landlord will eject us …'[45]

The Parish of Clondavaddog on the Fanad Peninsula in northern County Donegal was a hard place to live in the nineteenth century. Contemporaries noted the tough aspect of the terrain, remarking it was 'for the most part occupied by mountains of considerable altitude … separated by deep narrow vales'. Although there was some good arable country it was not generally suited to pasture, containing 'much waste and barren land' with many acres 'covered and destroyed by the shifting sands' of Lough Swilly. One of the families who lived there were the Coyles, who made their livelihoods on a small farm in Muineagh townland. The pension file that contains their story includes rare physical evidence of what remains one of the most emotive legacies of nineteenth-century Ireland – eviction.[46]

On 27 April 1869, Eunice Coyle made her way from her home in Muineagh to the nearest justice of the peace. Just over two weeks previously, Eunice and her husband John had received news that must have struck them like a hammer blow. Their landlord, William Sydney Clements, 3rd Earl of Leitrim, had decided to reclaim the land on which they lived, and served them with the following notice:

As agent to the Right Honourable WILLIAM SYDNEY EARL OF LEITRIM, I hereby give you notice to Quit and Deliver up to Me or his Bailiff, on the First day of November next, the Possession of ALL THAT AND THOSE, that Part of the Lands of Muineagh with the Houses thereon, and the Appurtenances thereunto belonging, situate in the Parish of Clondavaddog, in the Barony of Kilmacrenan, and County of Donegal, and all other Lands, Tenements, Hereditaments, and Premises, which you hold from or occupy under the said WILLIAM SYDNEY EARL OF LEITRIM, together with all and singular the Appurtenances thereunto belonging, situate in the County of Donegal, provided your Tenantcy commenced at that time of the year; and if otherwise, that you Quit and Deliver up the Possession of the said Premises, at the end of the year of your Tenantcy, which shall expire next after the end of half-a-year from the time of your being served with this Notice; and in case you shall neglect or refuse to deliver up said Premises, the said WILLIAM SYDNEY EARL OF LEITRIM will proceed to recover the Possession, and double the yearly value thereof, and all Costs attending such recovery.

Dated this 8th day of April 1869
To John Coyle

The 3rd Earl of Leitrim was a notorious landlord, and one who was strongly disliked by his tenants. Practices such as the constant raising of rents and frequent evictions meant that he was among the most hated landowners in all of Ireland. The eviction notice placed Eunice and John Coyle in an extremely vulnerable position. As both were in their mid-seventies their prospects for financial recovery were slight, and they now faced the very real possibility of spending their final years in utter destitution. It seems probable it was their impending eviction that prompted Eunice's journey that 27 April, as the couple sought to accelerate a process they had initiated some weeks previously. They needed to secure any financial aid available if they were to face the challenges ahead. The Coyles had decided to turn to the United States Government, applying for a pension based on the service of their son, who had died almost five years previously.[47]

Eunice gave a statement in which she recorded that her son, Hugh, had 'died of inhuman treatment while a prisoner of war at Andersonville Georgia'. Hugh had enlisted in the 8th Pennsylvania Volunteer Cavalry Regiment on 1 October 1861. He was part of a mounted force that fell upon elements of a Confederate wagon train at Monterey Pass, Pennsylvania on 4 July 1863, as the Rebels were retreating south following their defeat at Gettysburg. Taken during the fight, Hugh spent the next eleven months in captivity before succumbing to anasarca – a severe oedema that was likely a consequence of malnutrition – on 24 June 1864. His remains were buried at Andersonville, where they today rest in the National Cemetery, in Grave 2,399.[48]

Eunice and her husband John's 'small lot of land' was some 6 acres in size, which they held from the Earl of Leitrim year to year for a sum of £4 10s 10d. The earl would not allow the couple liberty of sale, but even if he had Eunice stated that 'it would not bring a penny' as it was 'very barren'. The Coyles' neighbours in Muineagh, Thomas Kerr and Matthew Morrow, had known the Coyles for decades and were happy to give statements to that effect. They highlighted an additional challenge that faced the couple – John Coyle's health. The elderly man had been physically unable to support his wife for some eight years, as he was suffering from rheumatism and general debility due to his age. His system was described as 'completely broken down', and this prevented him from performing any hard labour on his land.[49]

In addition to the statements and evidence they provided from Fanad, the Coyles knew that they would also need to source information about Hugh's life in America. Drawing on Fanad connections in Philadelphia, which included at least one of their children, they had statements prepared by Ann Coyle and Mary Dolan to support their claim. In 1869 these women said they had been living in the United States for twenty years, but that prior to that had known the Coyles well, as they were from the same neighbourhood in County Donegal. The two women claimed that prior to enlisting Hugh had worked for three years as a labourer, earning between $7 and $8 per week. They recalled him frequently sending money to Ireland for his parents' support; indeed just before enlisting he had given Ann

$22 to send to Donegal on his behalf. Both women recalled that Hugh told them he sent all the money he possibly could home for his ageing parents. This was something he continued doing during his military service. Just prior to his capture in 1863 he gave his sister in Philadelphia $100 to send to Ireland. There seems to be little doubt that Hugh's money was extremely important in allowing his parents across the Atlantic to make ends meet.[50]

As a final element in her pension application, Eunice included a personal appeal for the agent acting on her behalf in Philadelphia. In it she outlined what she felt were the Earl of Leitrim's motivations for issuing the notice to quit, and described the couple's reliance on the financial aid they had received from their son:

Munnagh April 28th 1869

To Joseph C. Devitt & Co. the military and naval agency No. 427 walnut street
Philladelphia

Dear Sir I confide in your honour that you will use all the efforts in your power to draw a support for me and my old & tender husband John Coyle in lue of our son Hugh Coyle and our only one son that left us helpless and tender to purchase a support for us in America and while he lived he sent us a help of support but alas he is gone and we have no support for I am doubtfull [apprehensive] the landlord will eject us out of the bit [of] land that we held under him for he wants it with others to put Black Cattle to graze on it
I place all my confidence in the good and generous government of the United States of Americ[a] that the[y] will take my case to a kind consideration for a support

yours respectfully unis coyle[51]

Eunice Coyle's efforts were rewarded with a United States pension based on her son's service. It is unclear if it was enough to stave off the impending hardships she and her husband faced. Conversely, the fate of their landlord, the 3rd Earl of Leitrim, remains well known in Donegal to this day. A little less than a decade after he issued his notice to quit to the Coyles, disaffected Fanad tenants played a central role in the landlord's demise. On 2 April 1878 a group of local Fanad men lay in wait along a road for the 72-year-old earl, killing him, his driver and his clerk when they passed. The assassins were never captured, and in the twentieth century a monument was erected to the 'Fanad patriots' who put an end to the despised landlord.[52]

THE KENNEDYS: OFFALY & OHIO

 'When he came back from the army, they would have a nice little farm.'[53]

In August 1861, Orderly Sergeant John Kennedy of the 10th Ohio Infantry wrote a letter home to his mother from western Virginia. The 22-year-old from Dunkerrin, County Offaly had been in the army for barely three months. Only weeks before he had been learning the tobacconist trade, which he plied in Cincinnati's 13th Ward. Now, that August, John was keen to calm his mother's fears – he was her sole family and support, and she was terrified as to what might become of them both in the months and years to come.[54]

John's mother, Catharine Talbot, had married Robert Kennedy in Dunkerrin Catholic church, County Offaly on 30 January 1837. John had been born around 1839, and spent his childhood years in Ireland. John's father Robert passed away in Offaly around 1850. Despite his young age, John immediately had to begin working to try and support Catharine and his baby brother Michael. Before long Catharine decided that the best prospects for her family lay in the United States, and following their emigration they settled in Cincinnati, Ohio. When they arrived, they entered a community that already contained some people from Dunkerrin – years later a number of other Cincinnati residents, such as Daniel Hickey and Denis Williams, would recall knowing Catharine in Offaly. Another, Thomas Irwin, remembered attending Robert Kennedy's wake in the County Offaly village. Ill health meant that Catharine relied on her son John for everything, from her rent to her groceries. The local grocery store owner, Mrs Hennessey, recalled how Catharine would buy her necessaries on account, with John coming every few weeks to pay off her bill. Catharine's landlord, James Bailey, remembered that John always paid his mother's rent for her, and described him as 'sober, industrious and much attached to his mother'. He also noted that after John joined the army, Catharine was unable to pay the rent until John received his army wages.[55]

John had initially enlisted for three months, in May 1861, but on 3 June, like most of his comrades, he committed to a three-year term. The unit he chose was initially known as the 'Montgomery Regiment', a largely Irish formation that would become the 10th Ohio Infantry. John had elected to march to war under the stars and stripes of the United States and the green flag of Ireland. Catharine was not pleased. Apart from the fact he was her only means of support, she was no doubt also terrified of losing him permanently. Catharine decided to take desperate measures, so before the regiment left its Cincinnati base – Camp Dennison – for the front, she persuaded a few influential citizens to help her get her son out of the army. They set off to see John's captain, Stephen McGroarty (from Mount Charles, County Donegal, later a brevet-brigadier-general). Catharine asked McGroarty to discharge her son, on the basis that he was her sole support. One can imagine the whole affair was somewhat embarrassing for John, who had only just been promoted to sergeant for good behaviour. In front of his commander, John now had to face off against his mother. He told her that he was 'anxious to go with the regiment' and reassured her that 'he would send her his money, and that it would be all the same to her' adding that 'when he came back from the army, they would have a nice little farm'. This was a reference to 160 acres of land that the men had been promised for enlisting. Captain McGroarty also told Catharine that even if John had wanted to leave, there was no turning back – he was now an enlisted man, and was compelled to go with the regiment.[56]

This was the backdrop to John's 11 August letter. By that date the regiment remained unpaid, but John reassured Catharine that the money was sure to come eventually. He was also keen to stress that he had not been in any real danger so far. The 10th Ohio had yet to be engaged in any major combat. In August 1861, such horrors still lay in the future.

Buckhannon Aug 11th 1861

Dear Mother

i take the plesure of writing you these few lines hoping the[y] may find you in as good health as this leaves me at present thank God. We have just got back from a long march through the Country sometimes marching all night. We are getting along very well now we may stop here for some time. there was six of our men shot coming through Bulltown on the 9th of aug we were there the day before the[y] arived there you see the Regiment is devided in three parts four Companys with Col Lytle four with Col Karff [Korff] and two with Major Burk [Burke] we are with Col Lytle. we may be at the Battle of Manassas Gap but i dont think we will however i know that we will have plenty of fighting for i supose it will take us some time to drive them out of Virginia. Perhaps i may get a furla [furlough] soon and go home for a week or two but i dont know how soon i may get it mother. i dont know what is the reason the [they] dont pay of [off] but one thing i do know that it is as shure as daylight and if you can get along for a short time it will be all wright. John Keller is going home tomorrow and i sen[d] this by him to you so he can let you know how i am. we have just as good a time here as if we were at home only the danger of being on gaurd at night as for me i dont have to go on any gaurd duty i have a very good

time here of cource i have charge of a Company and sometimes
i have a little trouble but it is not mutch. i wrote a great many
letters since i arived here and never got but two answered. Patrick
Hennessy and Hamilton Keown are well and sends their respects
to all the folks at home the[y] wish their friends would write to
them a little more than the[y] do. i will let you know that my
pay is raised five dolars more in the month. tell Mrs Ryan that
i was asking for her and Mrs Kilfoil also Mrs Comings and all
the folks. when John Keller is coming back i wish you would
send that white pants with him i want it those hot days.
No more at present

from your son
    John Kennedy
    Orderly Sergeant
    Company E 10th Regt
    O.V.M.[57]

Less than a month after John wrote this letter, on 10 September 1861, the
10th Ohio experienced battle for the first time. They 'saw the elephant' at
Carnifex Ferry, Virginia (now West Virginia), in an engagement that would
result in the regiment being referred to as the 'heroes of Carnifex' and 'The
Bloody Tenth'. Against a fortified enemy, Captain Stephen McGroarty led
his Company E forward to the attack. They were met with withering fire.
When it was finally over, ten of the regiment lay dead and fifty wounded. Just
how much John Kennedy ever knew of his first taste of action is unknown;
McGroarty remembered seeing the young Offaly man fall, shot through
the head.[58]

Back in Cincinnati, John's mother's worst fears had become a reality.
News of her son's death reached her before any of the army money ever
did. Not only had her child been taken from her, but now she was unable
to pay the rent on the 'scantily furnished room' which was her home in
Cincinnati. With her rent unpaid, she became reliant on relief committees
and friends for support. All that was left to her was to seek her son's bounty

and backpay, and apply for a dependent mother's pension, which she ultimately received.[59]

THE RIDGWAYS: DUBLIN AND WASHINGTON DC

 'So good a Government would not leave the widows of their soldiers dying in a Workhouse.'[60]

Many men were tempted by the apparent potential the American Civil War offered for financial betterment. The bounties on offer, combined with the prospect of regular pay, might be enough to kickstart a new life for themselves and their families. Such was the case with George Ridgway, who left his family behind in Ireland to pursue those goals. His actions did have a long-lasting impact on his loved ones, but not in the way he might have hoped.

Maria McDonald was born into the military life. Her father Edward was a soldier serving in Athlone when she entered the world in 1840. As her father moved around with his unit, so did his family; by the late 1850s the McDonalds were to be found residing at Beggar's Bush Barracks in Dublin. Another soldier stationed in the city at the time was Englishman Corporal George Ridgway. Born in Shropshire around the year 1835, George was a career soldier. Maria and George appear to have hit it off, and the two were married in St Peter's Church of Ireland parish church on Aungier Street, Dublin, on 30 February 1859.[61]

The couple did not have to wait long before celebrating the birth of their first child. Maria Honora was born on 22 November 1859, and a son, Joseph George, followed on 3 March 1862. It had been decided to raise the children in their mother's religion, and both were baptised as Roman Catholics in St James' parish church, Dublin. By the time of his son's birth, George was no longer with the family in Ireland. In 1861 he had been sent to Toronto, Canada with his regiment, the 30th Foot. The war raging south of the Canadian border seemed to offer promising prospects for someone with George's expertise, and was a potential means of improving his family fortunes. It was an opportunity that tempted many Canadian-based British soldiers. George made a momentous decision; he determined to desert from the British Army, and made his way south to join the Federals. It is doubtful whether Maria knew George was planning such a drastic step, one from which there could be no turning back. The only way the family would ever be reunited now was for George to succeed in gathering enough money to pay for his wife and children's passage to America.[62]

On 24 February 1863 George Ridgway entered United States military service in Washington DC. He was described as 28 years old with blue eyes, sandy hair and a ruddy complexion. Not wanting to draw attention to the fact that he had deserted, he had his profession recorded as 'laborer'. George became a private in Company L of the 1st United States Cavalry. As the Englishman headed to Virginia that spring, he no doubt hoped that he had made the right choice for his and his family's future.[63]

Four months after George's enlistment, the following letter was written to Maria from America, sent via the US consul in Dublin:

Sanitary Commission
Washington DC USA.
June 25th 1863
Mrs. Maria Ridgway
Dublin, Ireland

Madam,
It has become my mournful duty to inform you of the decease [sic] of your husband George Ridgway US Cavalry 1st Regt. Co. L. He was brought to this hospital from hospital at Aquia Creek very sick of chronic diarrhea [sic] on the 15th instant and died on the 19th inst. Was extremely feeble able to say but little. His last words were of you and his children. Tell my wife I die believing in the Lord Jesus. I hope the Lord will be a husband to her. Give my love to my wife and children. He had good care. Died in one of our best hospitals. Religious services were performed by the Chaplain in a grave in

the hospital ground. At his burial an escort followed the body which was buried in the National Cemetery provided for soldiers and his graves [sic] is carefully preserved having an inscribed and numbered head-board so that it can be identified at any future day. May God in his love and mercy minister to you and your children large consolations in Christ Jesus giving you beauty as ashes, the oil of joy for mourning and the garment of praise for the spirit of heaveness. Please accept my very sincere condolence in Christ.

Joseph M. Driver
Chaplain Columbian Hospital
Washington DC USA.

George Ridgway was buried at what is now the US Soldiers' and Airmen's Home National Cemetery, where his grave can still be seen. Maria, still only in her early twenties, was a widow. She successfully applied for a military pension from her then home in Goldenbridge, Dublin, which was awarded at the rate of $8 per month. It was later increased to take account of her two minor children. Maria Ridgway and her family had never been to the United States, and indeed may never have set foot outside of Ireland. Nevertheless the American Civil War had turned their lives upside down. The conflict and her husband's part in it would continue to be a central element of Maria's life for decades to come.[64]

As the years passed and Maria grew older, she continued to rely on the income that her US pension provided. Then, in 1893, changes to the pension system meant that this income was suddenly jeopardised. Measures implemented by an Act of Congress dated 1 March 1893 threatened to impact not only Maria, but all the pensioned widows and dependent parents of deceased American servicemen then living in Ireland. The act stipulated 'That from and after July 1st, 1893, no pension shall be paid to a non-resident, who is not a citizen of the United States, except for actual disabilities incurred in the service'. Maria and all other dependent pensioners in Ireland were informed that their payments would cease unless they could show that their loved one had been 'born in the United States, or, if not born in the United States, was at any time naturalized as a citizen thereof, it being held that his citizenship determines the citizenship of yourself'. Unsurprisingly, this was something that many Irish pensioners simply could not prove. Indeed, in many instances, their husbands and sons had not been naturalised citizens at the time of their deaths.[65]

Maria was among those who found it virtually impossible to prove her husband's naturalisation. Facing the prospect that her pension might be terminated, Maria embarked on a letter-writing campaign, first addressing the US Pension Bureau:

To the US Pension Agent

Most Honourable Sir,
This humble petition of Maria Ridgway, widow of George Ridgway Pvt. US Cavalry who is interred in the Soldiers burying ground in Washington DC with an inscribed and numbered headboard, the Reverend Joshua M. Driver Chaplain to the US Soldiers kindly sent me and my children my husbands dying words and where I could see his grave at any future time. Not having received my pension voucher No. 57226 to sign for the next quarter 4th September I have taken the liberty in addressing you and I knowing how good the Government has been to me all these years, in giving me means to live since the death of my husband who died fighting for them. I am sure so good a Government would not leave the widows of their soldiers dying in a Workhouse. I am now old and unable to earn my bread, with bad eyes and in a very delicate state of health, hoping the US Government would kindly take my case into their kind consideration and grant me for the short time I expect to be in the world what would keep me from the Workhouse. By so doing I shall always think myself as duty bound to pray for my kind benefactors. Sir I

have the honour to remain your most humble and obedient servant,

> *Maria Ridgway*
> *163 Gt. Britain Street [now Parnell Street]*
> *or US Consul*
> *Great Brunswick St.*
> *Dublin.*[66]

Just in case that letter did not work, Maria also took the precaution of writing directly to the then President of the United States, Grover Cleveland:

> *To the President of the United States*
>
> *Most Honourable Sir,*
> *The humble petition of Maria Ridgway widow of George Ridgway who was a private in the 1 US Cavalry and fought under the American Stars and Stripes for the American cause he is buried in the Soldiers burying ground Washington DC I his widow and two children was granted a pension on Certificate 57226, Act July 14–1862 and in March 19–1886 through the goodness of the American Government at which time I think you were President [Cleveland had been serving his first term as President in 1886] I got my increase to 12 dollars per month. Now through an Act of Congress July 1–1893, I am deprived of any means of support in my old age when I am feeble and not able to do anything for myself through rheumatism. Most Honourable Sir through your goodness of heart, should you take my declining years into your kind consideration and grant me a little to keep an American Widow from dying in a Workhouse, and my two orphans shall always think it our*

duty to pray for you. I have the honour to be Sir your most faithful servant,

Maria Ridgway
To Mrs. Alford [*her daughter's married name*]
6 Florinda Place, North Circular Road,
Dublin
5th March 1894.[67]

Maria also enlisted the help of her local priest, Fr Bernard Emmett O'Mahony. He wrote to the American authorities, asking, 'Is there any hope that this harsh if not unjust statute will be repealed?' In other correspondence relating to the suspension of her pension, Maria argued that she did not know if her husband George had been a naturalised citizen of the United States. She explained that in 1863 'he wrote to me and said if he got safe through the war America was to be our home, but God had it otherwise'. Maria then claimed that prior to her husband emigrating in 1862 he had already spent eleven years in the United States, at which time he may well have become a citizen. Given what we know of George's history, this was almost certainly a false claim, borne out of Maria's desperation to keep the vital payments. Eventually Maria's pension, along with those of the other Irish pensioners impacted by the 1893 Act, were reinstated. Her payments recommenced on 4 March 1895.[68]

Despite Maria's concerns that she may not have had long left to live in the 1890s, she survived well into the twentieth century. In 1911 she was still living at 163 Great Britain Street with her son Joseph, who had become a hairdresser, along with his wife Elizabeth and their eight children. Her daughter Maria had married cattle dealer John Alford and they and their nine children were living on Henrietta Street – Maria would eventually be a grandmother to no fewer than twenty children.[69]

Maria Ridgway's health finally began to fail in December 1918, with things taking a turn for the worse the following March. She passed away on the afternoon of 8 July 1919 at the home of her daughter, in No. 2 Synnott Place, Dublin. The official cause of death was cancer of the liver. Her entire effects, which consisted of 'a few pieces of old furniture and old clothes', were left to her daughter. The American Civil War widow's funeral mass was held at St Joseph's church on Berkeley Road before her remains were laid to rest in St Bridget's Section of Prospect Cemetery, Glasnevin, County Dublin. In April 1920, almost 57 years after Private George Ridgway's death in Washington DC, the US Government made its final pension payment to the Dublin family, when it contributed towards the expenses of Maria's funeral.[70]

THE DURICKS: TIPPERARY AND VERMONT

 'Entirely incapable of earning a subsistence.'[71]

Every few months for much of the 1880s the octogenarian Timothy Durick travelled from his home in Lackamore, Castletownarra, County Tipperary, to the nearby town of Nenagh. He made the journey to visit the post office and collect his pension. In order to secure those payments, Timothy had travelled across the Atlantic, following in the footsteps of his son, Jeremiah. Timothy was entitled to them because of the sacrifice Jeremiah had made on what remains the bloodiest day in American military history.[72]

Timothy Durick had been born around the year 1801. He married Mary Hogan in 1827 and the couple went on to have five children including Jeremiah, born around the year 1835. The dangers of childbirth were ever present in nineteenth-century Ireland, and Mary died from the effects of her fifth labour during the early 1840s. The family did not have significant means, and life appears to have been difficult. It was little surprise when Jeremiah decided to emigrate to America in the mid-1850s. His motivations are unknown, but it is interesting to note that on 23 May 1853 a Jeremiah Durick of Lackamore was found guilty at the Nenagh Court of Petty Sessions of 'assault and threats' towards one John McDonald, for which he was given the option of paying a fine and costs, or serving fourteen days in prison with hard labour. If, as seems likely, this is the same Jeremiah, it may have been this brush with the law that made up his mind to seek the emigrant boat.[73]

As was so often the case, Jeremiah made his way to friends in the United

States. His destination was Rutland County, Vermont, where a large North Tipperary community was already based, mainly working in the region's slate quarries. When Jeremiah arrived he went to stay with John Barrett, who had known him since he was a boy and had attended his mother's funeral in Ireland. The young man went to work in the marble quarries, making sure to send his father in Tipperary money whenever he could.[74]

When war came in 1861, Jeremiah decided to enlist. The regiment he chose was the 88th New York Infantry, one of the units of the Irish Brigade. He mustered in as a private in Company C on 28 September 1861, at the age of 26. A steady wage seems to have been one of Jeremiah's main motivations, but his selection of the Irish Brigade also suggests that he wanted to serve with his countrymen in an ethnic unit.[75]

Throughout his service Jeremiah put money aside for his father, at one point sending $30 back to Nenagh via his brother John. The Irish Brigade in which he served first saw action on the Virginia Peninsula in 1862, in a campaign which the Tipperary man survived unscathed. That autumn witnessed the first Confederate invasion of the north, when Robert E. Lee moved his army into Maryland. Lee's advance culminated in the Battle of Antietam on 17 September 1862. The Irish Brigade played a prominent role in the fighting, assaulting a Rebel position dominated by a sunken road – a road which would ever afterwards be known as 'Bloody Lane'. Captain William O'Grady of Jeremiah's regiment described the 88th's part in the battle:

We forded the creek, by General Meagher's orders, taking off our shoes (those who could, many were barefoot, and some, like the writer, were so footsore that they had not been able to take off their shoes, or what remained of them, for a week), to wring out their socks, so as not to encumber the men in active movements, and every man was required to fill his canteen ... the bullets were whistling over us as we hurried past the general in fours, and at the double-quick formed right into line behind a fence. We were ordered to lie down while volunteers tore down the fence ... then, up on our feet, we charged. The Bloody Lane was witness of the efficacy of buck-and-ball at close quarters. We cleared that and away beyond ... when our ammunition was exhausted, Caldwell's Brigade relieved us, the companies breaking into fours for the passage as if on parade ... by some misunderstanding, part of the Sixty-third New York with their colors were massed on our right for a few minutes, during which our two right companies, C and F, were simply slaughtered, suffering a third of the entire casualties of the regiment.[76]

Jeremiah Durick was one of the unfortunate members of Company C caught in this exposed position. He was killed on the field, one of thirty-five men of the regiment who lost their lives as a result of Antietam. Another sixty-seven were wounded as the 88th New York lost, according to Lieutenant-Colonel Patrick Kelly, 'one-third of our men'. In total the Battle of Antietam resulted in almost 23,000 casualties; a single day's military losses that have never been exceeded in all of American history.[77]

In April of 1867 Jeremiah's father Timothy, now 66 years old, sought to secure a pension based on his son's service. His initial efforts in this regard had been unsuccessful, and so he had to make a choice that faced a number of elderly parents of Union servicemen in Ireland. In order to press his claim he had to make the journey to the United States, where he could be assessed to prove that he was no longer physically able to work.[78]

Timothy made his way across the Atlantic to Vermont. There he was welcomed by old friends from Nenagh, including John Gleason and John Barrett, with whom Jeremiah had lived. They gave statements to show that Jeremiah had provided upwards of $100 per year in support of his father. They claimed that Timothy was very poor, with no property of any kind except his personal clothing, and no income or means of support except that which he earned by manual labour. Dr Backer Hayes, in the city of Rutland, examined Timothy, reporting that he suffered from long-standing hypertrophy of the heart, which had caused rheumatism in his back, right arm and shoulder. In the physician's view, these ailments rendered Timothy 'entirely incapable of earning a subsistence by manual labor', and this had been the case for at least five or six years. The old man's efforts were successful, and his pension application was approved in March 1868.[79]

Timothy remained in Vermont for some time after securing his pension, living in Castleton. In November 1868 he sought to have his pension backdated to the time of his son's death in 1862, although it is unclear if he was successful. Eventually he decided to return home to Tipperary. By 1883 he was collecting his pension in the local post office. Despite his ailments he lived well into his eighties, eventually passing away near Nenagh in 1887 at the age of 86. His son's service, which had ended in Maryland on America's bloodiest day, helped to provide vital financial assistance for an elderly man living out his final years a world away, in rural County Tipperary.[80]

THE GALVINS AND HORANS: ROSCOMMON, KERRY AND MASSACHUSETTS

 'He sacrificed his life … volunteering to nurse his comrades.'[81]

Long before the outbreak of the American Civil War in 1861, the armed forces had been an attractive option for Irish emigrants. At one point in the 1850s, as much as 60 per cent of the United States military was made up of Irish-Americans. Little changed following the war's conclusion, as the army still offered the prospect of continuous employment and a measure of security. Not all the Irishmen who saw service in the immediate post-war period were veterans; many had chosen not to volunteer during the Civil War, or had arrived just after its conclusion. This did not mean that they faced no dangers, however. As the families of two Irishmen found out in 1866, the war years had not held a monopoly on soldiers' deaths.[82]

Denis Horan grew up in the family home at No. 5, Boherbee in Tralee, County Kerry. One of ten children, he needed to earn a living from a young age; his father Edmond was incapacitated by a long-term illness and one of his brothers suffered from a severe intellectual disability (he was referred to as an 'imbecile' in contemporary parlance). At the age of 11, Denis went to work as an assistant in Tralee's mineral-water factory, where he earned 9 shillings a week. The young man didn't pocket any of the earnings himself: he gave them to his mother Mary instead, so they could benefit all the family. If Denis needed anything, his mother bought it for him. The young man grew to adulthood in the factory, spending a total of thirteen years as an employee there. Finally, when he was 24 years old, Denis decided that he might be able to earn more money elsewhere to help his parents and six younger siblings. He headed for America, emigrating to Boston around the beginning of 1866.[83]

A little over 200km north of the Horans, William Galvin and his family made their lives in and around that part of Athlone to the west of the River Shannon, then part of County Roscommon. The Galvins rented a small farm of about 5 acres, which helped to support William's mother Catharine, his sisters Margaret and Maria, and brothers Thomas and Martin. As with the Horans, the Galvins could not rely on the support of their father, albeit for different reasons. Patrick Galvin had left his wife and children for America sometime in the late 1840s, where he got work on a boat plying its trade between Albany and Boston. Patrick never wrote home, and never sent any money back for his family. They received word that he had moved to New Orleans, but that was the last they ever heard of him. Having for all intents and purposes abandoned his family, he apparently died in Louisiana in the mid-1850s. Like Denis Horan, William Galvin was 24 years old when he decided his future lay in the United States. He left Athlone for Boston a few years before the Tralee man, arriving there in February of 1863.[84]

As with so many other Irish emigrants, both Denis Horan and William Galvin went to Boston because other members of their local communities in Ireland were resident there. At least three of Denis' siblings had made their homes in the United States, but it was his maternal uncle, a resident of Boston from the early 1850s, with whom he seems to have linked up. Denis soon found employment in an oil and guano factory where he spent six weeks before taking a position as a longshoreman, where he would work for the next six months. William also had family in Boston as his brother Thomas had emigrated around the same time, if not on the same boat. The brothers went to live in the boarding house of Catherine Curley in Roxbury, who had known both of the brothers in Athlone. Among the other residents was another Athlone native, Mary Watson, who had been the Galvins' neighbour in Ireland. Having arrived in 1863, William could have elected to join the army there and then. Indeed his brother Thomas did enlist in the autumn of 1863, sending $100 of his bounty money home to Ireland. Instead, William decided to continue in agriculture, taking up a job on a farm in Brookline, where he was able to earn $20 a month. William lived with Catherine Curley and Mary Watson for the next two years, often sharing with them his plans and his hopes to send money back to his family in Athlone.[85]

With the effective end of the American Civil War in 1865, William Galvin's brother Thomas came home from the army. Finding work more difficult to procure due to the flood of recently demobilised troops and perhaps influenced by his brother's military experience, William decided to try life as a career soldier. The Athlone man enrolled in Boston on 5 August 1865 and became a private in Company C of the 2nd Battalion, 11th United States Infantry. He was joined in the same unit by his brother, who elected to once again return to martial life. By the autumn of 1866 the Galvin brothers were part of the military garrison in Camp Grant, Richmond, Virginia, former capital of the Confederacy. Despite the fact that the war was over, the brothers would find that death could still stalk the land.[86]

On 3 July 1866 a recruit in Fort Columbus, New York Harbor, fell ill. The new soldier, originally from Minnesota, had been in the army for only three days. He was quickly taken to the post hospital, where he was joined within an hour by another patient. Both had the unmistakable symptoms of cholera, likely contracted as part of a wider outbreak then underway in the city. This was the first case of an epidemic of cholera cases that swept through different US army posts in the last six months of 1866. The Galvins saw the first man drop with the disease at their Camp Grant base on 12 August. In total, 271 soldiers contracted the illness in Richmond over the following weeks – 215 in September alone. When it was over, 113 of the garrison were dead. William Galvin was among those victims, dying on 17 September. Tragically for his mother in Athlone, another of the men who succumbed at Camp Grant was his brother Thomas.[87]

Shortly after the deaths of the Galvin brothers in Richmond, Kerryman Denis Horan followed in their footsteps by enlisting in the army at Boston. On 29 October 1866 he became a trooper in the 8th United States Cavalry. His unit was then serving in the west, and to join it Denis had to travel by ship around South America, bound for San Francisco. His first stop was New York, where he joined other recruits and set sail on 20 November. For nearly a month of the passage all went well, but as they headed up the San Juan river in Nicaragua, on 16 December, cholera broke out. They arrived in La Virgin on Lake Nicaragua four days later, where they quickly established a hospital. Denis helped to care for the sick, but soon became one of the fifty-four men who contracted the disease. He died on 26 December. Denis and the twenty-six other soldiers who succumbed in Nicaragua were the last men to die in the army during the six-month cholera outbreak. Immediately after Denis' death, another group of passengers arrived in La Virgin carrying civilians from California who were making the same journey, but in the opposite direction. Some of them also contracted the disease, and a number died the following January. Their fate was recorded by one of their fellow passengers, who was spared the sickness – a certain writer by the name of Mark Twain.[88]

The cholera epidemic that swept through the army during the last six months of 1866 led to the deaths of over 1,200 men. Its impact travelled all the way back to Athlone and Tralee. In the years that followed, Catharine Galvin would continue to dwell on the west side of Athlone, living in Baylough and Connaught Street. Her surviving children were divided between Boston and Ireland, and were able to provide her with only limited support due to both their married circumstances and the nature of their work (as labourers and domestic servants). The pension which she received based on William's service would prove invaluable in the years ahead.

In Tralee, Mary Horan had further trials ahead as she sought a pension for Denis' service. Her relatives in Boston arranged for her dependent mother's application to go through a Massachusetts solicitor, who appears to have defrauded her of some money. The issue was eventually resolved, and like Catharine in Athlone, Mary was able to rely on her US pension for more than twenty years. All that changed in 1893, when they were informed of the new Act of Congress that effectively meant their payments would be stopped. As we saw with Maria Ridgway in a previous chapter, women like Mary Horan and Catharine Galvin had little option but to write letters of appeal. Mary – by this date living on the Mill Road in Killorglin – opted to write to the commissioners, and she was clearly unhappy:[89]

I received a circular stating that my pension was stopped, but being very ill I was unable to answer before now. I have received the pension since January 27th 1866 and any government that was in office since then never interfered with my pension until now. I am sure my papers and affidavits must have been lost or burned in the disaster at Washington or this government would not have interfered with me more than others.

It is through the death of my son, Denis Horan I received the pension. He sacrificed his life at Virgin Bay, Nicaragua by volunteering to nurse his comrades in an outbreak of cholera.

I received a letter of condolence from Washington and a form of application for a pension. I satisfied the government in all information they required of me and they granted me the pension. I had neither land, stock or property and my husband was old and infirm. The doctors certificate of his ailment ought to be at the pension office in Washington.

He is now 87 years old and I am 73 years. So we are unable to work for our living. Six of my children died since my son Denis left me and there are three of my children in the United States who do not write to me or give me any help. So it is a great hardship to deprive us of a pension now when we are old and helpless. My husband or myself were never in America.[90]

Catharine Galvin was among the threatened Irish pensioners who wrote directly to Grover Cleveland, President of the United States. She begged:

… leave to state for your kind consideration that your humble applicant was awarded a pension under the act of congress approved July 14th 1862 eight dollars per month for the loss of her son William Galvin who died of his wounds received in action while serving with the Union Army.[91]

Given that William had not fought during the Civil War, nor died of wounds received in action, this statement is clearly incorrect. Perhaps Catharine, who was then 86 years old, had become confused about her son's time in the military, or perhaps the text of her appeal was composed for her by a friend or relative unfamiliar with all the details. In any event, Catharine ended her appeal with a request that it would meet with the president's 'kind consideration' in 'not depriving her of her support the few remaining days that providence had left to her in this world'.[92]

Although both women's petitions were initially turned down, eventually the Irish pensions were reinstated. Unfortunately, this came too late for Mary Horan, who had passed away in the interim. On 16 January 1894, her husband Edmond took up his pen:

> As I have now grown old and unable to do any work for a considerable time past the withdrawal of the pension placed me in very needy circumstances indeed. Her [Mary's] long illness and the necessary expenses attendant on it brought me so low in this world that were it not for aid received from some kind neighbours, I would have been under the painful necessity of getting a pauper's coffin for my later dear wife. I hope you will see the great necessity as well as the justice of relieving me in my present distress by sending me the amount of her doctor's bill and funeral expenses which were £26, the greater portion of which is yet due me.
>
> I have only to say that if you aid me you will have my good wishes and those of my son who is an imbecile and my only companion in this world now ...[93]

Irish associations with the United States military, strong both before and during the American Civil War, remained in place in the years that followed the conflict. Many young Irish emigrants continued to see the army as a means of securing a stable income in an often-volatile labour market. But as the stories of Denis Horan and William Galvin demonstrate, such a life still carried with it inherent risk. Their deaths during the 1866 cholera outbreak did help to secure their ageing parents in Ireland with a source of income over the next three decades, though they were forced to fight hard for their reinstatement after 1893. Vital as these payments were, it is unlikely they assuaged the extreme sense of loss that both families experienced when disease carried away their emigrant sons.

TWO
Community and
Society

The widows' and dependents' files offer us much more than details on the American Civil War. In their pages can be found the social history of families across decades. In 'Community and Society' we see how chain migration could influence people from the same parish across multiple generations, or tempt groups of skilled local workers to relocate across the Atlantic. We follow the lives of families from their origins in Ireland – where some suffered personal loss in the Great Famine – to new but not necessarily better futures in the United States. Emigration did not mean an abandonment of those at home. Duties and obligations remained, particularly when it came to the remittance of money to help those who had remained behind in Ireland. We see the seemingly endless struggle of some families to escape a cycle of poverty and reliance on charity, while others suffered the consequences of domestic violence, alcohol abuse, bigamy and perceived sexual misconduct.

THE O'DONNELLS: DONEGAL AND PENNSYLVANIA

 'The Congressmen from this City … all know me well.'[1]

When Charles O'Donnell emigrated with his parents from Donaghmore, County Donegal to Philadelphia, he was travelling what was already a well-worn path. Decades before Charles's birth, another Donaghmore man had journeyed to the City of Brotherly Love, where he created a link between Pennsylvania's textile industry and his part of north-west Ireland; a link that led to significant chain migration. The pension file relating to Charles O'Donnell's military service in the United States Marine Corps includes significant details regarding these connections, revealing just how important they were for Donegal families on both sides of the Atlantic.[2]

Charles O'Donnell was born in the townland of Tievebrack, Donaghmore, County Donegal around the year 1844. More than sixty years earlier, in 1779, a man called Dennis Kelly had been born in the same parish. Dennis had lost his father at a young age, which led him to seek employment in the linen trade, a major industry in Ulster. Despite humble beginnings, he appears to have been a natural businessman. By the time he reached his late twenties, he had saved enough money to take his wife and child to a new life in America. Arriving in Philadelphia on 18 June 1806, he soon had his family loaded on a Conestoga wagon and headed west towards the frontier. They were only a few miles into their journey when Dennis made what would prove a momentous decision. One of their travelling companions seems to have been somewhat foul-mouthed; indeed his profanity was so extreme it outraged the Irishman, who promptly hauled his family off the wagon, returning to Philadelphia in disgust. Deciding to abandon the idea of settling on the frontier, he instead found work on a nearby milldam. By 1808 he was back at what he knew best, making his own 'bagging' cloth for the linen industry. He soon began to accumulate substantial wealth, which allowed him to buy up mills and enter the horse- and cattle-breeding business. So successful was he that the community that grew up around one of his enterprises – Clinton Mills on Darby Creek – would become known as Kellyville. By the 1860s, Dennis was a major contractor for the Union war effort, owned 800 acres in Philadelphia, Montgomery and Delaware counties, and operated no less than six mills. His success would have a lasting impact on his home parish in Ireland.[3]

Dennis Kelly employed a large number of Irish emigrants in his linen and other industries, and was also keen to look after other family members from Donegal. Most notable among these was his nephew Charles Kelly, born in Ardnagannagh townland, Donaghmore in 1808. Charles emigrated to Philadelphia and joined his uncle in 1821. He soon became Dennis' protégé and proved an adept businessman in his own right. By the outbreak of the American Civil War, Charles was also a major textile manufacturer and supplier to the Union army, and his success in turn created yet more opportunities for Donegal emigrants.[4]

It was the achievements of the Kellys that led the future US Marine Charles O'Donnell to America. His family were related to the textile magnates, as were a number of other families who left Donaghmore for Pennsylvania. Charles' parents John and Jane O'Donnell (*née* Kelly) had taken their family from Donegal to Philadelphia in the late 1840s. Although events such as the Famine may have played a part in their decision to emigrate, their destination was undoubtedly decided based on Jane's family connections – Dennis Kelly was her uncle (and by extension Charles O'Donnell's great-uncle). On leaving Ireland, they had the added security of knowing a number of other Tievebrack relatives were also living in Pennsylvania. The 1860 Census found the family in Precinct 3 of Philadelphia's 24th Ward, where their reliance on the Kelly textile empire was apparent:

Name	Age	Profession	Born
D. O'Donnell	24	Manufacturer of Wool Goods	Ireland
John O'Donnell	60	Laborer	Ireland
Jane O'Donnell	50	–	Ireland
Edward O'Donnell	23	Spinner	Ireland
John O'Donnell	21	Weaver	Ireland
Margaret O'Donnell	18	Weaver	Ireland
Charles O'Donnell	16	Wool Carder	Ireland
James O'Donnell	13	–	Ireland

Catharine O'Donnell	10	-	Pennsylvania
Sarah O'Donnell	8	-	Pennsylvania
Alice O'Donnell	6	-	Pennsylvania
Dennis O'Donnell	3	-	Pennsylvania

O'Donnell Family in the 1860 US Federal Census.[5]

In the 1860 Census, John and Jane O'Donnell's family were living with a 'D. O'Donnell' – almost certainly Dominick O'Donnell, another relative. Dominick and Edward O'Donnell were leasing a cotton and woollen mill in the 24th Ward, the mill in which all the O'Donnell family worked, including the later US Marine Charles, who in 1860 was a 16-year-old wool carder. The only member of the family not employed by the mill was the patriarch John, who was recorded as a labourer. However, in reality by 1860 John was unable to work. He had been struck by a violent sickness the previous year, which affected him in both mind and body. Indeed it so devastated him that he was admitted to the Pennsylvania Hospital for the Insane on 6 May 1859. Although he was released from that institution on 10 August, he was never able to undertake physical labour again. It was this disability that ultimately led him to seek support based upon his son's military service.[6]

That military service had begun on 22 July 1862, when 19-year-old Charles O'Donnell had enlisted in Philadelphia as a private in the United States Marine Corps. He was described as 5 feet 7½ inches tall, with dark eyes, dark hair and a dark complexion. On 7 August he wrote to his mother, who was concerned that he may not be getting everything he needed in the military. He let her know that he expected to get some leave in Philadelphia before he went to sea. Charles assured her that he was enjoying his new career, and was getting 'plenty to eat', and that 'every one hase [sic] a bed to himself'. He was even able to get to church every Sunday. He signed off by reminding her to 'right so[o]n and dond [sic] forget'. Charles was stationed in the Marine Barracks in Washington DC awaiting his posting. Two weeks after he wrote the letter, on 23 August, he began to suffer with a pain in his head. For several days he 'complained of little else', before his symptoms suddenly worsened and it became clear he had typhoid fever. He was moved to the Marine Hospital while his mother rushed to get to his beside from Philadelphia. She arrived in time to spend the last thirty-six hours of his life with him – Charles passed away on 9 September 1862.[7]

By the late 1870s, Charles' father John, now living at 2026 Christian Street, was struggling to make ends meet. His wife Jane had died on 27 April 1874 and he had to turn to his son's United States Marine Corps record in search of a pension. Extended-family members living in Philadelphia – all of whom were from Donaghmore Parish – rallied around John to help him secure the pension. Along the way they revealed the extent of the ties between rural Donegal and some of Pennsylvania's major textile production industries. John O'Donnell's first cousin, Mary, provided one of the affidavits. On 16 June 1879 she recorded that she was then 70 years of age and had emigrated to Philadelphia about thirty years before. She related how:

> … the said John O'Donnell and the said Jane Kelly and myself were reared in the same townland Teevebrack [Tievebrack], I knew them well, I remember when the said John and the said Jane were married, they were living in the said townland at the time, their marriage was known to all their friends and neigbors. I know they lived and cohabited there as man and wife and several children were born to them.[8]

John's daughters (Charles' sisters) Maggie and Catharine also gave statements. Catharine told how she only had partial use of her limbs as a result of an accident in her youth, which impacted her ability to aid in the support of her father. They also described how John had not been able to earn above $15 per year since his 1859 illness. Another Donaghmore family in Philadelphia who sought to help John O'Donnell were the Sharkeys. One of the Sharkeys noted in his statement that he was also from the same townland of Tievebrack in County Donegal. He related the O'Donnell family's close ties to the Kelly textile trade (both Dennis Kelly and Charles Kelly were by now dead). For good measure he highlighted the extended family's political connections, noting that the 'Congressmen from this city … all know me well', providing an indication of how high the Donegal family's stock had risen. He described how the Sharkeys were also related to both the Kellys and the O'Donnells; Dennis Kelly's mother and Sharkey's grandmother had been sisters. More than that, he also set out the sacrifices the Donegal Sharkeys had laid at the feet of the Union – one brother had died in the 1870s as a result of a disease contracted in the Union army; a second had fought as a draft substitute, while a third had been serving on the *USS Hatteras* when she was sunk by the famed Confederate raider *CSS Alabama* off Texas in 1863. Captured, he was afterwards deposited in Kingston, Jamaica.[9]

The efforts of Philadelphia's Donaghmore emigrants helped to secure John O'Donnell a US pension based on his unfortunate son Charles' brief war service. He was awarded a payment of $8 per month backdated to the date of death of his wife on 27 April 1874. The level of documentation he had to provide in order to receive that pension opens a window into the stream of emigration from Tievebrack, County Donegal to Philadelphia; emigration which was in large part due to the achievements of one man – Dennis Kelly. Kelly's success story opened the door for generations of his nineteenth-century relatives and friends to gain work upon their arrival in America, and it also ultimately led to the service of a number of these Donegal men in the Union military during the American Civil War.[10]

THE KEEGANS: WICKLOW AND PENNSYLVANIA

 'I send my love to you all.'[11]

The Keegan story begins in Bray, County Wicklow. It was there, on 11 September 1848, that Joseph Keegan and Mary Burns became man and wife. The couple were in their early twenties at the time, and were embarking on married life in the midst of the Great Famine that was devastating large parts of the island. Joseph had trained as a mason, but despite his having a trade he and his wife still found life tough. Their first child, Margaret, arrived on 3 January 1850, and her birth presaged a new chapter in the young family's lives. Joseph and Mary had likely taken the decision to leave Wicklow sometime in 1849, a year in which their hometown of Bray suffered sixty-eight deaths as a result of cholera. That they didn't go until 1850 was likely down to Mary's pregnancy. Once baby Margaret was old enough, the trio headed north to Dublin where they took ship for Liverpool, the great gateway port for many Irish emigrants to the United States.[12]

The Keegans left Liverpool aboard the SS *William Penn*, taking their place in steerage. All their possessions for the start of their new life were packed into two trunks. On 9 July 1850 they arrived in Philadelphia, the city that would ultimately become their home. They were part of a huge influx of immigrants there during the Famine years – by 1850 there were 72,000 people who had been born in Ireland living in the City of Brotherly Love. Before long, Joseph and Mary's family began to grow. Matthew Robert was born on 16 December 1851 and baptised in the church of the Assumption. The family may have had a short-lived effort to make a future in Ohio, as their next child, Frances Josephine, appears to have been baptised in the church of St Thomas, Cincinnati on 9 March 1856. However, by the time of the 1860 Census they were back in Philadelphia's 9th Ward, where the family were enumerated on 25 June 1850. Joseph was recorded as working as a labourer.[13]

During the 1860s the Keegans had their home at 1515 Melloy Street, between 15th and 16th and Market and Chestnut. When the war broke out, Joseph elected not to enlist, likely hoping that more opportunities would come his way at home. However, something had changed by late 1863. Perhaps drawn by the large bounties then on offer for joining up, or due to the seasonality of his work (labourers often found it difficult to get work in the winter), the 37-year-old Wicklow man decided to become a soldier. At the time the Union League Association – a patriotic society formed in 1862 to support the Union – were recruiting their 4th regiment for the front. On 8 December 1863 Joseph presented himself at one of their recruiting stations and was signed on by Lieutenant Egbert for three years' service. In so doing he became eligible for a bounty of $300, $25 of which was paid upfront. On 13 January 1864 Joseph mustered in as a private in Company A of the 4th Union League Regiment, otherwise known as the 183rd Pennsylvania Infantry. His first weeks of military life were experienced almost on his doorstep, as the unit was initially based at Frankfield Depot on Broad Street, only a few minutes from the Keegan home. It is probable that Joseph had an opportunity to see his wife and family while the 183rd completed its organisation. Then, in March 1864, they marched out of Philadelphia, bound for the Army of the Potomac on Virginia's Rapidan River.[14]

On 4 May 1864 the Army of the Potomac crossed the Rapidan to begin the Overland Campaign. The 183rd Pennsylvania had joined the famous 2nd Corps under Winfield Scott Hancock, forming part of Nelson Miles' 1st Brigade of Francis Barlow's 1st Division (the 2nd Brigade of this division was the Irish Brigade). Joseph Keegan's career as a soldier on campaign lasted a little under five days – considerably longer than those of many other recent recruits to the Army of the Potomac in 1864. At around 10 p.m. on the evening of 3 May he had broken camp with his comrades at Stevensburg, Virginia, marching towards the enemy. He crossed the Rapidan at Ely's Ford the next day, arriving on the Fredericksburg Road that afternoon and encamping on the old Chancellorsville battlefield. One wonders what he made of the sights that surrounded him from the harsh fighting of a year before. The next day, General Robert E. Lee's Confederate Army of Northern Virginia barrelled into General Grant's advancing men in the Wilderness, commencing the first major battle of the campaign. Although not seriously engaged, that was the day Joseph experienced being under fire for the first time, as his regiment continued their move through the wooded landscape from which the Wilderness took its name. The battle raged again on the following day, with Joseph among those ordered to fortify the left of the Army of the Potomac's line. He spent 7 May on picket duty, before again resuming the advance the next day. They were halted for rations near Todd's Tavern that afternoon when the Confederates attacked. Joseph's regiment formed in a field beside the Irish Brigade to fight off the advance, losing four men in the process. This was his last full day at the front. The next day, the 183rd Pennsylvania marched on to the Po, crossing that river at about sundown. Although his regiment was not engaged, 9 May 1864 was the day Joseph was captured by the Rebels. Perhaps he was taken while on picket duty, or had become disoriented or lost on the march. Whatever the circumstances, his time at the front was over.[15]

Joseph Keegan was taken south as a prisoner of war. Eventually he and around 1,400 other Union prisoners began a two-week journey to Camp Sumter, Georgia, the soon-to-be infamous site that is now better known as Andersonville. It was originally opened in February 1864, and by June more than 26,000 prisoners had been placed in an enclosed stockade designed to accommodate just 10,000. Andersonville was in existence for some fourteen months. During that time almost 13,000 of the 45,000 Union prisoners incarcerated there died. But Joseph Keegan wasn't one of them. In an intriguing story of survival, his pension file contains a letter that the Bray man wrote home to his wife, from within the confines of the prison:

Camp Sumter, Andersonville, Georgia

Dear Wife, I write you these few lines hoping you and children are well as I am at present thank God. Dear Wife I was taken prisoner on the 9th at Spotsylvania I was in 2 battles and 2 skirmishes and came out safe without a scratch thank God I am well in health and strength I have not being sick for one hour since I left Philadelphia thank God. I am comfortably situated and have quite enough to eat having nothing to do here but keep myself clean and there is opportunity enough to do so as there is a good stream running through the camp. There was fourteen hundred prisoners of us brought here the one time it took 2 weeks to get here, we are anxious to be exchanged. It is very warm down here. I send my love to you all write soon and tell me how you are getting along. Direct your letter to Joseph Keegan, Camp Sumpter [Sumter], Andersonville, Georgea [sic], prisoner of war.[16]

Although undated, this was likely written in late May or early June, given the time it would have taken Joseph to get to Andersonville. By then things were just starting to deteriorate in the prison, a reality that contrasts with the relatively upbeat tone of his letter. Perhaps Joseph had little idea of what was to come, and felt confident that his stay would be short. Maybe he wanted to put on a brave face for his family. But there is one other factor that likely played into the general tone that Joseph took in his correspondence – he knew the Confederates would read it before they decided whether to send it on or not. No doubt anxious to let his family know he was still alive, did Joseph downplay the situation in order to get the letter past the camp guards? A former Union POW in Andersonville, Dorence Atwater, described how the mail system in the camp worked:

A large box with lock and key was stationed near one of the gates, inside the stockade. Every few days the prisoners were told by the rebels that a mail was going to be sent north, and all those who wished to write to their friends must have their letters in the mail box by a stated time. Men traded their clothing and rations for bits of paper, envelopes, and postage stamps. The rebels claimed it was necessary to have two envelopes, the first containing the letter addressed to the party for whom it was designed, with a three-cent United States postage stamp. These letters were taken from the mail box to Wirz's [camp commandant] headquarters and examined. A few letters were forwarded to Richmond to give a color of appearance that the letters were duly sent, but most of them were destroyed, under the pretext that they contained information detrimental to the southern confederacy. Our three-cent postage stamps were worth a dollar apiece in rebel money, so that the rebels realized a dollar and ten cents for each letter written by our prisoners.[17]

Clearly Joseph was fortunate to have his letter delivered, but it doesn't appear to have arrived in Philadelphia until January 1865. Although Mary probably wasn't aware of it then, Joseph was already dead. Another soldier of his company, George Neill, later told her what had happened. George had been taken prisoner at Spotsylvania on 11 May, and on being escorted to the rear met other men from the 183rd, including Joseph. Afterwards they were 'constantly together'. George travelled to Andersonville with him, and was able to tell Mary that in September 1864 they were among a group moved to Florence, South Carolina, where a new prisoner stockade had just been constructed. Leaving Andersonville did not mean there were better times ahead. Another former Union POW who experienced both Andersonville and Florence, John McElroy, said of the latter place:

… the physical condition of the prisoners confined there had been greatly depressed by their long confinement [at Andersonville] … I think also that all who experienced confinement in the two places are united in pronouncing Florence to be, on the whole, much the worse place, and more fatal to life.[18]

Very shortly after they arrived at Florence, Joseph became sick, and in October he was sent to the camp hospital. George, still in the main camp, tried to keep track of his progress. When two soldiers of the 2nd Delaware Infantry who had been in the infirmary came back to camp about two weeks later, they told him that Joseph hadn't made it. George himself survived to be exchanged, ultimately returning to the 183rd around July 1865, when he was promoted corporal just days before mustering out.[19]

Mary Keegan began the process of applying for her pension in 1865. In so doing she provided further evidence of the close ties that Irish people maintained with those from their home localities after emigration, something which is a near constant feature of the files. The now 42-year-old widow called on Michael Boyland (Boland?) and Ann Kelly to give statements in Philadelphia. Both of them were able to say that they had known Mary 'all her life', since they had been children in Bray. Both had also been present at Joseph and Mary's wedding in Bray in 1848, and they recorded how their close relationship had been maintained after they had all moved to the United States. Mary ultimately received a pension based on her husband's service. She died on Cuthbert Avenue in the 9th Ward on 31 March 1880. The Keegan story is a fine example of just how much detail can be breathed into the lives of ordinary Famine-era emigrants when using the widow's pension files as a starting point. It also offers a rare opportunity to explore how soldiers tried to communicate with loved ones from the most notorious prison camp of the American Civil War.[20]

THE DELANEYS: LAOIS AND PENNSYLVANIA

 'He used to speak of you in the most affectionate manner and says it was you that taught him how to say prayers …'[21]

Not all Irish emigrants to nineteenth-century America were headed for the major cities. Some, especially those with specific skill sets, hoped to find a way of life in the United States that was similar to what they had known at home. Such was the case for many families around those parts of Kilkenny and Laois that specialised in coal mining. When they crossed the Atlantic, they travelled to the regions where their talents were in demand – places like the coalfields of Pennsylvania. One such family was the Delaneys.[22]

Thomas and Catharine Delaney were married in Rathaspick, County Laois by the Revd Father Grace in 1824. Samuel Lewis described the region's most notable asset in the 1830s:

> Here are the extensive coal mines of Doonane, worked by a company; they are drained by a steam engine, and supply stone coal to all parts of the surrounding country, which is principally conveyed by carriers. There are about five other works in the same range: the shafts are first sunk through clay, then succeeds a hard green rock, and next slaty strata, in contact with which is the coal: it is worked on either side by regular gangs, each member having a specific duty: the number of each gang is about thirty, and when the pit is double worked there are sixty; each crew works ten hours, but they are particularly observant of every kind of holiday.[23]

Although not explicitly stated in his pension file, we know from Thomas' subsequent history that he almost certainly spent decades as a miner in the locality. Through their years in Ireland he and Catharine went on to have twelve children, eight of whom (four boys and four girls) survived to adulthood. Then, in 1854, the couple decided to take their family to America. When they arrived, they quickly made their way to Schuylkill County, the heart of Pennsylvania's coal region.[24]

The Delaneys were joining large numbers of Irish miners in Schuylkill who were working the anthracite coal mines scattered throughout the area. They likely knew many of them – a large proportion of the Irish miners in 1850s Schuylkill had emigrated from the coalfields around Castlecomer, County Kilkenny, only a few miles from where the Delaneys had been married. As a result, the family were surrounded by former neighbours, work colleagues and friends from Ireland in their new home.[25]

Almost immediately upon their arrival, Thomas went to work in the industry he knew so well. He became a miner extracting coal from the

Black Heath vein, but within two years of the family's arrival they already faced a major setback. An explosion in the mine blinded Thomas in one eye, leaving him with only partial sight in the other. Although he was still able to work, his capacity to provide for his family would steadily diminish over the following years.[26]

The 1860 Census found the family in the largely Irish Cass Township in Schuylkill County, where Thomas and his eldest boys were all recorded as miners. One of the youngest, Thomas Jr, was then 15 years old and was just setting out on his mining career. Sometime in 1860 he began work in the nearby Forestville mine. The Delaneys were among the 1,590 miners who called Cass Township home at the time, living in a location that has been described as 'the most turbulent area in the anthracite region throughout the 1860s'. Townships like Cass would develop a notorious reputation during the Civil War.[27]

Miners were not afraid to organise themselves in order to achieve what they viewed as their working entitlements. This was nothing new – it was likely a propensity for organising themselves that Samuel Lewis was alluding to when he noted in 1837 that the Irish miners were 'particularly observant of every kind of holiday'. By 1862, the miners in Cass Township were fed up with their conditions and many of them went on strike in search of higher wages. In an effort to keep the mines functioning, the militia were called in to restart the mine pumps, but were forced to withdraw when they were attacked by rioters. Eventually over 200 troops had to be summoned to quieten the situation. Not long afterwards, the Militia Act of 17 July 1862 authorised the implementation of state drafts to supply the Union with badly needed men. Again Cass Township responded. Up to 1,000 miners marched to a nearby town, where they stopped a trainload of draftees heading towards Harrisburg; again troops were needed to restore order. The miners were as angry with their employers as they were with the prospect of the draft. In December 1862, up to 200 armed men from Cass Township attacked the Phoenix Colliery, beating up a number of men connected with the mine's operations. The following March, when enrolling officers arrived in Schuylkill to record the names of men in the area for the Enrollment Act draft, they were driven off. One of the officers recalled how 'it was uncomfortably warm, as the Irish had congregated, and, as we found, were determined to resist, and did by giving us four shots from a revolver (luckily none hitting us)'. Disturbances continued in the region throughout much of the war, and although they were by no means restricted to the Irish community, the Irish were frequently singled out as those culpable. Often exaggerated and almost hysterical reports were being sent to Washington. In July 1863 Brigadier-General Whipple reported that 'the miners of Cass Township, near Pottsville, have organized to resist the draft, the number of 2,500 or 3,000 armed men'. Eventually, the provost marshal sent officials backed with troops to seize the payrolls of mine operators, so their employees' names could be added to the draft. Those restless years of the 1860s would witness the continued rise in Schuylkill County of a secret organisation known as the Molly Maguires, who would later dramatically leap to national prominence due to their associations with violent acts in the region during the 1870s.[28]

The Delaneys found themselves in the midst of these turbulent times. We don't know what their views were, but it would seem likely that they shared many of their fellow miners' concerns regarding their employers and the draft. Either way, they bore witness to life in one of the most agitated areas of the Union during the Civil War. But they also had problems of a more personal nature to contend with. Chief among them was the death of Catharine Delaney, who passed away on 14 March 1862 in Minersville. Then, after four years in the Forestville Coal Company, Thomas Jr was enrolled in the Union army at Philadelphia on 15 October 1863. The young Laois man became a private in Company F of the newly formed 19th Pennsylvania Cavalry. That winter he and his comrades were stationed in Union City, Tennessee. In January 1865 they had to endure picket duty in what were bitterly cold conditions, the weather being so severe that it froze one of the men to death. Thomas Jr did not escape the conditions – both his feet were so badly frozen that he was sent to a hospital in Mound City, Illinois, his military career seemingly over. That February he wrote home:

US General Hospital
Mound City Feb 9/64

Dear Father,

I now think it near time that I would let you hear from me and how I am. I am here in the hospital with me feet pretty badly frozen, other ways my health is good and I trust in God these few lines will find you in the enjoyment of good health. Let me know when you heard from Dennis how he is getting along. We had pretty bad times of it down here and there was a great [number] of the soldiers frozen one man of or regiment was froze to death. The Regt has now started on an expedition which is to do some thing great. Let me know how is Catherine and Patrick and James. Give them my best love and I want you to send me Katys likeness. I don't know what they will [do] with me here as yet they may discharge me or probably send me to the Invalid Corps. I have not received any pay yet but I expect it about the middle of next month and when I get it I will send it to you. I want you to write to me as soon as you receive this letter.

I will send you all my money except what I want for tobacco. Give my love to brothers and sisters and all inquiring friends and accept of the same yourself. No more at present but remains your,
Affectionate Son,
Thomas Delaney.

PS Let me know if John is home yet. When you write direct your letter as follows

Thomas Delaney
US General Hospital
Mound City Illinois
Ward J Bed No. 17
Write soon.

The Sisters of the Holy Cross, based in Indiana, served as nurses in the Mound City hospital during the war. It was located in a series of warehouses, and each building was designated as a ward, with twenty or thirty men assigned to each. On 22 March 1864, Sister Mary Anne sat down to write the following letter back to Pennsylvania:

US Genl. Hospital
Mound City Illinois
March 22d 1864
Mr. Thomas Delany

Respected Sir,
It is my painful duty to inform you of the death of your son Mr. Thomas
Delany of the 19th Pa. Cav. which sad event took place in this hospital at
four o'clock on yesterday afternoon.

It must be a great consolation to you to hear that he died a happy and
a holy death. He received all the rites of the church and was fortified by
the sacraments in his last moments. He used to speak of you in the most
affectionate manner and says it was you that taught him how to say prayers
and his catechism. I send you a lock of his hair in memory of him. May his
dear soul rest in grace amen. If you write to Dr. H. Wardner the surgeon
in charge of Mound City Hospital he will send you his money or any other
effects he may have had.

Yours very resp.
Sister Mary Anne
A Sister of the Holy Cross.[29]

In 1867, 64-year-old Thomas Delaney Sr was living in Philadelphia when he started the process of applying for a pension based on his deceased son's service. He claimed that all his sons had served in the Union army (it is unclear if this was true or not) and were all now labourers and mechanics.

All his children bar his youngest daughter (14-year-old Catharine) were now married. It seems he had left the mining life in Schuylkill County behind, but was now living in extreme poverty. His application was successful, providing him with a modicum of support in his final years. The Delaney family's story in America was interwoven with some of the most turbulent times in nineteenth-century Pennsylvanian history, but, more importantly for Thomas, these years were also a period of personal loss, of both his wife of four decades and a beloved son.[30]

THE BOWLERS: CORK AND NEW YORK

 'As good a chance to escape as any other …'[31]

Emigration could split families, as husbands and wives often felt they had little option but to leave spouses and children in Ireland as they sought to trailblaze the family's future in the United States. Usually the intention was that funds be sent back across the Atlantic to enable the remainder of the family group to emigrate, but sometimes the longed-for reunification never took place. The American Civil War saw many Irishmen leave their homes to enlist in the federal army, hoping that the bounty money available for service would help to pave the way for their family to follow. One such man was Thomas Bowler, who left his wife and child behind as he sought to secure all their futures by donning Union blue.[32]

One obstacle that Thomas and other emigrants had to surmount when seeking to send money to Ireland was a way of getting it there. Many of the dollars that travelled back during the years of the Civil War did so because of the efforts of the Irish Emigrant Society. Founded as a charitable organisation in 1841 to assist new arrivals from Ireland, it provided important advice to newcomers on where to go, what to do and what to avoid. The society also facilitated the sending of money orders and prepaid passenger tickets from New York to family back in Ireland. In 1850, members of the society petitioned for a bank charter, and on 10 April that year the 'Emigrant Industrial Savings Bank' was born. Its founders envisioned it serving a dual role in 'furnishing the means of safe remittances to the distressed people of Ireland and of distributing in charities whatever of profits may arise therefrom' and 'affording our people a safe deposit for their hard earnings'. In 1850 alone, the modern equivalent of $4.6 million was sent back to Ireland via the society.[33]

The Emigrant Savings Bank was still going strong in 1864. Many men of the Irish Brigade (and indeed other units) put aside money in the bank that spring. Some were veterans, but many others were new recruits, brought into the brigade to refill its depleted ranks. All of them knew that a crucial campaign was coming. One was Captain (soon to be Major) Thomas Touhy of the 63rd New York, who had money deposited on 8 March. He left instructions on who was to receive it in the event of his death – Thomas would be mortally wounded at the Wilderness two months later. Thomas McAndrew, who had enlisted in the 69th New York in November 1863, had his money put away in the bank on 16 April. Like Major Touhy he was wounded less than a month later at the Wilderness, but survived to see the end of the war. Twenty-one-year-old Thomas Blake was not as fortunate. He made his deposit on 9 April, the same day he mustered into the 88th New York. By 12 June he was dead, succumbing to disease in Washington DC.[34]

Another Irish Brigade soldier who was making plans with his money that April was Thomas Bowler. The 35-year-old was also a new soldier, having enlisted in Brooklyn on 26 February 1864. For some reason Thomas chose to join up under an alias, using his mother's maiden name of Murphy. It was under this name that he would be recorded in the 69th New York. Thomas was not among those supporting a family in America. Instead, his wife Ellen (*née* Hubbert) and 6-year-old daughter Abigail were living on the other side of the Atlantic, in Youghal, County Cork. It is probable that Thomas was paving the way for his family to join him and he likely hoped that the large financial incentives on offer for enlistment in the spring of 1864 would hasten the arrival of his family. However, Thomas' first problem was how to get the money home to Ireland. Unable to get to the Emigrants Saving Bank himself, he entrusted his money to the regimental chaplain, who saw that it got to the bank in New York. Thomas then used Youghal broker Thomas Curtin as an intermediary to get the money to Ellen. Curtin can be found in an 1867 street directory, which lists him as a 'Ship-Broker' on Grattan Street in the Cork town. As April wore on and signs grew that the campaign was about to commence, Thomas became anxious to learn if the money he had sent had arrived in Ireland. On 17 April he wrote this letter to Ellen back in Youghal:

Camp Near Brandy Station
April 17th 1864

My Dear Ellen

I sent some time ago through through [sic] the priest attending this regiment 80 dollars which will I trust bring you 10 pounds of your money I sent it to Thos. Curtin broker in Youghal I hope you will have no difficulty in getting it. I hope you will not neglect answering it as soon as you receive it as it is natural to suppose that any man who sends so large a sum feels uneasy until such time as he receives an answer to it. I like soldiering very well, I do not know the moment we will go to the field of battle their will [be] great fighting this summer but of course I have as good a chance to escape as any other man. I am enlisted for three years or during the war. If it was over in the morning I would be discharged, but their is only a very poor chance of that but God is good and merciful. When you are writing let me know how all the neighbours are. I have no more to say but remain your affecttionate Husband Thomas Bowler.

Let me know how the child is getting on and all other things also let me know how is my brothers and sisters.

Address your letter

Thomas Murphy Company A
69th Regt N.Y.V. 1st Division
2nd Army Corps Washington D C

also let me know how is James Coughlan[35]

Just over two weeks after this letter was written, on 4 May 1864, the Army of the Potomac crossed the Rapidan River to commence the Overland Campaign. Thomas was proved right about the 'great fighting' that the summer would bring. The Irish Brigade was among those units engaged during the Battle of the Wilderness on 5 and 6 May. Their corps commander, Winfield Scott Hancock, would remark of the brigade's actions there that 'although four-fifths of its numbers were recruits, it behaved with great steadiness and gallantry, losing largely in killed and wounded'.[36]

There would be little pause to draw breath over the coming weeks of hard fighting. Back in Youghal, Ellen grew concerned when she heard no further news from Thomas. The weeks turned into months, and eventually even the war itself ended. Still Ellen was unsure as to Thomas' fate. Then, in 1866, a man called Michael Carroll travelled from New York to Youghal to visit his family. He met Ellen there, and told her that he had heard Thomas had been wounded in the war and died in hospital. A few months after that, a Mrs Meaney in New York wrote to her sister in Youghal, one Mrs Ahearne. In the letter Mrs Meaney stated that 'Mrs Bowler['s] husband Tom Bowler was dead … he died in hospital of wounds received in action'. In her application for a pension, Ellen stated her husband's death had occurred after 17 April. She knew this because that was the date of Thomas' last letter to her, the last word she ever had from him. Despite what friends said, there is no evidence to suggest that Thomas had died in hospital of wounds. He was reported missing in action on 7 May 1864, following the Battle of the Wilderness. Two weeks after his final letter to his wife, Thomas had entered the woods of Virginia for what was his first battle – it would seem he never reemerged.[37]

Ellen's pension was finally approved more than four years after her husband's death, on 14 April 1868. In a postscript to their story, Thomas' little girl Abigail would seek a continuation of the pension many years later. Now going by the name Alice, and using her married surname of Lynch, she wrote from Youghal to the commissioner of pensions on 29 August 1890. She stated how her father was 'killed in one of the bloody battles of the war' and how she was the 'only child of the man who lost his life in the service of the United States leaving [her] an orphan unprovided for'. She also cited her own ill health and destitution as reasons she should receive payment, before signing off as 'Alice Lynch, otherwise Bowler, otherwise Murphy'. Her application was refused. The 1911 Census of Ireland records Alice as a 56-year-old charwoman living on Cork Lane, Youghal, with her two sons, Thomas (a fisherman) and Daniel (a farm labourer). Her family story poignantly highlights the efforts that many Irish soldiers went to in order to provide for their families, and how the Civil War could forever shape the lives of those touched by it. Had Thomas Bowler avoided death in Northern Virginia's Wilderness, his little girl may well have been giving her name to a census enumerator in New York in 1910, rather than in Youghal in 1911.[38]

THE MADIGANS: KERRY AND NEW YORK

 'ye have made … faithful promises but slow performances.'[39]

The Madigan family story is one that began in the north Kerry Parish of Rattoo. It was here that, on 21 November 1835, James Madigan and Mary Costello were joined in marriage by Revd F. Collins. Mary could not have imagined at the time where subsequent years would take her. She was destined for a life that would be altered irrevocably by a procession of Famine, emigration, violence and war. Although Mary's experiences must have been far from unique, what is unusual is the extent to which we can piece together fragments of these experiences as a result of the American Civil War.[40]

Initially James and Mary's life in County Kerry developed as they might have expected. They had at least three children who would survive to adulthood: Thomas (born *c.* 1840), James Jr (born *c.* 1841) and Catherine (born *c.* 1845). Their future prospects changed with the failure of the potato crop and the calamity of the Famine, a disaster which James did not survive. He succumbed to 'dropsy' in March 1847, a year so deadly that it is still referred to as 'Black '47'. Dropsy is the common name given to an oedema, or an accumulation of fluid in the body. Nutritional-deficiency diseases such as starvation, marasmus and dropsy accounted for large numbers of deaths during the Famine years.[41]

James and Mary's daughter Catherine later remembered that the family emigrated to America around the year 1850, when she was about 5 years old. No doubt they were relieved to escape the difficult conditions life had brought them in Kerry. Catherine's widowed mother married again in December 1853, wedding a man called Maurice Kennedy. The family moved to Columbus, Ohio, and another child, Maurice Jr, was born there on 16 November 1854. But all was not well in the Kennedy household. Having taken her family out of Famine-ravaged Ireland, Mary now had to deal with yet another trial – a violent husband. Maurice Kennedy was described as an 'habitual drunkard and man of bad character' who was frequently arrested for disturbing the peace. Mary's daughter Catherine felt forced to leave the household due to the 'ill-treatment of her mother'. Finally, after six years of marriage, enduring constant 'ill-treatment and brutality', Mary could take no more and decided to 'seek the protection of her children'. In 1859 her son Thomas, who had stayed in New York and was working as a tinsmith, sent the money his mother needed to flee Columbus and Maurice's violence. Mary never heard from her second husband again. She would later hear rumours that he had died of yellow fever in New Orleans around 1860.[42]

Back in New York, Mary's son Thomas set up his mother with a place to live and got her established with furniture and the other necessaries of life. No doubt due to the abusive nature of the relationship, Mary, encouraged by family and friends, stopped using the Kennedy name of her second husband, and reverted to being called Mary Madigan. One can only imagine the emotional scarring that her life experiences up to this juncture had caused. As 1861 approached, Mary was living with Thomas (and presumably Maurice Jr) at 207 Mott Street in Manhattan. Despite having left Ireland as a boy, Thomas had clearly maintained an interest in the land of his birth. He demonstrated this by becoming a member of the 69th New York State Militia, an overwhelmingly Irish organisation. In 1860 its commander Michael Corcoran achieved notoriety for refusing to parade the regiment on the occasion of the visit of the Prince of Wales. Given the impact of the Famine on Thomas Madigan's family, this was a decision with which he most likely agreed.[43]

When war came in April 1861, the 69th New York State Militia answered the call for three months' service, and headed to Washington DC. Thomas enrolled on 20 April, and by 21 May he and his regiment were occupied in the construction of Fort Seward (later officially named Fort Corcoran) on Arlington Heights. There, Thomas took the opportunity to write to his mother:

> ... we took up our position on Arlington Heights and know [now] we are building a fort to be called Fort Seward it will be a large one and it will overlook the river Potomack [Potomac] and the City of Washington and if the enemy had it they could destroy Washington and Georgetown without losing a man. Dear Mother we are in the center of the enemy and in the enemys state. To day we were sworn in and we expect to be home marching up Broadway about the 9 or 10 of August.[44]

Precisely two months after this letter, on 21 July 1861, the 69th New York State Militia was engaged in the first major battle of the war at Bull Run, Virginia. The fight ended in defeat for the Union. As soldiers – and numerous civilian spectators – fled back towards Washington DC, many Federals wounded were left on the field. Among them was Thomas Madigan, felled by a bullet to the leg in his first engagement. Thomas' limb was amputated, probably by northern surgeons who had volunteered to stay behind with their charges. Meanwhile, back in New York confusion reigned as reports of the defeat filtered through. Newspapers tried to report the losses to those at home, but the fate of many of the captured remained unclear. On 12 August a number of Union surgeons were paroled, and they carried with them into Union lines lists of wounded men still in Confederate hands. When the *New York Irish-American* printed the list in its 24 August issue, one of the names that appeared was Thomas Madigan. It recorded that he had been in Centreville, but he had later been moved to St Mark's Hospital in Richmond. However, these details were already a few days' old. By the time his name appeared in print, Thomas was already dead, having passed away on 21 August. The 69th New York had returned to New York on 27 July, nearly two weeks before Thomas' predicted date. Unfortunately he never got an opportunity to go 'marching up Broadway' with his comrades.[45]

Before Thomas had left for the front he had made sure that his mother was set up with regular relief payments, supplied by the City of New York. His death demonstrates just how much of a 'second trauma' the American Civil War could be for Famine emigrants. By 1861, Mary had endured the loss of her first husband to Famine, had escaped the clutches of an abusive second husband, and then experienced the death of the son who had facilitated that escape. One wonders as to her thoughts when her other son James decided to enlist in the 158th New York Infantry – part of 'Spinola's Brigade'. The 21-year-old became a private in Company K on 12 August 1862, but thankfully survived to muster out with his company at Richmond on 30 June 1865.[46]

The laws which entitled Mary to a dependent mother's pension had not been in place when Thomas died, and Mary initially thought that because he was one of the militia's 'three month men' (as opposed to a later three-year volunteer) she would not be entitled to any payments. She started her pension application process in August 1862, when she was recorded as being 50 years of age. She was then living at 16 Mulberry Street in the notorious Five Points slum district of Manhattan. It was an area teeming with fellow Irish immigrants, many of them from her native Kerry.[47]

Mary had made a crucial error in her application, one that would be a factor in delaying her pension approval for many years. She recorded her name as Mary Madigan rather than Mary Kennedy. Cruelly, the name of her second husband, a name discarded because of the pain the man had caused, had come back to haunt her. The pension bureau sought clarification as to why she had not used it, and wanted information as to the whereabouts and fate of Maurice Kennedy. In addition, they wanted proof of her marriage to James Madigan in County Kerry. In order to obtain that proof she wrote to one of her Costello siblings back in Ireland. The response she received illustrates how those who had succeeded in emigrating, no matter what their circumstances, were looked to for aid by those still at home. Although it is not apparent from the letter if the correspondent was Mary's brother or sister (the latter seems more likely), what is evident is that the writer had helped to fund the journey of another family member, 'Jimmy', to the United States. It appears that Jimmy had then also decided to become a soldier in the Union army. Despite having received news of Tom's death in battle, the writer doesn't hesitate to chide Mary for having made 'faithful promises but slow performances':

Tralee March 31st 1863

Dear Sister I received your letter of the 17th I was sorry to heare of the death of poor Tom may the lord have mercy on his soul. Dear sister when I heard your letter was at the causeway [Causeway, Co. Kerry] I went for it but could not get the lines you required untill now [the proof of Mary's marriage]. Dear Sister you should suceed in getting this money I hope you wont forget poor Thomas soul get masses said for him and pray [for] him constant as he went so suddenly. Dear Sister I had to leave Mr Masons a long time ago in bad health which was a grate loss to me and to set down and spend what I earned during the time I was with them. Dear Sister I am sorry I ever sent you Jimmy or lost the few [pounds] to him that I did to be the manes [means] of sending him to the war, I would want what I lost to him verry badley now myself for I am getting into bad health every day. I am laid up at present with a scurvey in my feet and I fear I will have to leave my p[l]ace in concequence of them. I have a very good place at present if I could keep it I am living with Mr George

Hillard...Dear Sister I thought I would have got some assistance from you and Jimmy before now ye have made as I thought faithfull primisses [promises] but slow performances.

Dear Sister I hope you wont forget sending me some money for I feare I will want it very soon in concequence of my health which will cause me to leave my place. If it was the will of God to leave me my health I could do without from any one and as it not I crave you[r] assistance may the Holy will of God be done in all things, Amen.

Catherine Brien will be going to America and she will tell you all about me direct your letter George Hillard Esq. Madgestrar Tralee Dea place.[48]

By the time the war ended, Mary was living with her daughter Catherine. She would eventually have her pension application granted on 25 July 1868. With the award the Madigan story once again fades back into obscurity. However, their remarkable pension file provides us with insight into one family's arduous journey from Famine-ravaged Ireland to an America which, at least initially, did not prove to be the promised land. It also offers a rare glimpse back across the Atlantic, towards the obligations that many Irish emigrants had towards those who had been left behind.

THE CONWAYS: OFFALY AND NEW YORK

 'A noble fellow/He was so cruel ...'[49]

On 18 October 1862, the *New York Irish American Weekly* brought its readers news of 'The Dead of the Brigade'. It had been a month since the bloody Battle of Antietam – America's bloodiest single day – and the remains of those Irish Brigade soldiers who had fallen in the struggle for the Bloody Lane were still being laid to rest. Now the newspaper was reporting on the funerals of three more 'gallant fellows' who had just been taken to New York's Calvary Cemetery. The journalist remarked that it was little more

than a year since these men had 'marched out under the green banners of the Irish Brigade, full of life and energy, inspired by the most fervent devotion to their adopted country, and hoping still, as only Irish hearts can, for the future of their native land'. Clearly, these men were seen as fallen heroes, but was that a view everyone held?[50]

One of the bodies that had arrived in New York from the Maryland battlefield was that of Lieutenant John Conway of Company K, 69th New York Volunteers. His remains had travelled with those of a fellow officer, Captain Patrick Clooney of the 88th New York. Both had been placed in well-made metallic coffins, which were initially brought to the headquarters of the Irish Brigade at 596 Broadway, where they lay in state. From there they were taken in a military cortège to the cemetery, with the large procession of carriages and mourners headed by a band. Each hearse was drawn by four white horses covered in the stars and stripes, while the coffins themselves were draped in Irish and American flags. Twelve officers of the brigade operated as pallbearers and a military escort was provided by men the 69th New York State Militia, who fired a salute over the fallen men before they were laid in the vault. In describing the character of Lieutenant John Conway, the *Irish American* was unequivocal:

Lieut. John Conway was born in Tullamore, King's County, Ireland, and arrived in this country in 1840. Foremost among those who sprang to arms at the formation of Gen. Meagher's 'noble little Brigade,' he served in it with distinction and honor on every battle-field to the hour of his death; when, like many of his brave companions, he was struck down, on the 17th of September, at Antietam, leading his command to the charge. Courteous, affable, loving and truly brave – he was as much beloved in social life by all who knew him, as in camp by his fellow-officers, who esteemed him as a 'noble fellow,' and mourn him to-day as an irreparable loss. Aged but thirty-six years, his young life is another sacrifice of Ireland for America, in the annals of which, as a staunch and trusty soldier, the name of John Conway should be cherished.[51]

It is unsurprising that a newspaper such as the *Irish American Weekly* would remember the fallen of the Irish Brigade in such heroic terms. It was a common feature of contemporary journalism, and given the political motivations of the publication, it was going to take every opportunity to advance the cause of Ireland and the Irish in America. Often such glowing printed eulogies are all that is left to us as we seek to imagine the character and personality of such historical figures. However, it is worth remembering that all these men, including the celebrated fallen of the Irish Brigade, were not simply heroic martyrs – they were flesh-and-blood people, with their own flaws and foibles. Just as they were loved by some, they could be loathed by others. Less than two weeks prior to the publication of the above account by the *Irish American*, John Conway's brother-in-law, Charles Brady, wrote a letter to his sister regarding the Irish Brigade officer's death. Unlike the mouthpiece of the New York Irish, Charles had not mourned the loss of a hero when he heard of John's passing.[52]

As the newspaper recounted, John Conway had emigrated to the United States from Tullamore, County Offaly around the year 1840. On 7 January 1846 he was married to Catherine Brady in Auburn, New York, by Father O'Flaherty. The couple, who had no children, appear to have tried their hand at farming before heading to Brooklyn. There they entered the employment of Henry C. Bowen, a successful New York merchant. Bowen was the internal revenue collector for the 3rd District (Brooklyn), but was also a prominent abolitionist. He had founded the *Independent* in 1848, a congregational antislavery weekly that at one point was edited by Henry Ward Beecher. John worked as Henry Bowen's gardener while Catherine served the family as a nurse. The Offaly man was around 36 years old when he became a Lieutenant in Company K of the 69th New York in 1861. At the time he was described as being 5 feet 10 inches in height, with a dark complexion, dark eyes and black hair. Catherine, then 34, was still in the Bowens' employ when she learned that the Battle of Antietam had made her a widow.[53]

After the funeral of her husband, Catherine faced the practical issue of her own financial future. In 1862 she was living with the Bowens at 76 Willow Street in Brooklyn. She needed to prove her marriage to John in order to become eligible for a pension, so she asked her brother, Charles Brady, to travel to Auburn to see if he could get evidence of the marriage. Charles was a farmer living in Skaneateles, Onondaga County. When her brother wrote back, he took the opportunity to offer his own form of consolation to his sister. His opinion could not have contrasted more starkly with that of the *Irish American*. Charles made it clear that John's 'bad actions' had severely damaged his opinion of the fallen soldier. Indeed, Charles did not even feel it was worth Catherine trying to get John's body home, although as reported by the *Irish American* this is something that would subsequently take place. Charles also made sure to tell his sister to avoid the 'low Irish' who might lead her astray, and encouraged her to stay in her present position:

Dear Sister

I received your letter the third. We were very sorry to hear of John deaths [sic], I don't blame you to feel bad but still he was so cruel to you, but I suppose nature comples [compels] you to feel so. Dear Sister I don't think he ever used you like a husband when you lived up on the lake [presumably Lake Skaneateles] on the farm, you know when you had to go out and milk all the cows and he would be away playing cards, and since yous went east by all accounts he was but worse and after he went away Mother wrote to me and told me that he never left you a dollar after selling all his things. When he was up here he had plenty of money spending around the taverns and was out at Auburn at two Irish dances but I will forgive him and I hope God will for all his bad actions. Dear Sister there had been many a good husband left their wives and children which falls on the field of battle and their family's must feel reconcilise [reconciled] now. Dear Sister you have know [no] trouble but yourself and as the Almighty gives you health you aught to be well satisfied and also you aught to feel happy to think you are living with such kind folks that takes so much interest in you. Dear Sister now I am going to give you advice to keep away from all the low Irish and not be led *away by them, you may think they are for your good they will bring you to ruin. Dear Sister I hope you will remain with the family you are living with ... the advice you get from them will be for your good. Dear Sister I went out to Auburn yesterday to see about your marriage lines the priest that is there now his name is Mr Creaton [?] he is the third priest since you were married. This priest can't find the record that priest had that married you, that shows how correct they are about keeping the record. This priest says as long as yous lived man and wife for so many years and there is plenty of witnesses for that. Dear Sister if you will live with this family my wife or myself will go down to see you the latter part of the winter for I know you have got a good home with them. Dear Sister I think it is so foolish to think to get John['s] body home for they can't tell one from the other after they are three days under the sand. Them that are advising you for that are doing you wrong you take advice from Mr Hodge and not from them, for he knows all about such business. If there is anything coming to you he will get it for you, if you get anything put [it] in the bank for old age. Myself and family joins with me in sending their love to you. I have no more to say at present but remain your affectionate brother,*

Charles Brady
Skaneateles Oct the 5 1862.[54]

It transpired that the priest that had married John and Catherine, Father O'Flaherty, had returned to Ireland. However, statements from family members and Henry C. Bowen were enough to prove the marriage and secure Catherine's pension. Despite the unflattering content of her brother's letter, she had little option but to include it with her pension application as it outlined her efforts to obtain proof of her marriage. Without its inclusion, it is unlikely that any contrary view of John Conway would have survived to paint a more human picture of his character than that extolled by the *Irish American*. Whatever of her brother's views, Catherine's opinion of her husband goes unrecorded. It seems likely it sat somewhere between the glorified memorialisation exhibited by the newspaper and the extremely low opinion of him held by Charles. Catherine received a pension based on John's service, which was paid until her own death in 1905. She was ultimately buried at St Patrick's Cemetery in Aurora, New York.[55]

THE DALYS: KILDARE AND NEW YORK

 '... *with niggard clutch robs a poor Irish widow of her just right.*'[56]

Some families in nineteenth-century Ireland found it virtually impossible to escape the grip of poverty and want. No matter what efforts they made, they appeared consigned to decades of struggle as they toiled against seemingly endless hardship. Their lives were often punctuated by major efforts to improve their lot, some of which may have brought them brief respite. But occasionally these efforts also brought great risk, as proved to be the case for the unfortunate Daly family.

On 5 June 1861, almost a month after the American Civil War broke out, Mary Corcoran and John Daly were married by the Roman Catholic curate Robert Wheeler in Celbridge, County Kildare. Both appear to have been in their twenties when they became husband and wife. The couple may have had little choice but to wed, as by the time they married Mary was already pregnant with the couple's first child. Their son, named John for his father, was born on 28 December 1861. The location of his birth belied the couple's economic situation, as the parish registers record that John Jr entered the world in Celbridge Union Workhouse.[57]

Despite their early association with the workhouse, John Daly was not without a trade. Sometime after the birth of their son the couple moved to Dublin, where John was recorded as working as a printer. Perhaps their lot improved for a time, but any success appears to have been short lived. By late 1863 Mary was pregnant again, and the couple's second son, Edward, was born in Dublin's Lying-In Hospital (now the Rotunda) on 8 April 1864, later being baptised in St Michan's church on North Anne Street. The arrival of a new child brought both joy and added financial pressure to the family. John, presumably out of work again, took the momentous decision to provide for his family in the United States.[58]

It is unclear if John Daly left for America with the intention of enlisting in the Union army, or if that was a decision he took (or felt forced to take) upon his arrival there. Many Irishmen were undoubtedly attracted across the Atlantic in 1863 and 1864 by the large bounties on offer for federal service. Whatever his reasons, John enlisted in the army on 23 August 1864 in New York. Two days later, the 28-year-old was officially mustered in as a private in Company A of the 51st New York Infantry. It may be that John was tricked or induced to enlist as a substitute, as he was recorded under an alias — John Ryan — and it would be as Private Ryan that he marched off to war.[59]

Following John's departure for the Civil War, Mary returned to Celbridge, where she no doubt hoped to seek the support of relatives while she waited for money to trickle back across the Atlantic. Less than a month after enlisting, John was already at the front, serving with his regiment near Petersburg, Virginia. From there he wrote Mary a letter, the content of which suggests he had a torrid time following his arrival in the United States. He told her a tale of betrayal by one Thomas Donnellan, suggesting that it was he who was responsible for his service under an assumed name. Thomas Donnellan may have been a friend, but it is more likely that he was a substitute broker who preyed on his fellow Irishman for profit. The way in which John refers to him suggests that he had left Ireland with the intention of meeting Donnellan when he got to New York:

Battlefield near Petersburg
23rd Septr. 1864
Mrs. Mary Daly
Celbridge County Kildare, Ireland

My dear wife,

I take up my pen in hand to write these few lines to you hoping you and my two sons [are] in good health and my poor mother and my brother Mat and my sister Mary – I hope they are all doing well. My dear wife, I met with Thomas Donelan in New York and he took me to his son's house and they seemed to be very kind to me and they drugged me day and night with the worst spirits and other mixtures and then he thought to rob me of 100 dollars and more. My dear wife I am going to send you the sum of £20 and I am losing 40 by sending it to you you will be please[d] to give £2 to my mother and 1 to my sister Mary & 1 to Revd. Father Wheeler to say masses for my father's soul and the remainder for myself and you will keep good clothing on yourself and the children and you must do the best you can until I return and it wont be long with the help of God. My dear wife I will leave the sum of £50 with a Priest in New York for you and the children if anything happens me and I will let you know the Priests name in my next letter. My dear wife it is now 4 o'clock in the morning and I am writing to you and I have no tent or any cover and it is raining very heavy and I hope this will be a warning to me while I live. My dear wife there is from ten to twenty men killed a day out of the Brigade that I belong to but not many out of my Regiment. My dear wife you will be very cautious how you will direct your letters for that Robber Donnellan gave in my name as Ryan and direct yr. letter for John Ryan, Co. A, 51st Regiment New York Vols, Washington, America.

No more at present from your affectionate husband,
John Daly.[60]

A week after John wrote this letter to his wife, the 51st New York went into action near Poplar Grove Church in Virginia. Although the battle was regarded a federal success, it proved a catastrophe for the regiment. Out of the 340 men and ten officers engaged, only one officer and fifteen men escaped capture when the unit was surrounded. John was among those who became prisoners. While the officers were by and large sent to Richmond, little was heard from the enlisted men. In January 1865 *The New York Times* reported that of 'the rank and file of the Fifty-first, consisting of some 350 men, captured at poplar Grove Church, we have no intelligence of. They are distributed somewhere in the Southern prisons'. It is not recorded how Mary learned of John's capture, if indeed she ever did. It may well be that months passed with no word of her husband, but eventually news did filter back to Celbridge. His comrades relayed the news that the Kildare man had not survived his incarceration, dying in Salisbury, North Carolina, sometime in 1864.[61]

John's death condemned his wife and children to a life of poverty in Ireland. Before long circumstances forced them once again into Celbridge Union Workhouse, where Mary began what proved a long process to secure a US Government pension. The American consul in Dublin, William B. West, wrote to the pension bureau on the widow's behalf in 1867. Describing Mary as a 'wretchedly poor woman', he related that her pension claim, like those of many others in Ireland, 'has been delayed or rather postponed from the difficulty which poor people in this Country almost invariably experience in obtaining the necessary legal evidence of their marriage and the births of their children'. Mary's pension application was eventually approved in 1869, though unfortunately it appears to have had little impact on lifting the Dalys from the poverty which plagued their lives.[62]

As is the case with many Civil War pensioners in Ireland, the Daly family next enter the historical record in the 1890s, when the new law enacted by Congress in 1893 threatened to deprive foreign recipients of their pension entitlements if they could not prove that their loved one had been an American citizen at the time of his service. Like the others, Mary had letters written to the commissioner of pensions on her behalf. In her case it was the guardians of Celbridge Workhouse who took up their pen, sending the following resolution, adopted on 29 December 1893:

Celbridge Union
Resolution

Proposed by Colonel Dease J.P.
Seconded by W.J. Kirkpatrick J.P.
And Unanimously Resolved

That in consequence of the stoppage of her pension Mary Daly is now
a pauper and has become chargeable on the public rates. John Daly her
deceased husband was born in Ireland and there never was any pretence
that he was a naturalized American Citizen and it appears to the
Board of Guardians of this Union that while it is within the rights of
the United States Government to alter the law in respect of pensions
prospectively it is a cruel and unjust act to withdraw the pension of
which this woman has been in receipt for nearly thirty one years and to
let her die in a Workhouse, while her husband lost his life in the service
of the American State.[63]

Despite the passage of time, Mary Daly's lot had clearly not substantially improved. The unjustness of her pension stoppage even made it into the American papers. In February 1894 the *New York Irish World* reported on her predicament:

A sad case is reported from the poorhouse of Celbridge, County Kildare, Ireland, of a Mrs. Daly, whose husband was killed fighting in this country for the Union, being by the present Administration deprived of her $80 a year pension. It is a curious commentary on the Pension Bureau, and a poor recompense for Irish valor. Mrs. Daly was forced into the hated workhouse to spend Christmas, and it is left to two English colonels to look after her claim on the United States Government … An Administration which with … niggard clutch robs a poor Irish widow of her just right must be held to account by every honest Irishman. In questions of American politics, I am like the young Irish fellow in the faction fight, he belonged to neither party, but blue-moldy for battle and having a good blackthorn, where he saw a head gone wrong he hit it hard.[64]

Although her payments were ultimately restored, the money appears to have proved of little service to Mary, as her long association with Celbridge Union Workhouse continued. This unwanted connection ultimately lasted more than four decades. Mary's first child had been born there in 1861, and by the late 1860s both she and her sons were completely reliant on the institution. Indeed, the pension bureau would report that Mary and her children were resident there 'for many years'. Little had changed for her by the time of her pension crisis in the 1890s, and it was 1904 before she finally left the workhouse for the last time. Unfortunately, it was not a move for the better. On 16 September that year she was transferred to Carlow District Lunatic Asylum, suffering from 'cerebral disease'. Mary Daly passed away in the Asylum on 29 December 1905 and was buried in St Mary's Cemetery in Carlow. The last entries in her file relate to the asylum's efforts to recoup the unfortunate woman's burial expenses. Her family story is one of a lifelong battle with poverty, undoubtedly a struggle exacerbated by John's premature death in North Carolina. For this unfortunate woman, it ultimately proved a trap she could not escape. [65]

THE NUGENTS: DUBLIN AND ILLINOIS

 '… if having sexual intercourse made us man and wife we were married.' [66]

On 29 August 1879 Ann Gallagher, a 40-year-old prisoner in the 'Bridewell', Chicago's House of Correction, prepared to give a statement. Ann was in the midst of a one-year prison sentence, which had been handed down for a violation of the pension laws. She was a Civil War widow, but had lost her entitlement to a pension when she decided to remarry. However, rather than give up her payments, Ann had sought to conceal her remarriage, continuing to collect the money under her widowed name, Ann Manning. Her deception had been uncovered, resulting in her incarceration. Now, ostensibly motivated by little more than a renewed sense of civic duty, Ann

prepared to accuse another woman – her one-time friend Isabella Nugent – of the same offence.[67]

The pension available to the widows of Civil War soldiers was an extremely valuable asset. By 1890, the payments equated to ⅓ of the annual wage of the average American worker. Many applicants were willing to stretch the truth in order to secure this money, while others thought little of submitting spurious and even fraudulent claims. Similarly, many women who had grown reliant on regular payments based on their husbands' sacrifice were reluctant to give them up upon remarriage. Despite the potential social consequences, some chose to cohabit out of wedlock rather than lose their pension entitlements, a state of affairs that the Bureau of Pensions regarded as unseemly. Throughout the 1870s and 1880s the bureau grew increasingly dogged in examining the marital status and moral conduct of Civil War widows. The day after Ann Gallagher pointed the finger at Isabella Nugent, Ann's husband Edward Gallagher approached a pension official in Chicago to tell them that Isabella Nugent had remarried 'and he wanted it reported'. The Bureau wasted little time. On 3 September 1879 a special agent sent a message via the Western Union Telegraph Company requesting the immediate suspension of Isabella's pension.[68]

Isabella Murphy had married Michael Nugent, a butcher by trade, in the parish of St Nicholas of Myra, Dublin on 16 September 1848. The couple emigrated to Chicago, where Michael had enlisted on 23 July 1862, becoming a private in the 72nd Illinois Infantry. The 41-year-old was described as 5 feet 7 inches tall, with brown hair, grey eyes and a dark complexion. During the conflict he sent money back to his wife whenever he could. However, with pay often sporadic, Isabella occasionally had to rely on the help of local relief committees. It was while seeking this relief during the war that she first became acquainted with her later accuser, the then Ann Manning. None of this might have mattered if Michael's regiment had not found itself among those holding the main Union line near the Carter House at Franklin, Tennessee, on 30 November 1864. When the position was attacked by the Confederate Army of Tennessee, the 72nd became embroiled in one of the most desperate struggles of the war. That day saw many of the regiment 'using the bayonet, and others the clubbed musket' as they attempted to drive the Rebels back amidst savage hand-to-hand fighting. The federal position at Franklin ultimately held, but Michael Nugent did not live to see it. Isabella was staying with her brother-in-law Patrick Nugent in Illinois when news arrived of Michael's fate.[69]

Shortly after Michael's death, Isabella took to staying with Paddy and Mary McKay, who had known her when they had all lived in the 'old country'. The McKays ran a boarding house and saloon near the Galena Elevator on North Water Street in Chicago. As well as beds and alcohol, the McKays also provided a washing service for nearby workers. In the late 1860s one of the men who availed of this was Thomas Mann, an employee of Wright's Livery Stable on nearby Kinzie Street. Thomas met the widow Isabella Nugent at the McKays, where they took to 'drinking and carousing' together. The two embarked on a relationship that lasted for a number of weeks, before Thomas apparently took some of Isabella's pension money. He soon after departed the area for good, never to be heard from again. Many years afterward, this brief liaison would be one that gave Isabella considerable cause for regret.[70]

But for now that was all in the future. In the meantime, the life of Isabella Nugent and thousands of other Chicago residents was transformed utterly by the events of 8 October 1871. That was the day on which the conflagration that became known as the Great Fire broke out. Started by accident, the flames, driven by a strong southwesterly wind, would burn for more than twenty-four hours. When it was over nearly 300 Chicagoans were dead and more than 18,000 buildings – including the McKay boarding house – had been destroyed. As a result of what everyone called 'The Fire', the McKays and Isabella Nugent joined the more than 100,000 people who were left homeless.[71]

Having lost everything, the McKays temporarily left Illinois for St Louis, Missouri. It may be that they were joining relatives there. Isabella went with them, which indicates the closeness of their relationship. On their return to Chicago the McKays built what was described as a 'miserable shanty' on the former site of their boarding house. Isabella made her home there as well, picking up work where she could; by 1873 she was an employee at Chicago's Continental Hotel. Meanwhile the McKays' shanty was developing a reputation as a 'bad resort' and 'low place', where alcohol-fuelled fights were commonplace.[72]

Isabella and the McKays spent the majority of the 1870s living together. Their relationship appears to have changed around 1879, when the McKays shanty was torn down 'on account of being a nuisance'. Both the McKays and Isabella seem to have moved in with Edward and Ann Gallagher (formerly Ann Manning), Isabella's later accuser. It was here, in the Gallagher shanty beside the railroad on North Water Street, that the relationship between the different parties began to break down.[73]

One of the common threads through the experiences of Isabella, the McKays and the Gallaghers over the following months was their abusive relationship with alcohol. Isabella, though not described as a habitual drunkard, did by her own admission tend to go on binges. Nonetheless she remained able to function, and her 1880s employer at Burns Restaurant on 11 and 13 Clark Street did not seem to think it adversely impacted her role as a kitchen woman. The McKays were also heavy drinkers. One man recalled how in years gone by he used to consider Paddy McKay 'a nice man ... but he got to drinking hard'. There seems to be little question as to the alcoholism of Edward and Ann Gallagher. The McKays remembered Edward Gallagher as 'a hard character and all the time drunk'. Isabella said the Gallaghers 'both drank hard'. One particular story highlights the Gallaghers' alcohol dependence. During the war, Edward Gallagher had served as a private in Company I of the 58th Illinois Infantry. In 1879 he received more than $1,000 in retrospective pension payments based on this service, but quickly set to work drinking his way through much of it. Presumably after an argument, his wife Ann made off with some of the money, later being caught 'drunk in a ditch' with '$400 on her chest' that she had stolen from her spouse. Police put her in the station house for the night, before Edward came the following day to pay her fine and secure her release.[74]

The motivations behind Ann and Edward Gallagher's accusation of pension fraud against Isabella would appear to have been driven by self-interest. They hoped to use Isabella's supposed indiscretions to get Ann out of jail, despite the fact that many years had passed since the events they outlined. One of the agents investigating the case noted that Edward Gallagher was 'under the impression I could help his wife to be released from prison' while another surmised they were very zealous in reporting Isabella and noted that 'a motive existed … to answer falsely'. More damaging to Isabella was the testimony of her long-time friends, the McKays. Why they chose to implicate their boarder in fraud is less clear. One possible motivation was the fact that one Sammy McKay, who may have been their son and was almost certainly a relative, was sent to the Bridewell around this time for stealing some of Isabella's pension money. Whatever their reasons, both the Gallaghers and McKays gave statements to say that Isabella Nugent had married Thomas Mann, the man with whom she had spent a few weeks all those years before.[75]

On 29 August 1879 Ann Gallagher claimed to officials that Isabella had admitted her remarriage to her. As Ann told it, Isabella had declared that she 'did not care a damn' whether Ann informed on her, as 'she would rather be married than be a whore to him'. Ann further stated that Paddy McKay had told her he had seen a marriage certificate at the time. On 4 September 1879 Ann's husband Edward Gallagher claimed that Isabella had been drunk at his home two months previously, and had shown him a certificate of her marriage to Thomas Mann. He confirmed his wife's testimony that Paddy McKay had also seen the certificate, adding that the McKays had been unwilling to allow Isabella and Thomas Mann to share a room without seeing proof of their marriage. Edward went further and stated that Mann had stolen $48 of Isabella's pension money, but when she remonstrated with him, her lover had threatened to 'squeal' to the authorities about their marriage. Finally, Paddy McKay claimed that during the winter of 1878–9 Isabella had sought charitable aid under the name Isabella Mann. The McKays testimony supported much of what the Gallaghers claimed, both in terms of the relationship and the apparent existence of a marriage certificate.[76]

So began a lengthy investigation, as pension agents sought to track down anyone who may have had knowledge of the events. The efforts of agents were hampered by the fact that no one had seen Thomas Mann in more than a decade. Eventually they did locate a Thomas Mann who had worked at the Livery Stable, but it transpired he was not the man who had been Isabella's lover, just someone who happened to have the same name. Efforts to procure official evidence of Isabella's supposed marriage to Mann were also fruitless, as the 1871 Fire had destroyed all such records. On 6 February 1881, Isabella, now 62 years of age, gave this statement:

> I admit that I have lived with Patrick McKay and wife at divers times for upwards of 15 years. I admit that I occupied the same room and bed with Thomas Mann for a month on North Water St in Patrick McKays house before the Fire ... Thomas Mann was working in Wrights Stable at the time ... Thomas Mann was drinking and carousing and we slept together had sexual intercourse in bed at divers times for almost a month. We were both drinking and carousing together at the time, I did not represent myself as his wife nor did he represent me to be his wife to my knowledge. Patrick McKay and wife saw him in our room and coming in and out Mrs. McKay did his washing. I deny ever telling Edward Gallagher or Ann Gallagher that I was the wife of Thomas Mann nor did I ever show a paper called a marriage certificate to them or to Patrick McKay. That is a false charge. I deny saying that I was married ... and that the certificate was destroyed. While I again admit that I had sexual intercourse with Thomas Mann so called at my rooms in Patrick McKays house for a month before the Fire at divers times ... if having sexual intercourse made us man and wife we were married.[77]

Isabella also stated that she had never seen Thomas Mann after the month they had lived together. Furthermore, she accused Edward Gallagher of giving false testimony against her because she refused to give him money: 'Edward Gallagher said if I did not give him ... $3 dollars he would stop my pension the same as his wife. Ann Gallagher had lost her pension and he carried out his threat'.[78]

In response to the allegation that she had used the surname 'Mann' to claim relief money, she said she gave her name as 'Mary Mane' because if the county agent had realised she was a pensioner she would have received no relief, and she had selected that name as she had an aunt called that in Canada. Clearly desperate to have her support restored, Isabella gave a commitment:

> If my pension is restored I promise not to spree it away as I generally have done, I have suffered a good deal this winter and intend to do better. I admit to have spreed away my pension generally but I swear I never have remarried since the soldiers [Michael Nugent] death.[79]

Eventually, after much hardship, Isabella's pension was restored to her. The agents investigating the case felt the potential motives of her accusers, combined with the failure to locate Thomas Mann and the lack of any marriage certificate left them with insufficient evidence to prove fraud. However, she was unable to enjoy the payments for very long, last claiming the pension on 4 September 1882. Eight days later Isabella became an inmate of the Cook County Poorhouse, where she is recorded as dying on 27 November. The pension bureau note on her file recorded that the 'pensioner was an immoral woman, who died … in a public institution of charity'. In the same year that Isabella died, Congress approved a new measure which meant that it would no longer be necessary to prove remarriage in order to terminate a widow's pension payments. From then on, demonstrating cohabitation with a man was deemed sufficient to bring the payments to an end.[80]

THE MURRAYS: DUBLIN, DOWN AND NEW YORK

 '… to solve the mystery surrounding this boy's parentage.'[81]

Michael J. Murray had not known his father well. He had been only 5 years old when John D. Murray left his wife and children and struck out for America. Michael would never see him again. Ten years after his death, circumstances would lead Michael to follow in his father's footsteps and travel to the United States. He settled in New York, where he made a new life for himself. As the years passed, Michael grew more and more interested in his father's wartime activities and was undoubtedly proud of his father's service. In the 1880s, he joined the fraternal organisation known as the Sons of Union Veterans of the United States, which had been founded in 1881. Membership was open to those whose fathers had served in the conflict, and Michael likely viewed the association as an opportunity to both remember his father's sacrifice and further his own prospects. He eventually rose to become adjutant of the R.V. Young Post of the Sons of Veterans, based in Brooklyn. It was while he held this position in 1887 that Michael began to make inquiries regarding his mother's eligibility for a widow's pension based on his father's wartime service as well as his own entitlements for the years when he was under 16. This led him on a journey of discovery that would eventually reveal some unexpected truths about his father's relationships in Ireland – revelations that are likely to have caused him considerable embarrassment.[82]

The Murray family were familiar with being on the move, even within Ireland. John, who was from County Down, had married Michael's mother, Annabella Rogan, at the Riverside Chapel in Sligo town in the early 1850s. The family subsequently moved to Portadown, County Armagh, where Michael was born. A younger brother and sister followed, and Annabella was pregnant with another boy when John left for America. Outwardly it seems economic necessity drove his emigration, although John's commitment to his family was questionable. It was nine months before they heard from him again; by that time he was reportedly working as a compositor in the offices of the *New York Herald*. John sent his family a total of three letters before all communication ceased. Meanwhile Annabella and the children struggled. All of Michael's younger siblings died, and Annabella left Michael with his Murray grandparents in County Down as she pursued a semi-nomadic lifestyle, moving on again, this time to Cavan town.[83]

Meanwhile, in America, John had elected to join the army. He is recorded as enlisting on 28 May 1861, mustering in as a corporal. The unit he chose was originally intended to serve as a 'Naval Brigade' and man gunboats that would cruise the Atlantic coast. However, in August 1861 they were organised as an infantry regiment at Fortress Monroe, Virginia, eventually becoming the 99th New York Infantry. During the war they were variously known as the 'Union Coast Guard', 'Bartlett's Naval Brigade' and the 'Lincoln Divers'. John spent the majority of his service in and around Fortress Monroe, and it was in nearby Camp Greble that he succumbed to dysentery around 5 October 1862.[84]

Back in County Down, John's father received notification of his son's death, and in turn informed Annabella, before passing on a small sum of money that John had left behind. She used this along with her own earnings to depart for New York in 1864, but left her son Michael with his grandfather. Not long after her arrival in the United States Annabella married her dead husband's brother Bernard, and the couple would go on to have a daughter. Michael continued to live in Down until his grandfather passed away in 1872. Michael then travelled across the Atlantic and made his home with his mother and uncle Bernard in New York. By 1887, when he started his pension inquiries, he was living with his mother on 31st Street in Manhattan, working as a machinist. Just how prepared Michael was for the response he received to his pension inquiries is difficult to ascertain. Whatever his expectations may have been, he was soon informed that his mother would not be able to claim a pension. When he asked why, he was told it was not possible because another woman – one Barbara Murray – was already in receipt of it.[85]

Michael appears to have greeted this news with a degree of outrage. On 6 August 1887 he wrote to the commissioner of pensions:

Sir, if I am not mistaken you are paying a pension to a woman by the name of Barbara Murray as the widow of my deceased father John D. Murray who fought in the late War. I cannot account for this as I am the only son of the deceased and my mother still living and she the real person who should get this pension and not the parties whom is getting it. I am Adjutant of the R.V. Young Post Sons of Veterans No 20 of Brooklyn and therefore I claim my mother is the proper custodian of any pension that is derived from the Government.[86]

An investigation was launched into the case. However, examination of the pension file failed to find any fault with Barbara Murray's claim. She had initially applied back in 1863, providing evidence of her marriage to John D. Murray at St Paul's Roman Catholic church in Dublin on 4 February 1844 – a number of years prior to John's marriage to Annabella Rogan. In addition to this, Barbara Murray also recorded that she and John had a daughter, named Sophia. Michael later realised that he had actually met Barbara in Ireland:

> The woman who alleges she is my father's widow and is now drawing a pension as I understand goes by name of Barbara Murray and I saw her in 1870 in Co. Down Ireland she was on a visit there at that time and resided in Dublin Ireland. I learned at that time that she claimed to be my father's widow but I was young and thought but little about it. She did not come to my grandfathers house while grandmother was living but after her death in 1862 ... I never had any talk with my grandfather about father's having another wife.[87]

It further transpired that John Murray's sister Jane, who lived in Norfolk, Virginia, may have had some information about this other woman. The special examiner dealing with the case for the Pension Bureau noted that 'she is the one and only one now living in America who is able to solve the mystery surrounding this boy's parentage'. It seems probable that Jane was well aware of her brother's past relationship with Barbara, but although Michael had visited his aunt several times in search of answers about his father's past, she had told him nothing. For Michael, realisation was beginning to dawn as to the reality of his father's marital relations. In the face of overwhelming evidence the Bureau confirmed Barbara Murray's entitlement to a pension. The entire affair must have been a distressing experience for Michael. On 17 October 1887 he confirmed that he would be dropping his request for a pension and would be taking no further action with regard to it. Instead of benefiting from his father's service, all that

Michael had achieved was to uncover him as a bigamist and to learn that his parents' marriage had been invalid.[88]

Bigamy was not uncommon in the nineteenth century. Indeed, in many instances, particularly those where marriages had broken down, it was often countenanced by friends, neighbours and family. Although Michael Murray does not appear to have been aware of his father's previous marriage, at the very least his aunt and grandfather had been. It is not beyond the realms of possibility that Annabella had also known of it; she did not allude to her husband's previous marriage in her own statement on the case, and perhaps tellingly had not made any application for a pension prior to her son's inquiries. The details surrounding John Murray's relationship with, and estrangement from, Barbara Murray remain a mystery and it is not known if Michael ever discovered further information regarding his father's first marriage. For her part, Barbara continued to collect a pension based on her husband's service in Dublin until her own death in the mid-1890s. In New York, Michael was left with little option but to revaluate what he thought he knew regarding his relationship with both his father and his family.[89]

THE MARTINS: DERRY AND NEW YORK

 'I could not remain with my mother, when under the influence of liquors she would be harsh and cruel and compel us to seek for safety elsewhere.'[90]

On 28 August 1864 Second Lieutenant Dean Wilson of Corcoran's Irish Legion found a few moments to pen a letter to New York from the front. The pages he wrote told those at home of disaster. Three days previously the 2nd Corps, of which the Legion formed a part, had been badly mauled at what would become known as the Battle of Ream's Station. The Corps was the most famed in the Army of the Potomac and had been consistently used as the army's strike force. But they had performed poorly at Ream's Station, and it would prove their worst defeat of the war. Wilson expressed

his wish that he would never again find himself in such a 'tight place' as he had been on 25 August, asserting 'this is the first time the old corps was ever whipped'. Many Irish were among the large numbers of 2nd Corps soldiers captured that day. One of the Legion men taken was Private Patrick Martin of the 182nd New York Infantry. His subsequent fate would create a documentary trail that detailed the harsh realities of addiction and abuse in nineteenth-century America, the unfortunate lot of his wife and children in the years ahead.[91]

Patrick had married Ellen Baker in St Columba Catholic church, New York, on 24 May 1851. They went on to have three children together, Patrick (born 1854), Margaret (born 1859) and Henry (born 1861). They made their home at 266 West 34th Street in New York. Patrick had spent the pre-war years as a baker before enlisting at the age of 33 on 9 October 1862. He was recorded as being 5 feet 8 inches tall, with blue eyes, a dark complexion and black hair. A fellow member of the 182nd New York was Fergus McCusker, who served as a private in Company E. Like Patrick, Fergus had been captured at Ream's Station. He later remembered how the prisoners were first taken to Belle Isle, an island in the James River outside Richmond, where they arrived on 30 August 1864. From there they were sent further south, destined for Salisbury, North Carolina. Patrick didn't last long in his new surroundings. By 17 October he was dead. Fergus remembered how he 'saw the body of ... Patrick Martin after death, after he had been placed in the dead house'.[92]

In 1865 the now-widowed Ellen and her children were still making their home in Manhattan. Following Patrick's death, Ellen successfully applied for a widow's pension of $8 per month, with an additional $2 per month for each of her minor children (those under 16 years of age). However, the family's troubles were far from over. The first outward indications that all was not well came in January 1871, when Ellen reported to the pension bureau that she had 'lost her pension certificate out of her dress in a manner she cannot account for'. The probable reason she could not account for it would soon become apparent – Ellen suffered from severe alcoholism.[93]

Ellen's disease was having a devastating impact on her children. By the beginning of 1872 matters had reached a crisis point. Her eldest son, Patrick

Jr, just 18 years old at the start of 1872, was forced into desperate measures to try to support his younger brother and sister. Patrick described his mother as an 'habitual drunkard' who was using her pension payments to finance her addiction. The moment she received the money she would squander it on the 'purchase of intoxicating liquors and by the association of vile and evil disposed persons'. Patrick, who had left home, was forced to return as he attempted to get his mother back on the straight and narrow. He remembered:

> I two or three times … attempted to live with her and tried to induce her to keep house and take care of the family but in each instance, after getting such pension, she would leave home and refuse to contribute their [his siblings] share of such moneys towards the support, education and benefit of such two minor children. Her intemperate habits have prevented her from giving to either of the children such care and attention which they reasonably required.

Patrick's sister Maggie was 12 years old at the start of 1872. She later recalled how she and her younger brother Henry often relied on neighbours to provide for them when Ellen left on one of her drinking sprees. Things were even worse when she was at home. Maggie recollected having 'to spend the whole night in an out-house because I could not remain with my mother, when under the influence of liquors she would be harsh and cruel and compel us to seek for safety elsewhere'. Maggie remembered her older brother Patrick's efforts 'to keep the family together' as he tried to get their mother to reform, but no avail.[94]

Patrick was clearly at his wits' end. On 31 January 1872 he made a complaint to the New York magistrate, stating that Ellen had abandoned the support of her children. It was not the first time he had to resort to such measures. Two years previously he had lodged a similar complaint, which had resulted in Maggie and Henry being admitted to New York's Catholic Protectory for almost a year. Originally organised in 1863, the Protectory was a charitable institution which took in the destitute children of Catholics with a view to saving their souls, while making sure not to alienate them from their parents. During their time in the Protectory Ellen had paid $35 to assist in Maggie and Henry's support, before their eventual discharge on 2 October 1871. Now, only a few short months later, the two youngsters found themselves back there.[95]

Patrick also reported his mother to the commissioner of pensions. She was claiming a total of $4 per month for Maggie and Henry, but was not supporting them. In March 1873 a special agent arrived to investigate the case. When he interviewed Ellen she claimed the children had only been in the Protectory a short time, and that she was paying that portion of the pension due them to the institution for their upkeep. But Ellen was lying. When the special agent went to the Protectory to make inquiries, he learned not only that the children had been there for many months, but also that during their second stint in the institution Ellen had paid nothing towards their support – the financial shortfall was in fact being made good by their brother Patrick. The special agent recommended that the payments to Ellen be suspended.[96]

When the children came out of the Protectory for the second time Patrick stepped in to make sure they didn't have to go back. He began to pay for the board of his younger brother and helped his sister to find work as a servant girl. By 1875 Patrick had decided to try and obtain direct payment of the $2 per month due to each of his siblings from the pension bureau. On 4 March 1875 all of the family were called to make statements to another special agent who had been assigned to the case. Patrick gave his version of events, as did his sister Maggie (now 15), along with the woman who Patrick was paying to look after Henry's board and education. Ellen arrived on the same day to tell her side of the story; one wonders if the now-estranged family encountered each other as they arrived. For her part, Ellen did not deny that she had failed to support her children, and admitted that Patrick had been doing so in her place. Perhaps she was aware that she had let them down. There is a certain poignancy about her testimony, as she sought to deny that she had a drinking problem. The agent asked Ellen if she had ever been admitted to a hospital as a result of her drinking, and also had reason to inquire if she had been drinking that very morning:

I am not a drunkard although I have occasionally drank a glass of intoxicating liquors; I have been in the habit too when our friends call on me of going out and purchasing perhaps ten cents worth of common brandy and a pint of beer to treat my friends. I was once in the Charity Hospital to be treated for a sprained ankle; I had fallen on the ice and hurt my arm and foot; this occurred this Winter – about Christmas time. I am at present staying with Mr. Traynor and have no money whatever, having borrowed money enough this morning to pay our car fare; I had a glass of brandy this morning.[97]

In his report of the day's events, the special agent noted that during the interview Ellen's 'appearance indicated that she had been drinking to excess'. Patrick's efforts to receive the pension payments were successful, and in November 1875 he also secured official guardianship over his sister and brother. The decision of the court recorded that 'by reason of intemperate habits she [Ellen] is an unsuitable person to have the custody of them'.[98]

In 1877 Ellen's youngest son Henry reached the age of 16. With no further minor children payments due, Ellen successfully reapplied for payment of her widow's pension. She also appears to have taken steps to try to remove herself from the environment which had so damaged her and her family. By 1883 she was back in the town of her birth, Coleraine, County Derry, where she was presumably staying with relatives. Her stay in Ireland was brief. On 1 August 1885 the Department of Public Charities and Correction at Bellevue Hospital, New York recorded Ellen's admission. The 50-year-old was listed as suffering from 'disease alcoholism and wound of forehead'. Somewhat optimistically she was discharged two days later, apparently 'cured'.[99]

Ellen was, unfortunately, far from cured. Her final years can be traced through the records of the city's poorhouses. On 7 August 1884 she entered the New York City Almshouse. Such institutions sought to establish the family history and moral character of those they admitted by asking inmates a series of questions upon admission. Ellen related that she was then 55-years-old, and had been in the United States for some 35 years.

Though she had been born in Coleraine, she recounted that her father, a plasterer, had been born in Rome, Italy and her mother was originally from Dublin. She had five brothers, four in Ireland and one in New York. All were self-supporting. The reasons for her admission were given as destitution and epilepsy, from which she had been suffering for six years. Her admission slip documented that she had been both in hospital and a charitable institution before, and it proclaimed the prospects of her recovery from dependence were 'doubtful'. It would appear this was correct. Ellen was readmitted on 17 June 1893, an entry which provides us with the final update we have on her life. The reason for her seeking entry was 'destitution' and the fact that she was 'subject to fits'.[100]

THREE
A Life in Letters

There are few more powerful echoes of the past than the letters left behind by those who experienced it. The widows and dependents pension files of Irish-Americans contain thousands of them. When combined with the wider story of a family's experience, this correspondence can offer an additional emotional layer to our understanding of their story. In 'A Life in Letters' we discover the importance of music and culture in the life of one young Irishman, and learn of the extraordinary connections some emigrants maintained with Ireland in the letters of another. We see how some Irish soldiers used their correspondence to discuss politics and society, while others preferred to relate their progress in learning to write or in dreaming of the girl they left behind them. Here are the words of one young assisted emigrant who struggled with the cost of war and longed to be reunited with his mother, and of another who fought personal battles with loneliness and isolation. Not all the soldiers who fought in the war were young men. We examine the story of one middle-aged Irishman who fought for one of the war's most famous regiments but worried about the future of his ageing parents, and follow another from pre-Famine fair days in Ireland to the Mexican and Civil Wars while learning of the secrets he kept along the way. As the Civil War ended, ruthless efforts to suppress the Native Americans were redoubled. The final set of letters demonstrates that Irish homes were not immune from discovering the brutal realities of that struggle as it unfolded.

THE KELLYS: GALWAY AND MASSACHUSETTS

 'I send my love to John and tell him I am a soger.'[1]

Patrick Kelly left Ireland with his parents when he was still a boy. Having grown up among the Irish community in Boston, when the war came he wanted to serve in a regiment that underlined his heritage. In 1861 he enlisted in the 28th Massachusetts Infantry, an ethnic Irish 'green flag' formation that ultimately served in the Irish Brigade. During his service he wrote frequent letters home to his parents. His words reveal a young man steeped in culture, from his interest in reading to his deep love of music. Patrick was also a man fiercely proud of his origins, of his regiment and of its Irish affiliation.[2]

Martin and Mary Kelly were married in Ballinasloe, County Galway on 29 November 1840. Their son Patrick was born in Ireland soon afterwards, and was followed by at least one younger brother, John. After emigration, the family made their home in Boston's 7th Ward and by the 1860s were living at 3 Sturgis Place in the city. Prior to the war, Patrick had followed a path taken by thousands of his countrymen in Massachusetts, entering the leather trade as an apprentice shoemaker. Circumstances meant that his parents would soon come to rely on him for support. Patrick's father Martin, a fruit dealer by occupation, suffered an injury that left him with a severe limp. Although only in his early forties by the outbreak of the war, Martin was restricted to selling apples on the street during fine weather. The pain he suffered in his leg during inclement conditions drove him inside for much of the year.[3]

With the outbreak of the war, Patrick had an opportunity to contribute a meaningful amount of money to his parents' upkeep by enlisting in the army. Also eager to do his bit to preserve the Union, he joined up on 16 November 1861. Although he was recorded as being 22 years of age, he was undoubtedly somewhat younger. On 13 December Patrick mustered into federal service as part of Company G, 28th Massachusetts Volunteer Infantry. Less than a month later he was writing to his parents from the regiment's training camp at Fort Columbus, New York.[4]

Head Quarters 28th Regim.
Fort Columbus
Jan 15th '61 [sic.]

Dear Parents,

I now take the opportunity of letting you know that I arrived safe at my port of destination and had as pleasant a passage as circumstances allowed. We got payed off the day after coming to Fort Columbus. I got $19.50 cts. We did not get payed for this month at all. So I enclose $15 in this letter as that is as much as I can send now. Next I [will] send all my pay as I will not need it after this. This time I owed the sutler $1.25 and then we were asked to give as much as we pleased to the Captain and the Lieutenants to buy revolvers so I gave $1 as well as the rest. We have easy times in our new quarters but we are poorly accomadated as our quarters are too small, but we expect to be better fixed by and by. The Colonel said when we came here ... he would bring his men back to Boston again so we expect better room, we are too crowded that[s] all the matter with us. We ... [have] an appetite that would eat a horse. Jimy Naphin is the Corporal off our mess Jim has to do all the jawing for his mess. He is the best one in the place

*we have plenty ... [in] our mess when others are fighting for
theirs. Time is precious at present while I write I send my love
to John and tell him I am a soger [soldier]. Tell him I may
be home before him. Send my best respects to Mr and Mrs
Burns and the children and tell Larry O'Gaff I will shoot
Jeff Davis on a sour apple ... send my bests respects to Mrs
[and] Mr Guinen and to Hubert and to all enquiring friends.
No more at present from your affectionate son,
    Patrick Kelly.*[5]

As is often the case following the turning of the year, Patrick has accidentally
misdated his letter as 1861 instead of 1862. He began by getting the
business of money out of the way and noted his expenditure commitments
to the sutler, a civilian merchant who sold non-military goods to the
soldiers. Evidently Patrick also had to contribute towards the purchase of
presentation weapons for his officers, a tradition common at the start of the
war. Aside from his complaints regarding the cramped conditions, he seemed
to be enjoying his first weeks as a soldier, having quickly made friends. One
of them was 'Jimy Naphin'. Recorded in the rolls as James Naphan, he
enlisted as a 22-year-old shoemaker on 3 October 1861. Discharged on
18 December 1864, he would later serve in the 2nd Battery Massachusetts
Light Artillery. Though the 'Larry O'Gaff' mentioned may be a person, it
is perhaps more likely to be a song reference. It was the name of a popular
comic tune that charted the eponymous Larry's adventures in England and
during the Napoleonic Wars. The importance of music in Patrick's life was
confirmed by his allusion to shooting 'Jeff Davis on a sour apple'. 'We'll
hang Jeff Davis from a Sour Apple Tree' were lines from a contemporary
version of the famous 'John Brown's Body'. Patrick's next letter was sent
just four days after the first, written in response to correspondence received
from home.[6]

Head Quarters 28th Regim,
Fort Columbus N.Y. Januy. 19 1862

Dear Parents,
I received the letter you wrote and it gave me great pleasure to
know that you received it. I hope that you are better of that
cold you had, if not before now I hope you will be. I am still
in good health at present. You asked me how long we would
be on the island, that's a thing I can't say but I don't think
we will leave it before April so Pat Hoben says, he is one off
our teamsters. You need not be in a worry about coming out
to see me I'll be back in Boston after the war with the help of
God. So you need not [be] foolish spending money. The next
time you write let me know if you receive any money from the
State. I don't need much at present but you can send that box
if you want to and I should like you would [send] a guitar
and some song books if you can get the guitar cheap. I will send
$20 home the first of March if we get payed. We have good easy
times at present nothing to do and plenty to eat. I tell you
what it is a fine thing to be a Faugh for they are bound to clear
the way. Jeff Davis clear the way as the crazy sargent sung the
other night. The fire that blazed from Emmets Patriotic eye shall
lead us to our victory. So said the bard when Cass left for the
seat of war. I can't think of anything else only that [the] boys
are all well. O'Brien and Kileen and Jimmy sends their best
respects to you, send my love to Mr and Mrs Gafney and to
all the neigbors and tell Tom I won't get shot in the back.
    No more at present from your ever affectionate Son,
    Patrick Kelly.

Just as I was writing this letter the Pilot you sent came in.
You do not direct the letter right our Company is not H it is G
then direct it to Compy G.

The three soldiers Patrick mentioned in this letter serve to illustrate the destructive nature of the conflict, as none would see out the war with the regiment. Pat Hoben, a former teamster (someone who specialised in driving a wagon using draught animals), was killed in action on 30 August 1862 at the Second Battle of Bull Run; Patrick O'Brien, a shoemaker, died of disease at Beaufort, South Carolina on 8 July 1862; Patrick Killian, who also made shoes before the war, was discharged for disability on 29 June 1863. The State aid Patrick referenced was a financial support promised to the families of soldiers in order to reduce the potential impact of irregular military pay on their dependents. Patrick's reference to being a 'Faugh' relates to the war cry 'Faugh a Ballagh' meaning 'clear the way'. Originally the motto of the Royal Irish Fusiliers, it was used in reference to numerous Irish regiments and was also adopted by the 28th Massachusetts Infantry. Again, the importance of music to Patrick is apparent. The song sung by the crazy sergeant containing the lyrics 'Jeff Davis Clear the Way' and 'The fire that blazed from Emmets Patriotic Eye' is 'Fág an Bealach', which was written specifically for the 28th Massachusetts. This song is still being performed today, and would only have been a few days old when Patrick first heard it. The 'Cass' Patrick mentioned was Colonel Thomas Cass, commander of the first Irish regiment raised in the State during the Civil War, the 9th Massachusetts Infantry. The Boston *Pilot* was the leading Irish-American newspaper in the city, and was a staple for not only the Massachusetts Irish but many Irish-Americans across the United States. Eventually the 28th's training in New York came to an end, and the regiment was sent to South Carolina, where they were to join in operations against Charleston. Patrick's next letter was written in the Deep South.[8]

Hilton Head
South Carolina
July 18th 1862
New Port News Virginia

Dear Parents,

I received your letter which gave me great pleasure to hear from
you. I got your likeness the same day I got the letter and I got
the other things you sent. When we came to Hilton Head after
the battle the Regt got payed on the way here and I went and
put mine in a tin box I had in my pack. I was waiting for
the crowd to clear away so that I could give it to the Major
to send home before any temptation might cross me on land.
Well I went aloft on the ships mast and sat down there, well
I was sitting there about 5 minutes when I took out my pocket
handkerchief to wipe my face never thinking of the box, when I
suppose I pulled it out and that was the last I seen of the $26
since then. I know no one I keep by myself. Let me know if
you got the $15 I sent home in a letter. I have no more time to
write now. No more at present,

    From your son,
    Patrick Kelly.[9]

Evidently Patrick was extremely unfortunate with respect to his money,
although whether he was being truthful about how he lost it is another
matter. Though he had started this letter in South Carolina, it appears he
completed it at Newport News, Virginia on his return from the Deep
South. The battle he referenced was Secessionville, fought on 16 June 1862
as the Union sought to march on Charleston. The engagement ended in
Confederate victory. Having returned to Virginia, he and his comrades joined
the Army of the Potomac, seeing action during the Second Bull Run and
Antietam campaigns. Finally, November 1862 brought news the regiment
had long been anticipating – they were to become a part of the Irish Brigade.

Camp 28th Regt. Mass. Vol. Irish Brigade
near Falmouth Va. Nov. 27th 1862

Dear Parents,

I now take the opportunity of writing to you hoping to find
you in good health as these few lines leaves me in at present
thank God. I received your letter and although I am hard up
for writing material I cannot send for them now, for I would
never get them for we are always on the march. We now lay
opposite Fredericksburg, the rebels hold the city and we are on
the other side. We don't know the minute we will be called on
to cross the river or start off some way else. We joined the Irish
Brigade about one week ago, the Brigade gets as much beef as
the whole corps. Faugh a Ballagh is the war cry and no turn
back. Of course we will cross the river first but no matter trust
to Irelands bold Brigade to clear the road. We did not get payed
yet I think we soon will. Today is thanksgiving I hope we will
be in winters quarters before Christmas so that you can send
me a Christmas dinner. Patrick Killeen is tip top he is driving a
team now and gets 25 cts a day extra but he will soon be back
again, for we left the 9th army corps so all the detailed men
had to come back. Me and him slept together and fought side by
side and he never got a scratch. Mike Ney was taken prisoner at
Bull Run. The first volley that was fired at us he ran away and
hid in the woods so when the army left he was caught, I don't
know how true [that is], well thats what some of the boys said.
He is now at Camp Chase Ohio. The last time we were here we
left our knapsacks behind us so we never got one of them and I
left Longfellows works in the knapsack. The government would
not make the articles good except the overcoat. I want Father the
next letter he writes to write of the song called Mary Le More
I want to learn it. I have the same prayer book I carried from

home I will carry that home safe. If there is any signs of going in to winter quarters I will let you know. Let me know how times is and how dear is things I will send home $45 when I get payed that is 4 months pay. If they don't pay us until January I will send home $70. Let me know if you got the State aid yet.

Give my love to all the neighbors,

Direct your letter to me Compy G 28th Regt Mass Vol Washington DC 2d Army Corps

No more at present from Your aff. son, Patrick Kelly.[10]

As Patrick outlined, the men now found themselves opposite Fredericksburg, and the Irish Brigade was a little more than two weeks away from the most famed battle in its history. The immense pride the Galwegian felt in being part of the formation is apparent, as is his expectation that they would be to the fore in the coming engagement. When they did attack they would be without Mike Ney, a soldier who had been tainted with accusations of cowardice. Whether or not the 30-year-old former teamster had succumbed to the terrors of battle is unclear. Reported missing at the Battle of Chantilly on 1 September 1862, he was later paroled and returned to service. Civil War soldiers had to grow accustomed to constant risks to their personal property during campaigns. Regularly ordered to leave their knapsacks behind when going on manoeuvres or into battle, all too often they did not find them when they returned. The book Patrick particularly lamented losing was the works of the famous American poet Henry Wadsworth Longfellow. The most popular wordsmith of his day, Longfellow was noted for his lyric poems, which had a musical quality that would have appealed to Patrick. Further evidence for his cultural appetite can be found in his request for the music of 'Mary Le More', an Irish eviction song about an encounter with a woman driven mad by her experiences. It is not difficult to imagine Patrick playing it for his comrades later, particularly in the atmosphere of romantic nationalism that must have been prevalent in the brigade. Patrick's next letter was written in the spring of 1863. The horrors of Fredericksburg had occurred, and the Army of the Potomac was back across the Rappahannock, preparing for the campaign that would culminate in the Battle of Chancellorsville.[11]

Falmouth Va. April 27th 1863

Dear Parents,

I received the letter which ye sent me I am glad to hear that ye are all well as these few lines leaves me in at present thanks be to God for his mercy to me. I sent $30 home by the priest you will get by Adams ex[press]. You must excuse me for not sending home as much as I did before, but our clothing money for the year was stopped. What was stopped from me was nothing in comparison to others and we raised a subscription for the relief of Ireland and sent it to Donahoe. Killeen is gone to the Lincoln Hospital Washington. 4 Regts of the Brigade is gone to Kelly Ford to relieve some of the 5th Corps and our Regt is gone down to the river to do picket duty. I think we will go to the rear yet but if we don't we are able to do our duty in the field as we have always done it. Yes I got the papers ye sent. I hope this summer will end the war. I will go see Mr Murphy in Co. I but he is on picket now. So I have no more at present only give my best respects to all the neighbors.
No more at present,
From your aff. son,
Patrick Kelly.

PS I sent my likeness yesterday.[12]

This letter provides further evidence of Patrick's feelings towards his childhood home, as he contributed some of his pay towards the poor of Ireland. He did so against a backdrop of reports that the country was once again on the brink of famine, which caused relief committees in the United States and elsewhere to call for donations. Irish Relief Funds emerged across the war-stricken north, and in the first months of 1863 thousands of Union soldiers donated part of their pay to these efforts. It was a further demonstration of the keen interest that many Irish-Americans maintained in Ireland, and was all the more noteworthy given that many of the contributors would soon be facing mortal danger on the battlefields of the war. By August 1863, more than £20,000 sterling had been sent to Ireland from America. Units like the 28th Massachusetts and others proudly publicised their fundraising exploits in Irish-American newspapers, often specifically naming the contributions of individual donors.[13]

Patrick Kelly was evidently a good soldier. He was a corporal by the time of the Battle of Fredericksburg, and although he makes no mention of it in these letters, he was reportedly wounded there. He also presumably fought at Chancellorsville and Gettysburg with the 28th Massachusetts. But his April 1863 promise to send his likeness to his family is the last letter in his file. A few months later, on 3 December 1863, Patrick was on picket duty at Kelly's Ford, Virginia when he was shot and killed. Tragically for his family, it would appear that by this time his brother John was already dead. Patrick's letters were included in his mother Mary's pension application in 1864, and clearly demonstrated to the authorities that he had regularly sent money home to his parents. Mary would receive a mother's pension until her own death in 1894, three decades later, her husband Martin having predeceased her.[14]

THE FINANS: SLIGO AND NEW YORK

 'I feel very lonely and down hearted.'[15]

Second-class fireman Patrick Finan was a Union sailor serving aboard USS *Wabash*. During the Civil War his ship was one of those responsible for implementing the blockade of Confederate ports, service that could often be dull and monotonous. In his spare time Patrick wrote long letters home to his father. The correspondence had to travel all the way back to Sligo town, and demonstrates how it was possible for Irish emigrants to stay connected with their families in Ireland. In his letters, Patrick discussed emigration, community and life aboard ship, but he also touched on his personal feelings of loss and loneliness.

Patrick Finan first enlisted in the Union Navy in New York on 29 April 1861, signing on as a coal heaver. Although he was from Sligo, his place of birth was incorrectly inputted as Brooklyn. At the time he was recorded as being 23 years old, 5 feet 6½ inches tall, with blue eyes, light hair, a light complexion, and no profession. His first surviving letter home to Ireland was written off the coast of South Carolina in 1862.[16]

Hilton Head, Port Royal S.C.
October the 23th [sic], 1862

Dear Father,

I take the liberty of writing these few lines to you hoping to find you brother and sister in good health as this leaves me in at present thanks be to God for it.

Dear Father you must excuse me for not answering your letter sooner than this but I was waiting for the ship to go to New York until I would send you all particulars, but when the time came to go home I was disappointed, for in place of going to New York we were sent to Philadelphia and we received one weeks liberty on shore. I was thinking of going to New York from there but I changed my mind for I thought I might as well spend my time there as in New York. So you may think what a week I spent after being fifteen months at sea but I got sick of it at the latter end and I was glad to get on board the ship again, but we only remained fifteen days in Philadelphia until we left for Port Royal on the first of August again, and to make my liberty better I got sick on the passage out and I had to go into hospital on board the ship for two months before I got better, but I am quite well again and at my duty. Dear Father we expect to make an attack on Charleston very soon for we are to have a fleet of iron clad vessels as soon as our Admiral comes back, for they would sink all the wooden vessels that ever was built but our ship is too large to get in close on the Bar but I hope it is all for the better, for I don't want to be under the fire of them guns that is on them Forts but our iron clad vessels can stand anything so I think our vessel will have to remain outside the Bar and look on at the sport and I hope we will come out victorious.

Dear Father I have not heard one word from Patt Keen since he came out here or from Bartly Burns or the wife, but I expected Patt Keen would write and let me know how he was getting on but out of sight out of mind with them all, for they knew very well where to write to me, but I hope I will live to return them the compliment they have shown me since I left New York, but a stranger will think more of you here than your one friend. Well Dear Father I received a letter from one of Mrs. Short's sons that lived in Manchester and he is in the Navy about the same time as myself, his mother and brothers and sisters is living in Fall River where James Tindell was living, and he told me that Michael Flanigan [en]listed in the Irish Brigade under General Francis Magher, eight thousand strong, and he went into the battle that was at Richmond about a month ago and all the men he brought out alive was five hundred, so I suppose Michael Flanigan was killed in that battle.

Dear Father you must excuse me for not having something to send to you in this letter but you may expect it in the next, I will send to you in January next so try and do the best you can until then, for there is no money to be got in this ship at the present time. Dear Father you will make it your business to see Mr. Coggans and ask him if he has heard anything from his son Michael, for I was told by a prisoner we got on board our ship that come from Charleston and he told me he knew Michael Coggans, and that he got married and shortly after he [en] listed in Charleston and is now stationed in James Island the very place we are going to make an attack on, and give my respects to him and his daughter Margaret. Dear Father if I remain twelve months more in the navy you may expect me home for a few months as soon as I get paid off, for I never can let home out of my mind I am always thinking of home, I don't know the reason of it for when I was in England I never used to think half so much of home as I do now, but I am not the same since my Mother died. I feel very lonely and down hearted.

Dear Father you will be kind enough to tell John Gannon not to be uneasy ... for they are pressing men to [en] list all over the States but as soon as Rebellion is over we will have a good country here again and I expect this winter will finish it all. Give my love to my brother Michael and wife and child, and my sister Mary Ann, and to Martin Conlin wife and family, and tell little Patt Conlon I will bring him home a suit of Man O' War clothes and make a regular Jack Tar of him ... So I bid you all goodbye for the present but I remain your truly son Patrick Finan, until death.

When you receive this letter write by the return of post and let me know how you are getting on and how Michael is doing.[17]

The time at Patrick's disposal allowed him to write lengthy correspondence to his father. It is apparent that he had initially left Sligo to work in England, probably Manchester, prior to his emigration to the United States. Patrick was aware that many people in Sligo were keeping track of the war as they sought to time their own departure for America; for example he asks his father to tell John Gannon that 'we will have a good country here' once the conflict concluded. Patrick mentioned two other military men in the letter. Michael Flannigan served in the 88th New York Infantry, Irish Brigade, and survived the battles around Richmond. Captured at Chancellorsville in 1863, he was exchanged, but deserted in 1864. The reference to the other, Confederate Michael Coggans, is a remarkable demonstration of just how local the Civil War could be for Irish people. Here we have a Union sailor, stationed on a vessel off the South Carolina coast, writing a letter to the west coast of Ireland to discover if one of the men facing him in the Rebel ranks was a former neighbour. Patrick's information seems to have been surprisingly accurate. A Michael Coggins did serve as a private in Company D of the 3rd Palmetto Battalion, South Carolina Light Artillery, having enlisted aged 23 in Charleston on 14 November 1861. He was sentenced to forfeit two weeks' pay by order of court-martial in June 1862 and in July of the same year was listed as absent without leave, sick in the city (Charleston). On 4 October 1862 he was transferred to the Confederate naval service. An 'M. Coggins' is recorded as an ordinary seaman on the crew of the CSS *Chicora* for late 1863 and early 1864, and this may be the same man. The *Chicora* was an ironclad ram built in Charleston in 1862 – it was volunteers from her crew who became the first to serve on the famed Rebel submarine *Hunley*. It seems that Patrick was indeed facing an old friend from home along the South Carolina coast. This letter gives a real indication of Patrick's emotional state. His morale was low, as illustrated by the reference to his mother's death, his loneliness, and his sense of betrayal that friends from home had not made contact since their emigration to New York. Living a lonely life aboard a blockading ship, he turned his thoughts to Ireland and to all he had left behind. It is interesting to note that Patrick references his previous experiences in England, and says that during his time there he did not feel quite so far from home. His expressions of hope that he would soon return to Sligo and bring a little sailor's suit to young Pat Conlon in Sligo are also suggestive of this homesickness. Patrick was still stationed off South Carolina when he wrote his next letter, dated 25 January 1863.[18]

Hilton Head
Port Royal S.C.
January the 25th 1863

Dear Father,

I take the liberty of addressing these few lines to you to inform you that I received your kind and welcome letter on the 20th, and I am happy to hear that you are all in good health as this leaves me in at present thanks be to God for it. Dear Father I am sorry to inform you that it is impossible for me to send you the money home or I should feel very happy in doing so, for the money we get here that it is no use out of the country, for every pound in gold I would get here to send you I would have to pay two dollars discount on it so you see now how much it would take to send as much as would bring you all out here. Dear Father I am willing to pay your three passages in [to] New York, yours Mary Ann and Johnney Mullroony if you are willing for me to do so, for I don't know any other way in bringing you out here at the present time. I have the money on hand these three months and could not get no way of sending it to you. Dear Father when you receive this letter write as much as possible and let me know what you intend to do and tell Johnney Mullroony that if he is willing to come out here I will pay his passage along with yours, that is if his wife is willing to let him come here, but on no other condition. I would like to bring him out here.

Father ... when you and Mary Ann leaves we will be well divided, and if Michael had taken my advice when I was leaving Liverpool I would have him out here long ago but he has taken his own or else yours [advice] and let him abide by it, for I am sure he was time enough to get married these five years to come. Let me know how you stand, that is to say if you have got as much money as will bring you as far as Liverpool, and if not let me know in your letter and the sum you think will do you, and I will send it to you, I don't care how much I have to pay for sending it for I don't want you to be in debt to any man leaving Sligo, and for my part I am willing to do all that ever a son can do for you and more perhaps than them you thought more of. But at the same time it is no more than anybody to a Father and all I am waiting for now is the answer of this letter and if you are willing to come that way let me know and I will pay yours, Mary Ann and Johnney Mullroonys passage as quick as possible. Dear Father I intended to go to Sligo when I got paid off but all my hopes is blasted for the future of ever seeing … [my mother] lies cold in the clay that I would give all the world she was alive to be with you until I would see her face again but alas that day will never come in this world, and may the Lord have mercy on her soul, Amen.

Dear Father I have not received a letter from Brooklyn this twelve months, and I can't say how Bartly Burns and the family is getting along for like all the rest of them that is here he soon forgot me. But I hope I will live to return to New York to pay them back with the same coin, and I was greatly surprised when I heard Thomas Mullroony was married, but I suppose he took a foolish notion like all the rest of the Sligo boys. Let me know what young woman he got married to, Sligo can't be so bad when the young boys can support wives, and as for this country the widows and girls are going mad for men and can't get them, for the war has all the young men in the country away and any young man that comes home safe out of the war the young girls will be giving any amount of money to get a man, and plenty of money they have got. [It] is now the time for the young men of Sligo to come to this country, any of them that is able, for this will be a fine country when this war is over and as it is I hear they can't get men enough to do the work for them in New York. There is very few men in the citys at all but what is away in the army and navy. Dear Father there is nothing thought of a man here if he is not either in the army and navy fighting for his country. I have received a few letters from Patt Short since I come in the navy he is living in Fall River and his mother and brother and sisters sends their love to you and they wish to see you out here. Tell Johnney Michael Flanigan is still a prisoner in Richmond.

Dear Father I intend to be in a hot battle very soon, I expected it sooner than this but the weather kept the vessels from coming down here but the most of them arrived here this week, and we expect the rest of them here soon, all iron clads vessels and we expect to make an attack on Charleston, [in] the next month and I hope that will be our last. Dear Father give my love to my sister and brother, [his] wife and child and to my aunt Mary and family and Thomas Mulroony and wife, John Mulrooney and family ... Captain Steward and ... old sailors of the Shamrock ... I remain yours truly Patrick Finan and I bid you all goodbye and old Sligo for now and ever more,

Yours Respectfully, Patrick Finan

Send your letter for Patrick Finan US Navy Ship Wabash Port Royal S.C. New York America and send me Mary Ann's age.[19]

This letter is another example of the emotional depth visible in Patrick's correspondence. His efforts to pay for his family and relatives to come to the United States weighed heavily on him, as did the perceived poor decisions of his brother Michael. Interestingly he suggested it was a good time for young Sligo men to strike out for New York, where both work and women were plentiful due to the war. Patrick referenced upcoming military actions in which he expected to be involved. The USS *Wabash* on which he served was a steam-screw frigate, and spent most of the conflict on duty with the South Atlantic Blockading Squadron. Her main function was to prevent shipping from reaching Confederate ports. During the course of her service the *Wabash* took a number of prizes, including the *Wonder* on 13 May 1863. A little over a month after that capture, Patrick wrote another letter home.

Port Royal S.C.
June the 24th 1863

Father I take the liberty of writing these few lines to you hoping to find you in good health as this leaves me in at present thanks be to God for it.

    Dear Father I received your kind and welcome letter on the 20th and I am very happy to hear that you are enjoying good health and I am also very sorry to hear that Johnney Mulrooney is lying very bad, but I hope he will soon recover his health again and be able to come to see me in the land of liberty. Dear Father I am surprised at you for to sell all your things in such a hurry before you received your passage ticket, for I am sure you would have time enough to sell them after you received the order, and on the other hand you wanted me to pay your passage on a steamer but the passage is too high, it is 32 dollars in gold and 48 dollars in the US currency, so you must know how much it would be to bring you out on a steamer and to send you money home also, for I know you can't come out without sending you some money home and I think it would be very good on my part to be able to bring you out on a sailing ship, the same way as I come myself, not that I would think it too much to bring you out on a steamer, but for the way times is here at present that if a man wants a dollar in gold he has to pay one dollar and a half before he can get it, and that is what is keeping you in Sligo so long, for I think it very hard to lose so much money for nothing for it is my intention to save all the money I can while I am in the service, that I can be able to start you in business as soon as you come here. Dear Father it would take very near forty pounds to bring you and Mary Ann out at the present time so with the blessing of God remain where you are until the times takes a turn here for the better, and I hope that won't be long and I think you can't starve in Sligo as bad as you say it is.

Dear Father I wonder how the young men of Sligo that is coming out here will like to be drafted as soon as they land for they have passed a law here to draft all the young and married men from 25 to 45 years of age after they are thirty days in this country, or else they will have to leave the country again and I am very glad of it for there is a lot of young fellows around New York that won't fight for their country and they ought to be made fight or else clear out. But I wish to God it was for the freedom of Ireland I was fighting for in the place of what we are fighting for. Dear Father I wrote to Patt Short in Fall River to let me know of the first chance he can see that I can send for you, and I am very much surprised at you for not sending some account of John Gannon in your letter to his brother Michael for he was waiting to hear from him in your letter and he was greatly disappointed when he heard his name was not mentioned, and I felt ashamed myself when you did not send some news about him for I am sure you had plenty of place [space] in your letter. Dear Father I have ten months more to serve before my time is up but that won't be long passing, we are expecting our ships to go home very soon we are waiting for a ship to relieve us and as soon as she comes we start for home. Dear Father you have liberty to do as you wish with the pictures when you get them but be sure and give

Mrs. Flynn her pictures and tell her to receive them as a favour from me for her kindness to my mother, but you could not expect to receive them as quick as the letter for there will be a delay on them before you receive them. Dear Father tell Mary Finan I received her brothers likeness last week in a letter and I [am] going to send him my likeness this week. I receive a letter from him every week and he is getting along very well.

Dear Father we are making up a great deal of money in this country for the Poor of Ireland and on board our ships we made up near twelve hundred dollars on board this ship, you can see it in the last two papers I sent you. And I had to laugh the other day when I read in the papers about Patrick Davey getting eleven sheep killed on him with some of your mad dogs and about Patrick Kearns in Pound Street turning bankrupt, there is not a thing done in Sligo but I hear of it in one of your Irish papers. Dear Father cheer up and make out the best way you can until such times as I can bring you out, I am sure you would not know me if you seen me for my hair is getting grey. I am greatly changed since you last seen me, this is the country to take the blush off your cheeks. Dear Father when you write again you need not put yourself to the expense of paying the postage for I can pay for it here better than you can, let me know in your next letter if you received the pictures all right for I feel uneasy until they go to hand, be sure and let me know how Johnny Mulroony is getting along for I feel uneasy for fear anything would happen to him.

Dear Father give my respects to Patrick Flannery wife and family and tell him I feel very thankful to him for his kindness towards you, give my compliments to Patt Flynn wife and family and to Patt Feeney wife and family and give my love to my sister and brother, [his] wife and child, give my love to my uncle Johnney wife and family and to my aunt Mary and Martin Conlon and family and my aunt Peggey *give my respects to John Mulrooney wife and family, Patrick Kearns and family, Dan Riley wife and family and to Mrs Keen and tell her I never heard one word from Patt since he landed, give my love to James Hennesy and James Mulroony and to Bridget Mulroony. Give my respects to Michael O'Hara wife and family and to Patt his wife and family and to my good Father.*

No more at present but I remain your most respectfully Patrick Finan. Good Bye.

Direct your letter as before: Mr. Patrick Finan US Flag Ship Wabash Port Royal S.C. America.[20]

Once again Patrick's abortive efforts to try to get his family to America were a central theme of his correspondence. His father had sold some of his possessions in anticipation of the passage, but evidently Patrick was still not in a position to pay for the ticket. By now the Sligo sailor had changed his view on the prospects for young men in New York, primarily as a result of the decision to implement the draft. Though his political views are not to the fore in any of the letters, Patrick shared a view common to many Irishmen fighting in the Civil War when he remarked, 'I wish to God it was for the freedom of Ireland I was fighting'. References to the efforts he and his shipmates made in collecting for the relief of the poor of Ireland is further evidence for how widespread that campaign was among Irish immigrants in the military during 1863. The letter further demonstrates just how much information the Irish in America could receive from home. Despite Patrick's position on an operational vessel in the midst of a war, he was still able to obtain a local Sligo newspaper, presumably sent to him by his father.[21]

Unfortunately, Patrick's efforts to have his family join him in the United States were never realised. Just a few months after the above letter was written, he was dead. On 21 March 1864 the 27-year-old was examining water cocks beneath the boilers of the USS *Wabash*, still off Port Royal, South Carolina. An accidental discharge of hot water from the boilers caught Patrick, severely scalding him on the body and limbs. In the days following his horrific injury it first seemed he might pull through, but on 5 April an effusion of the brain occurred. He died the following night. His father John never did make it to the United States. A number of years later he sought a pension in Sligo based on his son's service. Having to prove that his son had helped to support him when he was alive, John included Patrick's wartime letters with his application, as they mentioned this financial assistance. John prepared an affidavit to accompany his claim on 12 May 1880, when he was 65 years old. He gave his postal address as West Garden Lane, Sligo and outlined his personal circumstances.[22]

I John Finan say I am a working butcher by trade but am now prevented by infirmity and ill health from earning my support by labouring at my trade. I was married in the month of July 1835 to Bridget Mulrooney but the Roman Catholic Register of the Parish of Sligo has been mislaid and I am unable to produce the certificate of my marriage. I say I had 7 children, but all are dead save two, one daughter living in the United States, of whom I have not heard for 5 years last past and one son in Australia, of whom I have not heard for the last 10 years – my son Patrick Finan was my eldest child and he left Ireland about the year 1859, and after residing some years in United States enlisted in the Navy of the United States and died on board the United States ship the Wabash until the year 1864 having been scalded to death by an accidental escape of steam – my said son Patrick Finan previous to his enlisting in said navy constantly remitted to me sums of money for my support, and I received from him in the year previous to his enlisting ten pounds sterling for my support, but in consequence of his being out at sea whilst on board the Wabash he was unable to remit money at regular or fixed times. I refer to his letter marked A dated 23d January 1863 and the letter marked B dated 24th June 1863, stating he had money for me, but was unable to remit same. My said son Patk. Finan whilst he lived afforded me my only means of support and was the only person on whom I could rely for support. From his death to the present time I have had no other means of support, than the sum of £90 the arrears of his pay and a subscription raised for me, which fund is now exhausted and which was remitted to me. I say I am incapacitated from work and am now trusting to the charity of my friends and neighbours for my support. I say my wife Bridget Mulrooney died 21 years ago and I remained since her death unmarried – I say my said son Patrick Finan never married.[23]

John Finan received a pension for the service of his son. The former butcher passed away in West Garden Lane on 20 December 1890. By then he had married again, as his widow Sarah was recorded as being present at his death. Despite his age being given as 65 in 1880, it was recorded as only 66 in 1890, which is symptomatic of an inconsistency not unusual when dealing with nineteenth-century records.[24]

Patrick Finan's letters are particularly revealing with respect to the process of emigration and the maintenance of community belonging in nineteenth-century Ireland. They demonstrate that departure for America did not necessarily mean a permanent severing of connections with home. Patrick Finan was able to regularly send and receive news about both Sligo town and Sligo emigrants, despite his position on a warship off the Confederate coast. Even in the midst of war, there remained a responsibility on men like Patrick to help their families get to the United States. The letters make apparent just how central emigration was to Irish life in this era. Those considering emigration and those who were already immigrants are frequently mentioned, including a number who fought in the Civil War. So intrinsically linked were they that Patrick could inquire, across more than 3,500 miles of ocean, if one of the Confederates he was facing in nearby Charleston was his former neighbour from home. Patrick Finan's letters not only open a window on the strong ties that could be retained between Ireland and the United States, but also provide a very personal insight into the thoughts and emotions of one Irish emigrant who had left his family to try to forge a new life across the Atlantic.[25]

THE WELCHS: IRELAND AND MAINE

 'the flag that has given protection to persecuted countrymen.'[26]

Perhaps one of the best known of all Irishmen to serve during the American Civil War was Buster Kilrain of the 20th Maine Infantry. Buster plays a major role in Michael Shaara's 1974 novel *The Killer Angels*, and was portrayed by actor Kevin Conway in the 1993 film adaptation *Gettysburg*. Kilrain, a loyal soldier and confidant of Joshua Lawrence Chamberlain, died of wounds received during the 20th's famed actions on Little Round Top at Gettysburg. Buster Kilrain is a fictional character – no one of that name ever served with the 20th Maine. But real Irishmen were present in the regiment's ranks. One of them was Tommy Welch who, like his make-believe countryman, was among the defenders of Little Round Top. Tommy shared other traits with Kilrain: both were among the older men in the regiment, and unfortunately both were destined not to survive the war. The pension file that was created as a result of Tommy Welch's death reveals much about his pre-war life and circumstances. It includes a letter he wrote home which not only explains one of his reasons for fighting, but also mentions the 20th Maine's actions at the Battle of Fredericksburg. Tommy's character is further revealed thanks to his popularity among the Maine men, which saw him remembered many years later by former comrades who sat down to record their memories of life during the American Civil War.[27]

It is not clear when the Welch family migrated to North America, but they may well have travelled via Canada in the late 1830s or early 1840s. The family group consisted of Robert and Mary Welch, their son Thomas (Tommy), a number of other sons and at least one daughter. On the eve of the war Tommy's parents were ageing. Mary Welch had been born around 1797, while Robert Welch celebrated his 77th birthday in 1860, having been born in 1783. Of their children, it was Tommy who bore chief responsibility for providing for them, foregoing starting a family of his own in order to see to their care, a not-uncommon occurrence among Irish-American families. A neighbour in Bangor, Maine, would later recall that his sister once asked Tommy why he had never married; he replied that he couldn't, as his father and mother depended on him for their support. Tommy provided this support by working in the lumbering business during the winter, and at a boom on the Nashwaak River rafting logs during the summer. A boom was a barrier placed in the river to collect timber that had been floated downstream from logging sites. This strenuous (and dangerous) livelihood saw Tommy travel some distance from Bangor, and he spent much of his time across the border. The Nashwaak is a Canadian river located in New Brunswick, where the town of Fredericton was home to a number of the extended Welch family. The seasonal nature of Tommy's work created a problem that was all too common for many Irish labourers – the unpredictability of wages. While he could hope to make $25–$30 per month on the river during the summer, this earning potential fell away to between $15 and $20 a month during the winter. Employment uncertainty and income fluctuation were factors that many Irishmen took into consideration when choosing whether or not to don Union blue during the 1860s.[28]

Whatever his ultimate reasons, it can't have been an easy decision for Tommy to enlist in the northern cause. He told friends that he was going into the army in order to better support his parents, but he was also motivated by a sense of patriotism towards the Union. There is evidence for both these economic and patriotic motivations in his subsequent actions. The latter are illustrated by views he expressed in correspondence with his brother, while the former are demonstrated by the fact that he sent at least $155 in bounty money to his family. Nonetheless, enlistment meant that he would be much further away from his mother and father than New Brunswick, and this must have been hard for a man so devoted to his parents' welfare. Tommy was probably around 37 or 38 years old when he enlisted at Houlton, Maine, on 6 August 1862, in what would become Company H of the 20th Maine Infantry. Within a matter of weeks he and his comrades were marching off to the seat of war, and their first encounter with the enemy.[29]

The 20th Maine Infantry initially became part of the 3rd Brigade, 1st Division, 5th Corps of the Army of the Potomac. They arrived at the front in time for the Battle of Antietam on 17 September 1862, but were kept in reserve and were not engaged. However, the Pine Tree State troops were involved in the pursuit of Lee's army as it made its way back across the Potomac. The 20th Maine crossed after them, but soon found that the number of Rebels they faced necessitated a swift retreat, forcing the men to dash back across the water to the other bank. One incident that occurred during this recrossing remained fresh in the mind of 20th Maine veteran Theodore Gerrish many years later:

In Company H was a man by the name of Tommy Welch, an Irishman about forty years of age, a brave, generous-hearted fellow. He was an old bachelor, and one of those funny, neat, particular men we occasionally meet. He always looked as if he had emerged from a bandbox; and the boys used to say that he would rather sacrifice the whole army of the Potomac, than to have a spot of rust upon his rifle, or dust upon his uniform. He was always making the most laughable blunders, and was usually behind all others in obeying any command. When our regiment went tumbling down over the side of the bluff, to reach the river, the men all got down before Tommy understood what they were doing. Then very slowly he descended, picking his path carefully among the trees and rocks, and did not reach the river until the rear of the regiment was nearly one-half of the way across. The officer who commanded our regiment on that day rode a magnificent horse, and as the regiment recrossed, he sat coolly upon his horse near the Virginia shore, amidst the shots of the enemy, speaking very pleasantly to the men as they passed him. He evidently determined to be the last man of the regiment to leave the post of danger. He saw Uncle Tommy, and although the danger was very great, he kindly waited for him to cross. When the latter reached the water, with great deliberation he sat down upon a rock, and removed his shoes and stockings, and slowly packed them away in his blanket. Then his pant legs must be rolled up, so that they would not come in contact with the water; and all the time the rebels were coming nearer, and the bullets were flying more thickly. At last he was ready for an advance movement, but just as he reached the water, the luckless pant legs slipped down over his knees, and he very quietly retraced his steps to the shore, to roll them up again. This was too much for even the courtesy of the commanding officer, who becoming impatient at the protracted delay, and not relishing the sound of the lead whistling over his head, cried out in a sharp voice: 'Come, come, my man, hurry up, hurry up, or we will both be shot'. Tommy looked up with that bewildered, serio-comic gravity of expression for which the Emerald Isle is so noted, and answered in the broadest brogue: 'The divil a bit, sur. It is no mark of a gintleman to be in a hurry'. The officer waited no longer, but putting spurs to his horse, he dashed across the river while Tommy, carrying his rifle in one hand, and holding up his pant legs in the other, followed after, the bullets flying thickly around him. Poor Tommy Welch, brave, blundering and kind, was a favorite in his company, and his comrades all mourned when he was shot down in the Wilderness. He was there taken prisoner, and carried to Andersonville prison, where he died of starvation.[30]

Although Gerrish's description demonstrates a stereotypical and somewhat patronising characterisation of the Irish common to the time, it also reveals a genuine affection for 'Uncle Tommy' within the 20th Maine. The regiment's first major direct experience of combat would follow a few weeks after this incident, at the Battle of Fredericksburg on 13 December 1862. The 20th Maine participated in one of the last attacks against Marye's Heights, and were forced to stay on the field through the night in front of the Rebel position. More than a month after that battle, on 26 January 1863, Tommy wrote home to his brother Robert, replying to a letter he had received from him. Robert was then living in New Brunswick, a fact that had caused a long delay in his letter reaching the front.

Falmouth VA Jan 26 63

Dear Brother I recived your letter dated Oct 20 a few dayes ago and am glad to hear from you but think you are a little unjust in not writing to me before. I have recieved but one letter from you the letter you wrote was delayed in Frederton [Fredericton, New Brunswick] about tow months. If you write they [there] will be now [no] trouble but what I shall get them. The postage must be paid before they can come.

I was very sorry to learn of Brother B. Albert['s] misfortune I hope he will be better in short time you must tell sister Mary to write to me as you can give her the directions I think she is a little ungratefull in not writing me before. I want you to let me now what [you] are doing this pleasant winter and the rest of my brothers I think I can see the hills all congealed with snow while I am in the sweat suny South.

But still I am not without trouble and trials but still I beare them willingly and more because the flag that has given protection to [our] persecuted country men. We are going to be paid of in a day or so and it will be quite a sum I will send it the same way I did before I am intitled to 55 dollars from the town of Houlton and in case it should be the will of God to call me from this world I oferise [authorise] you to collect it for me they are holden to pay it.

[illegible] is time I should tell you of the Battle of Fredericksburg we cross[ed] the Raperhanock the 13 Dec in the afternoon and marched doble quick into the citty and then we went upon the field and it was a bloody field I was struck with a shell we marched half a mile in front of the Rebles a rifle fire the shell struck me before we got on the field the Capt told me to go back and said I was badly hurt but I puut my trust in God and went forward.[31]

Tommy's letter indicates how his thoughts were turning to home (although there is perhaps a hint of sarcasm with respect to the weather) and also to providing for his parents. Given the horrors he must have gone through at Fredericksburg, his account of the fighting is remarkable in its matter-of-fact nature. Although the 20th Maine were not engaged at Chancellorsville, their finest moment of the war was to come later that summer. We know that Tommy was present with the 20th Maine on Little Round Top when they became immortal during the Battle of Gettysburg. Unfortunately, as indicated by Theodore Gerrish, Tommy's luck would run out during the bloody Overland Campaign of 1864. Although Gerrish states that Tommy was wounded and captured at the Wilderness, Tommy became a prisoner on 8 May, which suggests he was likely taken at Laurel Hill on the Spotsylvania Courthouse battlefield. He would ultimately end up in Andersonville, where he died of scurvy around the 16 August 1864. He is buried in Grave 5942 of Andersonville National Cemetery. As might be expected, his death had serious consequences for his parents back in Maine. Before long they were described as being in 'indigent circumstances' and had to take drastic steps to survive – in the words of one friend, 'necessity compelled their separation'. 67-year-old Mary went to live with her single daughter (also Mary) in Bangor, who supported her through work as a seamstress, while 81-year-old Robert, who required more care, was compelled to move to relatives in New Brunswick. They appear never to have been reunited. The 1871 Census of Canada indicates that Robert was by then a widower. Now 88 years old, he had been consigned to Fredericton Poor House.[32]

THE MCINTYRES: IRELAND AND PENNSYLVANIA

 'I think the Radicals of the Northeast want this Gov't broken up.'[33]

The widows and dependents pension files occasionally include groups of letters written by individual soldiers over a period of months or years. These can provide significant insight into the motivations, fluctuating morale and political allegiances of these men. One such example are the writings of William McIntyre, a young Irish-American from Philadelphia. Through 1862 and 1863 he told his parents of his experiences on the march, outlined what he thought of his generals, and gave his opinions on both the political situation in the north and the question of emancipation. His final letter home related his participation in the opening phases of one of the great campaigns of the war – a campaign that would ultimately cost him his life.[34]

Irish emigrants Hugh and Elizabeth McIntyre made their home in Philadelphia, north of Market Street in the city's 9th Ward. By the 1860s both had been in the United States for many years, and each of their five children had been born in the Keystone State. Hugh worked as a tailor, a job that gave his children opportunities not open to all. Principal among them was a chance to gain a degree of education. The couple's eldest son William, born around 1841, was sufficiently competent to take a job as a proofreader at the age of just 13. By the time of his 19th birthday, William was earning a decent wage, taking home $14 a week as an apprentice printer. With the coming of war, the young Irish-American enlisted, mustering in as a corporal in Company H of the 95th Pennsylvania Infantry (Gosline's Zouaves) on 24 September 1861.[35]

William's earliest surviving letters come from the time of the 1862 Peninsula Campaign, where his regiment first saw action. By the start of 1863 the now 21-year-old could count himself a veteran, having witnessed some of the toughest battles of the war. But January 1863 found him in low spirits. Defeat at Fredericksburg the previous December had been followed by the debacle known as the 'Mud March', a fruitless attempt by federal commander General Ambrose Burnside to renew the offensive against the Confederates, which came undone amidst horrendous weather conditions. William described his regiment's part in this memorable episode of the Army of the Potomac's history:

On Tuesday the 20th [January 1863] we started and at night the rain came down in torrents. The next morning we were on the march before daylight and were soaked through to the skin which made us feel anything but in the best of spirits. We marched three miles and as it was impossible to move, the artillery were stuck fast in the mud. We laid for two days in the mud like a parcel of hogs and on the fifth day Burnside made up his mind to turn our Brigade into jack-asses or some other kind of an animal for we were marched two miles stacked arms and started to pull the 'Ponto[o]n Boats' out of the mud. It was amusing to hear the boys as they pulled on the ropes for it made us feel like having hold of an engine going to a fire. We had a race with the New York Regts but every one of us pulled and beat them. You ought to have seen us after we were done. We were covered from head to foot with yellow mud and many were the 'jokes cracked' with each other about their personal appearance. If any one had told me a man could stand the hardships he has to stand now I would not have believed him. But the old saying is 'Live and Learn'.[36]

Irish and Irish-American letters in the pension files rarely make reference to politics, but where they do a clear preference for the Democratic Party is usually to the fore. There are two periods during the war which appear to witness an increase in political references in these letters – the autumn of 1864, when a hope that George McClellan would defeat Abraham Lincoln in the forthcoming presidential election is often expressed; and the first months of 1863, following the issue of the Emancipation Proclamation, a measure that was not popular among many of the Irish. On 30 January 1863 William set down his own position on the latter matter to his parents:

I see by the papers that there has been an exciting time in the United States Senate. What can be expected of the people when our representatives set such an example. If one is to judge by appearances of the different State Legislatures the present administration sits on a very shaky basis. I think the Radicals of the Northeast want this Gov't broken up and they think by so doing they will get the Middle States with them, but they are mistaken. Pennsylvania, New York and New Jersey will never take up with such a set of hypocrites and defamers of a country's rights as the Abolition [Republican] Party are. I have had time and means to look into the question at issue [slavery and the emancipation proclamation] and in a clear and candid view I have come to the above conclusion. If a State has laws they ought to be respected and there is no Institution in any State that ought to be interfered with unless *it is the wish of the majority of the inhabitants of that State but I have let myself too loose now, but if I was home I could tell you better what I think and feel since I came out here.*[37]

On the face of things, William's views would not appear out of place had he been serving with the Confederate Army of Northern Virginia, but his was a perspective shared by many others in Union blue. Although it may seem he had sympathy for the south, his enlistment was almost certainly at least partly motivated by a strong desire to destroy the rebellion. Like for so many other Irish-Americans in northern service, his primary ideological motivator for service was the preservation of the Union – not the emancipation of the slaves. William's general despondency with the state of affairs in early 1863 was at least tempered by the fact that the Army of the Potomac would not be led by Ambrose Burnside any longer. Following the 'Mud March', William wrote: 'I believe it is the last move he [Burnside] will make of the Army of the Potomac and I am glad of it'. But he was not happy about the general selected to succeed:

I suppose you have heard of Gen. Hooker taking charge of the Army of the Potomac. He is not the 'right man'. It ought to be either Gen's Franklin and Sumner as I think they are better engineers than Hooker. The latter is more like Stonewall Jackson. Lay out the plans for him and he can carry them out if fighting is what is needed. But Franklin and Sumner have been removed and it is left for Gen. Hooker to annihilate the little Army of the Potomac. 'So Mote it Be' [a Freemasonry term]. But I think the Almighty will interfere if more importance is not attached to his creatures by our Govt leaders.[38]

William clearly did not hold out much hope for an upturn in the fortunes of the Union. Unfortunately for him, on a personal level, his prediction of annihilation would prove prophetic.

Within a few weeks Major-General Joseph Hooker commenced what would become known as the Chancellorsville Campaign. William's 95th Pennsylvania played a key role in one of the opening manoeuvres, helping to seize a bridgehead over the Rappahannock at Franklin's Crossing, below Fredericksburg. This was part of a move on the army's left flank, aimed at threatening the Confederate right. At first light on 29 April assault parties from the 95th and other regiments crossed the river through a thick fog, charging up a steep bluff and dispersing the Rebel defenders with little difficulty. As Joseph Hooker personally led the main strike force across the river into the Wilderness a few miles upstream, William McIntyre took the opportunity to write to his parents on 1 May. His letter is a rare instance of a pension-file letter penned by a soldier in the midst of the very campaign that would cost him his life.[39]

May 1/63

Dear Father & Mother –

I write to inform you that I am safe and sound since I have come across on the Fredericksburg side of the river. We took up the line of march on Tuesday after noon and at 4 o'clock on Wednesday morning our Brigade was put in Pontoon boats and rowed across the river. It was a complete surprise to the 'Rebs'. They did not see us until we had got to the shore when they gave us a volley but it did not hurt very many. I did not expect to get across so easy. We soon sent some leaden pills at them that made them 'skedaddle'. They keep up a very strong front. We have not had any firing since Wednesday but our boys have had it on the right and left. We had a note read to us that our troops had turned their left flank. I don't know whether to believe it or not as we have been bamboozled so much by orders from Headquarters that we don't give them much credit.

Our Division still occupies the front. I don't know how long we will stay here, but I think we will get relieved by another Division tomorrow. There was nobody hurt in our Company. The weather has been pretty rough since we started out but to day it is warm as any summer day.

Billy Boyds Regt was not engaged so he is all safe. Jack Eberle is well and sends his best respects to you all. Give my love to Kate, Eliza, Nalty and Tommy and all inquiring friends. I sent the Adam's Express Co's receipt the day we moved. No more at present. Write soon. I remain,
    Your affectionate son,
    Wm McIntyre

Enclosed you will find $5 as I have no use for it and if I want any before I get paid again I will send for it.
    Your son,
    Wm McI.[40]

The following day, on 2 May, Stonewall Jackson launched his famed flank attack against Hooker's troops at Chancellorsville. Fighting continued to rage on 3 May, and William and his comrades were once again called upon. The force of which they formed a part, under General John Sedgwick, was ordered to advance on Chancellorsville to assist Hooker. Moving to the attack, Sedgwick took the famed Marye's Heights outside Fredericksburg before advancing his men westwards towards his commanding general. That afternoon they encountered significant Confederate resistance, ultimately culminating in a major confrontation on a ridge around Salem church on the Plank Road. The action became general around 5.30 p.m., as the Yankees advanced on the enemy along both sides of the thoroughfare. William and the 95th Pennsylvania were among those who surged forward on the north (or right) side of the road. William's divisional commander, Brigadier-General William Brooks, later described the action.

> Immediately upon entering the dense growth of shrubs and trees which concealed the enemy, our troops were met by a heavy and incessant fire of musketry; yet our lines advanced until they had reached the crest of the hill in the outer skirts of the wood, when, meeting with and being attacked by fresh and superior numbers of the enemy, our forces were finally compelled to withdraw … in this brief but sanguinary conflict this division lost nearly 1,500 officers and men.[41]

William McIntyre died during this attack, shot through the head. His father Hugh succumbed to a long battle with heart disease a year later, causing William's mother Elizabeth to apply for a dependent mother's pension. In so doing she submitted a number of her son's letters as evidence of her partial dependence on him, thus preserving them for future generations.[42]

THE SHARKEYS: IRELAND AND NEW YORK

 'I am sory [sic] *that I could not dance the divil out of her.'*[43]

In September 1863 young Irish-American recruit James Sharkey wrote a series of letters home to his family in New York. He was a newly minted cavalry trooper. The correspondence distinctly reveals the character of the young man. A picture emerges of a soldier who was hardworking, jovial, determined, and loving, but one who was also extremely young.

James Sharkey's parents Martin and Margaret (*née* Gibbon) were married in Ireland on 14 December 1837 by Father Peter O'Connor. In the early 1840s they emigrated to Canada, where they initially settled and where their first two children were born. As was often the case with Irish immigrants who first arrived in Canada, after a few years they moved on to the United States, where they decided to live in Rochester, New York. It was in Rochester that their third child James arrived around 1846, the first of six American-born additions. A mishap that occurred in 1854 meant that Martin and Margaret Sharkey would increasingly have to rely on their children for financial support. That year Martin fell from a building, an accident that broke his right hip and rendered him crippled. He would need a cane to walk for the remainder of his life. Although he was still able to work sporadically as a gardener, the injury almost certainly had a detrimental impact on Martin's outlook on life. From at least the age of 10 James had gone out to help bring home income. Likely through his father's influence, he obtained a position at Irish-born Patrick Barry's nursery, where he worked through the late 1850s and early 1860s. It seems that a number of the family found employment at the nursery.

James's brother John, two years his senior, also worked there. James kept none of the money he earned himself and instead gave it all to his mother, who controlled the family finances to such an extent that it was she who bought James his clothes.[44]

At first the outbreak of the American Civil War appears to have had little impact on the Sharkeys. All that changed in 1862, when James' Canadian-born brother John decided to join the war effort. John enlisted in Rochester on 28 August that year, becoming a private in Company K of the 140th New York Infantry. Although he claimed to be 21 years old, he was no more than 19 at the time. While his brother marched off to war, James remained at home, continuing his work in the local nursery. In the months that followed he likely wished he was off with his brother at the front. July 1863 brought the Battle of Gettysburg, where John's regiment played a vital role in the defence of Little Round Top under the guidance of Colonel Patrick Henry O'Rorke from County Cavan, who was killed during the engagement. How his brother's service influenced James is unclear, but he was certainly eager to escape his home life and his increasingly difficult father. A little over a month after Gettysburg he decided to follow his brother into the army. James was probably 17 when he enlisted in Rochester on 11 August 1863. Unlike John, he had decided to become a cavalryman and on 28 August he mustered in as a private in Company C of the 21st New York Cavalry. That September he sent at least three letters home to his mother, to let her know how he was faring. The first was sent from Camp Sprague, Staten Island on 4 September.[45]

In Camp on Statten Island
Sept 4th 1863

Dear Mother
I received your letter of Aug 24th in Troy and I have wrote
to you once since and sent you fifteen dollars and I would like
to know if you have got the money I would like to have you
write and let me know if you have got the money yet we are in

camp on Statten Island in Camp Sprague there is above five thousand soldiers here in this camp we are having a goodtime here and we are enjoying ourselves fine we have plenty to eat and drink and nothing to do but to drill once a day and a parade once a day and that does not amount to over one hours work a day my health is good and I am getting fat as a bear I expect to get some more money before I leave here and I will send it home for I don't want to use it I can not get the furlough that Capt Jennings promised to give me so you see I cant come home you may say to Miss Lyng her brother John is well and enjoying himself fine give my love to Mary Ann Giligan and Kate and tell them I want that matching they was going to give me give my love to all of my folks and my best respects to all inquiring friends no more at present so goodbye from your affectionate son

James Sharky[46]

This letter was written in a different hand to the others and was likely penned for the young Irish-American by a fellow soldier. At the time he dictated it he was still early in his military career and was clearly enjoying himself. The sentiments he expressed with respect to his health and diet are a feature of many recruits' letters in the Union army. Unsurprisingly, money is the first item addressed. James had taken a risk by physically enclosing fifteen dollars with his letter rather than arranging for its transit to Rochester through more secure means such as Adams Express. The letter also contains the first reference to a young woman who was very important to James – Mary Ann Gilligan. She was the 20-year-old Irish-born daughter of tailor John Gilligan and his wife Mary, who lived in Rochester's 6th Ward. Evidently Mary Ann was a friend of James' eldest sister Kate (who like John had been born in Canada; she was 21 years old in 1863). James appears to have been smitten, and was already looking forward to getting home on leave so he could see her. He referred to two other members of his regiment in the letter. The first was Captain John S. Jennings who had organised the company and had evidently made some promises to recruits about leave when they enlisted, which he was now unable to keep. The other was 20-year-old private John Lyng (also sometimes Lynn and Ling). Born in Ireland, Lyng had previously served in the 26th New York Infantry, and before the war had been a tobacconist in Rochester. James and John were quickly becoming fast friends. James' next letter was written six days after the first, while still in Camp Sprague. Unlike in his initial correspondence, this time he wrote the message himself.[47]

Camp Sprague Sept 10th 1863

Dear Mother

I now take the opertunite of writing you a few lines containing my health and welfare I am in good spirits now and I like it very well down here I have received your kind letter and I have seen that you are well wich I did like to hear. you want to know how I have sent you the mony I have sent it in a letter last week and I am sory that you did not receive it. you want yo know how I did like Jonys letter it was pretty good but I do not like to say that I have to live the life of a dog but we have not hat it very hard yet but once or twice we did not get enough to eat wich I did not like. you have tolt me of that party I would like to be there and engoy myself once more but I canot do it as you know yourself now. I would like to have Kate letter with her photograph I hope that I will get it and Mary An[n] Gilligan photograph I would like to have two. dear Mother I would like to know if you have got them photographs that I have left you in Rochester. We expect to go to Wachington in a few days and then to Texas to fight with the Indians. I do not like to go to Texas for it is a pretty hard place to go two. We expect to go to get our mony to morrow I will sent it to you as quick as get it and I hope you will recive it and not be chetet out of it as you did before. This is all I can let you know now at present I will remain you son

Write soon for we expect to leave here

James Sharkey[48]

It seems from this letter that the money he had sent enclosed in cash with his previous correspondence had been stolen. In the interim he had also received a letter from his brother John in the 140th New York. Based on James' reaction, it seems that John had suggested the life of a soldier was no better than that of a dog – an opinion formed following hardships that James had yet to experience. Up to this point, the worst James had to endure was missing out on social events like local parties and dances. His absence from the Rochester scene was made all the more difficult as these were events where Mary Ann Gilligan was in attendance. The regard in which James held both Mary Ann and his sister was underlined by his request for images of them. Rumours that his company of the 21st were moving out imminently for Texas proved false, and James would still be at Camp Sprague a week later. Before James fully finished his letter home he had an adventure about which he wanted to tell his mother, and so added a postscript to the original:

Dear Mother this is a nice place I hat a pass to go to New York yesterday and I was lost in the city it is a very large City and I hat a lots of fun there. Dear Mother tell Mrs. Lynn that Jony is all well and enjoying hisself down here. Sent my love to father and Kate and all the children sent my love to Mary Ann Gilligan...Dear Mother I will come to a close Jony Lynn is just like a brother to me and he likes me very well give my best respects to Jony tell him that I am well your obedient son

James Sharkey[49]

The passage once again gives a sense of James' youth and exuberance. The soldier's life had given him his first opportunity to explore New York City, presumably in the company of his friend John. As was standard practice in virtually all Irish letters of this period, James signed off by listing large numbers of friends and relatives to whom he wanted his respects to be given. The final letter in James Sharkey's file was written from Staten Island on 18 September, and is the most revealing of the three. Unlike his previous correspondence, it directly addresses difficulties at home, demonstrating the impact they had on him. Despite this, he still found time for some light-hearted references to his pursuit of Mary Ann.

Camp Sprague Sep 18th 1863

Dear Mother

I now take the opportunity of writing you a few lines containing my health and welfare I have received your kind letter of the 14 on the 17 and I was glad to hear that you are well which I was glad to hear and I was glad to hear that father is going to work in the nursery. My dear mother I am sorry that I did not send that money by the Captain but I thought that the Capt would go down on the boys for we think he has sold us for he does not come down here. Dear Mother I think you must be pretty hard up for money but you must not be discouraged for you know if I was home I would give you some money once in a while. Dear Mother when we get our money then I will send 60 Dollars which will come good for you this winter and then Johnny will send you some and tell father to work for he knows he has not much help now. Dear Mother if Eddy was home then he would help you a little. Dear Mother you must have a kind of open heart to have 4 of us left from home but you cant blame us for Father is so mean to us that we had to leave home. Dear Mother there is no use crying [over] spilled milk for we will all be home again for this war will be over before long.

Dear Mother I can spell pretty good now and I am studying to read every day. Dear Mother you have told me to trust in god I will do it and I have a prayer book and I say my prayers every night. Dear Mother tell Kate Duffy that I will home to stand up for another one of her sons ... tell Mary Ann Gilligan my best respects and tell her that I am sorry that I could not dance the divil out of her tell her that I m waiting every day for them photographs ... Tell Kate that I will send her a good present if I can get a furlough to go to New York. you say you have given Johnny my address but I have not received any answer from him yet if I go to Washington then I will be sure to see him ... tell Mrs Lynn that Johnny is well and in good health and as quick as he gets his bounty he will send her some money home. Dear Mother please give my best respects to ... all the folks around the Weigh Lock ... If I do go to Texas probably I will see Thomas Green. Dear Mother I am enjoing myself we get plenty to eat I got as fat as a hog ...[50]

The precarious financial situation his family found themselves in was again to the fore. The sporadic payment dates that were the soldiers lot throughout the war had impacted both James' and John's ability to assist their family in Rochester. These circumstances had forced their father to once again seek work in the Barry nursery. Here James provided an insight into just how difficult things had become since their father's injury, as his 'meanness' had caused four of the Sharkey children to leave (aside from John and James, the others were presumably Kate and their younger brother Eddy, who was around 15 or 16 at this date). It cannot have been easy for any of them.[51]

Despite the young cavalryman's stated reservations about Captain Jennings, the officer did rejoin his men and would muster out as major in September 1865. James was attempting to use his time in the army to improve his literacy skills, which he was proud to show off in his letter home. He had also acquired a name stamp (perhaps on his trip to New York City), which allowed him to liberally apply 'JA. SHARKY' to his correspondence. In his final letter James gave the strongest indications of his feelings towards Mary Ann, who he wanted to 'dance the divil' out of. She was just one of the members of the community around the Rochester Weigh Lock of the Erie Canal that James was missing. Despite some homesickness, he looked forward to the potential of seeing his brother John around Washington, and once again remarked how good the army food was for him.[52]

Company C finally did move on towards Washington DC. It was a little over a month before Margaret Sharkey next received word from her son. Unfortunately, rather than more news of his adventures, or an update on his progress with writing, it was a letter from Captain Jennings that came to her Rochester home at 15 Mount Hope Avenue.

Camp Stoneman DC Oct 26/63

Mrs Margaret Sharkey

It is my painful duty to inform you that your son James Sharkey of Co C 21 NY Vol Cavy died on Saturday Evening Oct 24th at the General Hospital of this Camp of Malignant Typhoid fever after an illness of about eight days.

I can assure you that in all the circumstances attending his illness he showed a remarkable patience and in all ways displayed a desire to give but little trouble to those around him. As a soldier, though so young, he was remarkable for his willing and cheerful attendance to duty, and I cannot but sympathise deeply with you in your loss of so good a son.

His death surprised us all. I had no idea that he was so near his end, and had charged the Surgeon on friday to notify me in case he should become dangerous – he promised to do so and seemed much surprised himself at the rapid progress made by the disease, when it was too late to arrest its progress.

The men of Company C have had the body embalmed and sent home for burial, thinking it may be a poor comfort to you his mother to have his body resting near your own. It is all the sympathy they can show you in your sorrow, but it is honest and earnest.

James had not an enemy in the company and altho' he has not been permitted to yield up his life on the field of honor yet the sacrifice is none the less glorious – His life's strength has been yielded up in the cause of Humanity, Liberty and Godliness and his reward is reached. Let his memory be kept ever green as one of the patriot martyrs of the day.

His effects have been forwarded to you with his body. Some $75 of Bounty remains due to him from the Government and pay from the 11th July at $13 per month the Govt therefore owes him $120.00 as follows:

Bounty $75.00
Pay $45.06
Total $120.06

Which you can get by applying thro the Sanitary Commission, without charge – let me advise you to apply thro the agent of that society instead of going to Lawyer agents.

His clothing &c are here they are not worth sending home. Should there be anything amongst his effects worth sending to you it will be forwarded by Express.

Hoping that you may be sustained and comforted in your day of affliction by 'He that tempers the wind to the Shorn Lamb' and that you may finally meet those called before in a happier and better Land I remain

Truly Your Friend
John S Jennings
Capt Co C 21 Reg NY Cavy
Washington DC[63]

James' life had been cruelly cut short. There would be no more dances or parties, no more fun with his sister Kate and Mary Ann Gilligan. The news must have come as a deep shock to all of the amiable young man's family.

James' best friend in the regiment, John Lynn, was not there to hear the news – he had deserted on 6 October. How the loss affected James' brother John in the 140th New York is unknown. He would provide the family with a scare of his own in the months to come, when he was shot during his regiment's charge across Saunders Field in the Battle of the Wilderness on 5 May 1864. He recovered, living a long life and dying in St John, Kansas in 1922.[54]

James Sharkey's letters provide an insight not only into one young man's personality, but also into his place in Irish-American society. Neither James, born in the United States, or his older brother John, born in Canada, are traditionally included among those figures for the 'Irish' who served during the American Civil War. But it is clear that they were intrinsically linked with the Irish community in America. James Sharkey's parents were Irish, his employer was Irish, his best friend in the army was Irish, and his prospective girlfriend was Irish. Had James been asked, he would surely have affirmed his own sense of 'Irishness'. By any measure he and those like him should be included when discussing the impact of the conflict on Irish people. With that comes the realisation that the story of the estimated 200,000 Irish-born men who served during the Civil War represents only a part of the Irish experience. To fully encompass it, we must include in our reckoning the tens of thousands of American-born Irish who felt just as much a part of the Irish community in the United States. In so doing, we dramatically alter our perspective on the true scale of Irish-American involvement in the struggle.

THE TIERNANS: ROSCOMMON AND NEW YORK

 'I am improving in writing if I knew all the capital letters I could do first rate.'[55]

Many of those who emigrated from Ireland in the 1840s and 1850s had to adjust not only to life in a new country but also to dramatically different environments. Such was certainly the case for Bridget Tiernan and her family. Bridget (*née* Hanly) had married Dominick Tiernan in the Parish of Kilgefin, County Roscommon on 1 October 1837. There were surely few more dramatic relocations than that which she experienced with her children, moving from rural Connacht to the heart of Manhattan's Five Points, the notorious slum district in New York's 6th Ward. Dominick died around 1850, either just before or just after the Tiernans' emigration. That left Bridget to fend for herself in the raising of their three sons, Dominick Jr, Martin and Thomas. As it transpired, Bridget had swapped one set of hardships in Ireland for a seemingly endless string of trials in America. By the mid-1860s, she may well have wondered if she had made the right choice in leaving Roscommon.[56]

By the time of the 1860 Census, Bridget's eldest son Dominick had already followed his father to the grave. That year the enumerator found her occupying some of the attic rooms in a two-and-a-half-story wooden tenement at 15 Baxter Street in the Five Points. The 45-year-old woman shared the cramped accommodation with her surviving sons Martin (19) and Thomas (17), both of whom were apprentice hatters. Bridget also rented space to boarders in order to make some additional money, and they shared the family's rooms. They were among dozens of occupants of the Baxter Street tenement, the vast bulk of whom were Irish.[57]

The cramped and overcrowded conditions in which the Tiernans lived made disease a constant risk. Bridget's youngest son became consumptive, which forced him to give up his trade due to his sickness and severe cough. His illness did not prevent him from entering the United States service following the outbreak of war, though his time in the military was apparently brief. Bridget's other son, Martin, also decided to try his hand at soldiering. He enlisted in New York on 10 October 1861, initially mustering in as a private in Company E of the 61st New York Infantry on 12 October. He quickly demonstrated his capabilities, and by 1 November the Roscommon man had been transferred to Company B to take up the role of corporal.[58]

A little more than a week after his promotion, Martin's regiment left for Virginia. He took the opportunity the army presented with both hands. Like for many other Irish soldiers, one his main aims was to try to improve his literacy. His first surviving letter is covered in evidence that he was practising his writing skills, repeatedly copying the letter 'B' of his Company on the page until he got it right.[59]

Virginia Janua[r]y 20th 1862

Dear Mother I recveed [sic] your letter on the 17th but I being on guard I could not answer you sooner I do not know what to think of Thomas as I have not heard from him since he cam[e] out he could come to me if he tried as for him be[ing] in bad company there cou[ld] be no worse than hims[elf] and as for him losing his money there is no fear of that as he can beat an[y] of them gam[b]ling and another thing they can[n]ot gamble much as they have no time Do not send him any more money I inquire[d of] Johny Shea if he heard anything of him and I will let you know Dear Mother there will soon be a great battle all the fighting will be done inside of three weeks but you must not be alarmed as there is no fear of me and Thomas with the help of god perhaps I may not have a chance of writing again for some time but do not be alarmed I thought to send 20 Dollars this time but I could send but 13 I am getting along very well and I have been promoted That will be $15 a month and less to do I am improving in writing if I knew all the capital letters I could do first rate I enclose Thomas[ ]s Letter and read it if you hear from him write as soon as possible no more at present

From your son Martin Tiernan Direct your Letter Martin Tiernan company B [the letter B repeated three times]

61st Regt
N.Y.S.V. camp
California
virginia or elsewhere
write soon send me a few stamps as they are very dear here [the letter 'B' is practiced a further 18 times] [60]

Evidently Martin was the more sensible of the two brothers, with Thomas having a reputation as a bit of a tearaway. Despite his expectations, it would be many months before Martin's unit would see any serious action. In the spring of 1862 the regiment moved with the Army of the Potomac to the Virginian Peninsula, where they settled in to a siege at Yorktown. The next letter was written from Camp Winfield Scott on 21 April. [61]

Camp Winfield Scott Virginia April 21st 1862

Dear Mother I recived your kind and welcome letter this day and it makes me feel glad to hear that the boss has got plenty of work as there is a report that we are going home and it is reported that the officers of our Regment has orders to report at Washington to be sent home and we think it true Dear Mother you talk about the South being strong now I do not know how you can belive those stories and what has happened there best general is killed and the half of them is prisnors and there is one hundred thousand of them in yorktown and we have them sure as we have two hundred thousand men and plent[y] of cannan and they have not Our Diveison is on the reserve and we are within three miles of yorktown and we can hear the cannans every day for a week you need not be afraid that

I will know much about the battle. I am out here now six months and never seen a Rebel but three that came in prisners. Tell Thomas to stay at work untill I come home and then he can work for me and I will give him more and ask him if he got a Letter from me and if he answered it Dear Mother tell Thomas to go to Paddy Meehan and tell that I got those papers from him on the 14th and that I am well and that I wrote four letters to him and got no answer

No more at present from your son Martin Tiernan give my respects to all friends. Dear Mother we have got no pay yet. I will have four months pay on the first of May.[62]

By this time Thomas had been discharged or had otherwise left the army, most likely due to his health. Again, Martin's sense of responsibility towards his sibling is apparent, as he suggests that Thomas could soon come to work for him as a hatter. His expectations that the war would soon be over were shared by many of his comrades, and clearly he felt he would be back in New York in short order. Certainly it appeared to him that his regiment was not needed for the fight. His next letter was sent following the capture of Yorktown in early May.

Yorktown May 9th 1862

Dear Mother I received your kin[d] and welcome letter on the 3rd and it gave me great pleasure to know that you are all well as this leaves me at present thank god for it. Dear Mother we have taken yorktown without losing a man and the army is in pursuit of the enemy and you may be sure that the war is over and we will soon be home Dear Mother I sent 20 Dollars to you by Adams Express we are in yorktown and expect to stay there until the war is over. We expect to get discharged at any moment. Dear Mother it would astonish you to see the guns *they have left here but I will tell you all about them when I go home No more at present from your son Martin Tiernan Let me know if there is any news from Ireland and what Thomas is doing write soon I was not in the battle.*[63]

The engagement Martin had missed was the Battle of Williamsburg, which took place on 5 May. His restated belief that the war would soon be at an end was misplaced. In reality his regiment were about to experience their baptism of fire, when the 61st New York engaged in their first major battle at Fair Oaks on 1 June 1862. Forming line of battle just after 7 in the morning, Martin and his 431 comrades stepped off towards the sounds of firing coming from the woods to their front. When they reemerged later that day, they had lost a quarter of their strength, suffering 110 casualties. Among them was Martin, wounded by a bullet during his first engagement. He died from his wounds the following day in the Regimental Hospital.[64]

Martin's death robbed Bridget of yet another son. While she continued to live at 15 Baxter Street, her only surviving boy, Thomas, moved to Washington DC in an effort to improve his health. In late 1862 Bridget, now around 50 years old, set about securing a pension based on her son's service. Unusually for an Irish emigrant to America, one of those Bridget was able to call on for an affidavit was her former landlord in Ireland. Elizabeth Flemming was able to confirm Bridget's marriage, as both husband and wife 'were tenents of hers' in Ireland. Elizabeth may have been a relative of Richard Fleming of Gorthlyon, County Roscommon, who advertised for sale the rental of a 604-acre estate in the baronies of Athlone and Ballintober in December 1853. An encumbered estate, it illustrates that the Famine also had a significant impact on many members of the estate-owning classes. Aside from her former landlords, among the others who rallied to Bridget's support were the residents of the Baxter Street tenements. In December 1862 Irish blacksmith John Sands and his wife Frances, who had lived in the same room of 15 Baxter Street with Bridget Tiernan and her sons, swore they had first-hand knowledge of Martin's efforts to financially support his mother. They had seen Martin give Bridget money every Saturday night when he came home from work and had seen the letters and money he had sent her after he enlisted.[65]

As if her trials were not enough, Bridget was now also suffering from a severe cough and pains in her chest, indications that she may have been developing the consumption that had afflicted her youngest son. Unfortunately further hardship lay ahead. At around 12.30 a.m. on the morning of Tuesday 11 June 1863, a fire broke out on the second floor of 15 Baxter Street, in the room of Mary Ann Daniels. Like many of the Five Points tenements, the building had no fire escape. The conflagration quickly began to sweep through the wooden building and up towards the attic rooms, where Bridget and another Irishwoman Jane Collins lived with their lodgers. By the time the alarm was raised, there seemed to be no escape for those on the upper floors. Before long the staircase was completely filled with thick smoke. Upon realising this, the attic occupants became 'frantic with fear and rent the stillness of midnight with their piercing shrieks, rendering the scene one of horror and despair'. A report recalled how 'the women groped their way through the halls, and from one room to another, and called upon the fireman to rescue them from the awful death which threatened them'. As the police arrived on the scene to try to help those on the lower floors escape, those trapped in the attic had a decision to make. At the time Bridget had eleven lodgers staying with her. Two women braved the stairs and managed to make it through the fire, but the majority jumped. Hugh Devier and his wife Catherine, who was blind, 'embraced each other and jumped from the window together; and miraculously escaped, with only a few bruises'. Not all were so lucky. Margaret Keating was seriously injured when she jumped. Two boys, aged 11 and 15, managed to leap onto a shed from the rear windows and escape. But their mothers were among the four people who died in the building. The body of 35-year-old Alice Murphy was later found in a doorway, with her 4-year-old child held in her arms. That of 35-year-old Sarah Gray lay partly dressed on the floor, while the remains of 30-year-old Mary Jane McMasters were found in her bed. All the victims were Irish. Bridget Tiernan was one of the lucky ones, managing to throw herself out the front windows of the attic space. Her friends the Sands, who only months before had supported her pension application, weren't so fortunate. By the time John and Frances jumped into the street, John had suffered severe burns to his body. He died from his injuries the following day in New York Hospital. An inquest was held into the tragedy, at which Bridget and a number of other residents gave evidence. Bridget testified:

> … that she was lying in bed in the attic of the house, but had not been asleep when she saw the fire in Mrs. Daniels' room; she subsequently got out of the house without saving anything; Mrs. McMasters and Mrs. Gray (two of the deceased) were drunk; there were eleven lodgers in the three rooms occupied by witness; Mrs. Murphy (another of deceased) was also drunk; all who were sober got out but the little child of Mrs. Murphy.[66]

Bridget Tiernan was living temporarily in 14 Baxter Street when her pension application was approved on 13 August 1863. The financial aid must have offered her some comfort following the sequence of misfortunes she had endured. Over a few short years she had lost two sons, watched the other become incapacitated by illness, and become sick herself. What few personal possessions she enjoyed were then taken from her in a fire. For Bridget, life in the United States had proved to be every bit as tough as what she had left behind in Roscommon.[67]

THE CARRS: DERRY, NEW YORK AND ILLINOIS

 '… these are hard times nothing but fighting every day and killing of men.'[68]

On occasions the information contained within the widows and dependent parents pension files can be combined with other sources to provide a much wider picture of one family's nineteenth-century emigrant experience. The file relating to the Carr family is a case in point, charting as it does their journey from poverty in Ulster to a life of hardship and separation in 1850s New York. It is a story that continued into the American Civil War, as an

Irish soldier fought not only to reunite the Union, but also for the right to be reunited with his family. It continued into the post-war period, as the family tried to forge a new life in the 'Gateway to the West'.

On 18 August 1860 the following advertisement ran in the 'Information Wanted' section of the *Boston Pilot*:

INFORMATION WANTED OF BERNARD (or Barney) CARR, who left Ireland and landed in New York in 1851, with his mother and her children. Being unable to support them she was obliged to send three of the boys to Ward's Island, from which place a person named Fenton Goss, from New Jersey, took one of the boys (Bernard, or Barney) to West Liberty, Logan county, Ohio. The unfortunate and disconsolate mother, who is now in certain circumstances, offers a reward of $20 to any person who can give her any information of her son Bernard Carr. Address Mrs. Ann Carr, Walton, Delaware county, N.Y.[69]

There are hundreds of ads like this scattered across newspapers like the *New York Irish American* and the *Boston Pilot*. They often provide tantalising glimpses into the hardships experienced by many Irish emigrants, but in reading them, we are often left with more questions than answers. Where in Ireland had they come from? Why had they emigrated? Was the advertisement successful? What became of them afterwards? Remarkably, in the case of Ann Carr and her son Barney, we are in a position to answer all of these questions. Surviving records allow us to give voice to the Carr family, representatives of Ireland's poorest emigrant class, and to hear from Ann and Barney in their own words.

The starting point for investigation is an Irish place name, phonetically transcribed in 1865 by a clerk in Hudson, New York. As he listened to Ann Carr recount details of her family's past, the clerk did his best to capture where he thought Ann was from. This manifested itself in his notes as the word 'Belmosgreen', a location that does not exist in Ireland. However, the Catholic Parish Registers record the marriage of an Arthur Carr and Nancy Mulholland in Ballinascreen, County Derry on 10 November 1835. Given that Ann's husband was called Arthur, and that the historical records demonstrate that Ann was variously known as Ann or Nancy throughout her life (a not-unusual interchange), there is a strong likelihood that Ballinascreen was the Carr family's place of origin. Ann would have been around 22 years old at the time of her marriage, and the couple had at least five children prior to Arthur's death around 1850. Although it is not known what caused Arthur's demise, what is apparent is that it left Ann and the children utterly destitute. They were so poor that they could not have contemplated passage to the United States were it not for the intervention of others. Ann later related that in 1851, 'I and family were sent to America and our expenses paid by the local authorities in Ireland' indicating that they were assisted emigrants. The family clearly escaped penury in Ireland only to be faced with pauperism in New York. The 1860 advertisement that Ann placed in the *Boston Pilot* demonstrates this, as she had been forced to place her sons in institutional care due to an inability to afford their support.[70]

We know that Ann's 1860 advertisement worked. By 1862 Barney, now 17 years old, had moved from Ohio to Illinois, where he was working for William Gillis, a farmer in Embarrass, Edgar County. It was around this time that Ann reestablished contact with Barney, though they had not yet been reunited face to face. The prospect of them doing so anytime soon seemed remote, particularly as by the end of 1862 Barney's movements were no longer his own to dictate. By then he was a Union private serving in the Army of the Cumberland. Having found himself with no money, Barney had enlisted in Paris, Illinois on 19 July and mustered into Company C of the 79th Illinois Infantry on 18 August 1862. He was variously described at this time as 'under 18-years-of-age' and 'quite young'. Despite the circumstances, Barney seemed happy in his new role. He started to correspond with his mother, who was living with his younger brother and two sisters in the village of Walton, Delaware County, New York (there is no mention of his third brother after 1860). In one of his early letters, written in camp near Nashville, Tennessee, he asked his mother to:

> pray for me continually I hope that you and me and the rest of the folks at home ... see each other once more before I die. If it is the will of God that he may spare my life to get home to embrace my mother as we haven't seen each other for about 9 years or more.[71]

Barney became a regular correspondent with the mother he had not seen in so long, and his letters reveal much about his character. Despite the fact that he had not seen his family in many years, he still managed to have an argument with his younger brother John via their letters. It seems that John (around 15 years old by 1863) thought that it was not very 'manly' of Barney to be sending some of his money to a friend to mind it for him. In a letter written in the fortifications of Murfreesboro, Tennessee on 31 March 1863, Barney sent some money for his mother and sisters, but raged that:

> John can do very well without any money for what he said in his letter, Sis I want you to tell him that he can keep his pen and paper and I will do the same if he thinks that it don't look very manly to send money home to a man. I would thank him to keep his mouth shut and I will send my money how I please and if he wants to know the reason of [it] I want to have some money when I get home ...[72]

As with other Irish soldiers whose primary motivation for enlisting appears to have been economic, Barney nonetheless displayed considerable patriotism in his writings, demonstrating that preserving the Union was a strong motivator for him. However, life's simple pleasures were important to Barney too, and absolutely nothing seems to have been more vital in this regard than tobacco. This is demonstrated in a letter to New York from Chattanooga, Tennessee on 14 November 1863, written at a time when Union forces in Chattanooga had faced shortages in supply.

> ... Mother I want you to send me by mail one round of fine cut chewing tobacco just as soon as you can send it to me, for that is the only way I can keep from spending my money and if you don't send me plenty of tobacco, why then you will have to send me my money to buy it [he was sending home $30] for I can't do without the article in no shape nor form ... as for tobacco you can buy me a number one quality there and

not cost near so much as it would here, I have to pay $1.00 for one plug of tobacco and it won't weigh half a pound and it is musty after I get it so that I can't chew it.[73]

Barney was also in need of a new uniform cap, and wanted to avoid drawing one from the army stores: 'send a good soldiers cap … I am out of a hat and I will have to draw from Uncle Sam or else go and pay $7.00 for a hat and I would rather send you the money … the kind of cap that I wanted a soldiers cap one that the top leans over on the bill and the bill sticks straight out'. Just in case his mother had forgotten his sustained appeals for tobacco, Barney signed off the letter with 'please don't forget what I told you and send them all right along'.[74]

On 18 November Barney wrote a letter from Chattanooga that suggests he was keen on word play. In describing an early morning skirmish with the Confederates, he equated the whole affair to a quest for breakfast.

… this morning directly after I got up our boys and the Rebels had a knock down before breakfast and I think that our fellows gave them a breakfast of hot lead, just all that they could eat for I guess they have not had very much to eat for some time and it took a good deal to fill them for they are big eaters. Any how when they have not had anything to eat for some time I guess that they were a trying to get back across the river to get at our cracker boxes and our fellows are a little hungry this morning and did not like to issue rations before they got what they wanted themselves, and Mister Rebs had to stand back until Yanks got his share for they feed our bull dogs double rations of canister and grape and the Rebs could not eat that when they throwed it across to them, and I guess it was [a] good deal of trouble for them to catch them kind of crackers throwed the distance that our boys had to throw them and that distance was across the river and when they got across they were pretty well scattered and it was a little cold and the Rebels thought that

their fingers might [get] cold to pick them up and concluded they had better left that alone ...[75]

Although the fighting experienced by Union and Confederate soldiers in the first years of the war was horrendous, the conflict entered a new chapter in May 1864, when Grant's strategy of applying sustained pressure was implemented. That summer the 79th Illinois marched with Sherman's army in its long, painful advance towards Atlanta. The 79th took casualties at Rocky Face Ridge on 9 May, at Resaca on 14 May, at New Hope Church on 27 May and at Muddy Creek on 18 June. The Yankees had gradually been forcing the Rebels back towards Atlanta, but now they faced the Confederates most formidable defensive line yet – Kennesaw Mountain. As the jostling for position around this daunting Confederate fortified line continued, Barney wrote the below letter to his mother on 20 June. It is a remarkable note, and is here reproduced in full. It was not only written under fire, but it expresses sentiments that demonstrate the mental toll that fighting of this nature took on the men.

Headquarters 79 Regt Ills Vols. Camp in the field in front of the enemys breastworks and they are a shooting at us all the time, this date June the 20th 1864.

Dear Parent, once more I take the pleasure [of] writing to you a few lines to let you know that I am still alive yet. As I suppose you are well aware that Shermans army has been a fighting ever since last May and that I am still in his army. So as I have not wrote to you in a good while I thought you would be uneasy about me and thought that I would write you a few and let ... [the letter stops at this point, and continues as below]

Dear Mother I have had to stop writing, we are a lying on the line [of] battle and there are 12 pieces of cannons in front of us and they are a shelling the Rebs and that draws the Rebels fire and it is a horrible place to be in. Cannonballs are a flying thick around us and the shells are a screaming in the air and through the woods, cutting the timber and earth in all directions, but thank [God] Mother I am still safe and unhurt, but how long I may still remain so I can't tell anything about that yet. God only knows how long it may last, I am sure I can't tell anything about it now that by the grace [of] God I still live yet and am well and hearty in the bargain and I hope that when this few lines reaches you that [they] will find you all well and doing well.

Dear Mother these are hard times nothing but fighting every day and killing of men I am a getting tired of it but then I want to see them keep those Rebels a moving to Atlanta and I guess that it is the only way of putting down this Rebellion and the sooner it is down the better it is for them that lives to see it. But Mother pray for me that I may live to see it over and live to see you all, so Mother I want to see you before I die and I want to see all of the Carr family.[76]

Seven days after Barney wrote this letter, on 27 June 1864, Sherman ordered his men to assault the Confederate line at Kennesaw Mountain. Lieutenant-Colonel Terrence Clark of the 79th Illinois described how the regiment formed:

> in double column at half distance on the third line of battle, Capt. O. O. Bagley temporarily commanding. He advanced the regiment to the front line, when he, on account of the troops on the right falling back, was compelled to retire, losing, in commissioned officers, 1 wounded, 1 enlisted man killed, and 11 enlisted men wounded.[77]

The Union assault at Kennesaw ended in a bloody repulse. The next day Captain H.C. Beyls of Barney's company sat down to compose the following letter:

Mrs Nancy Carr

Madam,

I have to report the most painful and sorrowful duty to perform, to notify you that your son Barnard Carr of my company was killed while in the discharge of his duty. On the 27th inst our brigade was ordered in connection [with] others to charge the rebel works. Many were lost – but Barnard was the only one of my company – he [was] a noble, brave and patriotic soldier never flinching from duty but always on hand ever ready to lend a hand to assist me – I sympathize deeply [with] you and his friends
I am with respect
your obedient servant

H.C. Beyls Capt –
Co 'C' '79' Ill Infty[78]

Ann Carr would never be reunited with her son. Barney was ultimately interred in Marietta National Cemetery, where his body lies in Plot I, Grave 9311. Back in New York Ann was comforted by her three surviving children, Mary Jane, Ann and John. She would go on to seek a pension based on her son's service, citing his financial support of her and the fact that her advancing age (she was around 51 years old when Barney died) prevented her from carrying out as much paid housework and washing as she used to do. As additional evidence, Ann included 'eight letters rec'd from my said son while he was in the army and which will show his feelings towards me'. She claimed that there had been no time since she had landed from Ireland that she needed the money as much as she did now. Ann's pension request was granted. In 1865 she moved to Hudson City, New York, before going west and settling in Omaha, Nebraska in 1876 with her three children. The surviving members of the Carr family would all live out their days in the 'Gateway to the West'. Ann's death was recorded by the *Omaha World-Herald* on 17 March 1898:

Died. CARR – Mrs. Anna Carr, age 90 years, at the residence of her daughter, Mrs. Stephen Rice, 963 N. Twenty-fifth street. Funeral Friday, March 18, at 8.30 a.m. to St. John's church; services at 9 a.m.

She is buried near her three children in Omaha's Holy Sepulchre Cemetery.[79]

THE DEVLINS: TYRONE AND INDIANA

 'Let William know there are cows here as well as in Ireland.'[80]

One May morning in the mid-1840s, Charles Devlin made the 5-mile journey from his home in Rylands, Gortin, County Tyrone, to the fair in Newtownstewart. He and his family were experiencing hard times. Charles had until recently been employed as a labourer on the Beltrim Castle demesne, home to the local landlord family the Cole-Hamiltons. But Charles had lost that job when his employer, Major Arthur Willoughby Cole-Hamilton, had left the estate. Try as he might, Charles had been unable to secure more work. Travelling to Newtownstewart that day, he determined to spend some of the money he had left on a cow to help support his family. However, his wife Margaret was unhappy with the purchase. Likely upset that the buy diminished their already finite resources, she had him return the beast. Charles was running out of options. In order to provide for his wife and two children he took the decision to obtain passage to America. Discussing it with Margaret, he told her of his hope that 'with God's help I shall do something for you and my children'. A neighbour, David Graham, visited Charles on the Saturday before he left Gortin for the last time. The two men drew out manure on the land for the setting and planting of the family potato crop, leaving it ready for spreading. One wonders what went through Charles' mind that day as he worked his field. By the time Margaret planted the ground he had prepared, the Tyrone man was already sailing across the Atlantic.[81]

Charles and Margaret Devlin had been married by Revd Bernard O'Neill in the townland of Meenadoo, County Tyrone, on 18 December 1836. They would go on to have three children, Catherine born in February 1839, William born in the autumn of 1841 and Peter born in August 1843. When Charles left around 1845 there was nothing to indicate that he would not be able to send for his family, and it appears that it remained his intention to do so for a long time. Within a year of his departure a letter arrived for Margaret from America. Unable to read herself, she took it – unopened – to her neighbour Peter Devlin. Together they brought it to the house of Dan McKelvy, who outlined its contents. Inside was a bill for £5. Dan read out the note from Charles that accompanied it: 'Let William [Charles's son] know there are cows here as well as in Ireland'. Peter Devlin and Margaret took the money and bought a cow, an acquisition that would prove vital in sustaining the family over the Famine period.[82]

Within a couple of years of his arrival in the United States Charles had his first taste of military life, enlisting in the army during the Mexican–American War. He is likely the 'Charles Deavlin' who was recorded as joining Company A of the 2nd Dragoons at Philadelphia on 4 December 1847. That man was a clock finisher from Tyrone, who was described as 5 feet 11 inches in height, with hazel eyes, brown hair and a ruddy complexion. He served through that conflict, being discharged on 13 August 1848.[83]

The years passed and Charles continued to send money back to Ireland. Margaret brought the American bills that arrived in the post to Patrick McCullough's General Merchants in Gortin to be exchanged. The drafts often carried with them suggestions from Charles as to what the money should be spent on. Charles and Margaret's daughter Catherine remembered them being used to buy necessaries and provisions, but also occasionally something special. At one time her father requested that she should have a suit of clothing out of the sum sent. Catherine also recalled her father's desire that the family soon join him in America: 'On one occasion I heard read a letter in which he requested my mother to go to the United States and for me or one of the boys to go also'.

The regularity of the letters varied a great deal – they sometimes arrived quarterly and sometimes less frequently. But all in the locality agreed that without the money sent home by Charles his family would have required charitable support. Still, Charles never seemed to have gathered the money required to allow his family to join him. Some fifteen years after his emigration, around 1861, he sent a sum of £10 home with the intention of assisting their passage. He told Margaret to use the money to come out with the children if possible, but if not to come herself and leave the children well secured in Ireland until they could send for them. While she was still deciding what to do, Margaret received a letter from Charles. As he was unable to write, the correspondence was penned for him by another member of the regiment.[84]

Camp Morton Dec 6th 1861

Dear Wife I take my pen in hand to inform you of how I'm situated in this country I'm now joined in the first Irish 35th Indiana Vullinteers for three years or sooner discharged and dear wife I received your last letter which it gave me great pleasure to hear that you and the children are all well and Dear wife don't be uneasy about me for I am getting along very well for soul and body I hope for I attend to my duty as good now as ever I did before if not bet[ter] and Dear wife we got an Irish Catholic clergyman his name is Father Cowney [Cowney] and we attend mass every Sunday and the two thirds of the regiment has taken the pledge from one to three years and meself among the rest and he is giving them all scapillers [scapulars] and says one mass in the month for those belong[ing] to the society and we expect to have the best regiment that ever gone in to the field and with that that we have marching orders not knowing what day we might be leaving here and going into Kentucky in the battle field and Dear Wife I'd very well like to know from you how are all the children and how they are getting along an[d] how are they situated and also let me know the state of your own health and Dear Wife I did very well like to have you remember me in your prayers and to have one or two masses said for me and Dear wife life is uncertain but if the lord spares me out of this I'll expect to see ye once more in Ireland and Dear Wife in case that any accident might happen me I have all particulars testified between me and the colonel and the adjutant general for you to get my pay my pay is thirteen dollars per month clothing and board and 100 dollars bounty at the end of the war and 160 acres of land and I want to have you see after all of this if you never hear from me any more Dear wife the colonels name is John C Wa[l] ker and the captains name is John P. Dufficy and first Leutenants name is Christoper O'Brien and belonging to company B and Dear Wife in writing about all there particulars write all of your letters to the parish priest of Indianapolis in the state of indiana his name is Revd Father Besoney for Father Cowney that is our chaplin name as before mentioned and Dear Wife I'm three month in the service this very day but we got no pay as yet we expect to get it after we leaves for Kentucky and as soon as I get paid I'll send a portion of it home as money is no use to me here now and Dear wife I'd like for you to let me know how is sister Mary so no more at presant but send love to you and Catherine William and Peter farewell but I hope not forever

Farewell Dear Wife and children but I hope not forever May God bless and care for you all and for me for two with the blessing of God.

Direct your letter to the Rev. Father Bessoney for Revd Father Cowney from I'll receive it

Indianapolis in the state of Indiana

Marian County[85]

Charles had become a sergeant in Company B of the 35th Indiana Volunteers, often called the 'First Irish', an ethnic Irish regiment organised in Indianapolis in late 1861. At the time of his enlistment his residence was given as Washington, Indiana. News of him joining the army came as a shock to his wife at home in Ireland, and affected her decision on travelling to America. Margaret would later remark 'when I heard of his being enlisted I declined going to him fearing that I might be left desolate in a strange country in case of his death'. The offer of a $100 bounty and 160 acres of land seems to have been a particularly tempting offer for Charles, who was also clearly proud to be serving among his fellow countrymen. Evidently a religious man, he referenced his membership of the regiment's Temperance Society and his wearing of a scapular provided by the regiment's Catholic chaplain, Father Peter Cooney from County Roscommon. Father Cooney was a member of the Holy Cross community in Notre Dame and was immensely popular with the men of the regiment. Charles' next letter was sent a month later, by which time the unit had moved into Kentucky. By then he had heard back from his wife, who had expressed her surprise at his decision to enlist.[86]

> *January 11th 1862*
> *Camp Morton Kentucky*

Dear Wife and children I take my pen in hand to let ye know that I'm in good [health] at present thanks be to God for his mercies to us all. Dear Wife I have written you two letters and got but one and in that was stated that you would not believe that I was enlisted. Dear Wife it is so for truth I'm stationed here in Camp Morton in the state of Kentucky 40 miles from Louisville the regiment I'm in is an iris[h] from the sta[te] Indiana the[y] is to be attach[ed] a brigade of 20 thousand strong and now I mean to give a scetch of camp life we live like fighting cocks here the flower is rolled into us by the barrels and that every man may cook it to his own taste as particular cooks we mus[t] do our own cooking and besides I'd to tell of the food that we get we get coffee twice ¾ lb of pork once a day the day we don't get that we get ¼ lb of fresh beef besides beens rice ... sugrar millasses coffee ... and soap and salt and so you may believe we live well besides their 14 of us in each tent and our principle bed is the hard wet ground wherever we encamp at this present time we have a little straw like as you shake under your cow of a cold snowy night and as for our bed clothes we cant brag of them for we only have one blanket and we can under it or over it which ever we please Dear wife were here now about 60 miles of the enemy and their supposed to be about 400000 strong and our forces are supposed to be about 200000 thousands strong Dear wife you spoke to me about sending you a newspaper and its impossible for me to get as such aint allowed for soldiers were dispersing the[m] pretty good and we expect to have a big battle before 3 weeks Dear wife I'd like to write more to you now but I aint got time or much ro[o]m in this ... I got promoted from a private to a sergeant and my pay is 17 dollars per month and we expect to get paid now pretty son for we were mustered in for pay 8th of this month and their 4 months pay coming to me now Dear Wife let me know how you and the children are getting along and in case that anything might occur to write to the priest that is going with the regiment and his name is the Revd Father Cooney and write about all of this to Louisville in state Kentucky to the Revd Bishop Spawlding and he'll get my pay for you if the above mentioned might occur to me and tell him for employ a lawyer for you and you pay him for getting it and you must have set your marrage lines and a certificate from the parish priest and you get the parish priest to write about all of this to the Bishop So no more at present from your beloved and affectionate husband Charles Develin but I hope the children will [be] good obedient children to their mother I have no more to say at presant God care for you all and for me too.

Dear Wife farewell but I hope not forever ... Dear wife

get some masses said for my soul and offer up daly prayers for me.[87]

Aside from painting a picture of camp life, Charles was also taking care to let his wife know the process by which she might claim a pension if anything should happen to him. Charles' next letter followed in March:

Camp Wood
Munfordsville Ky
March 9th 1862

Dear Wife and children I write these few lines to you hopeing to find you and the children in as good health as I am at present thanks be to god for the same. Dear wife I wrote a letter to you on the last of December and have not received an answer from you yet let me know if you got it or not our Regt have been paid off on the 8 of this month my pay came to $65.16 cents for three months and thare are two months more pay coming to us yet I have sent $50 dollars or ten pounds of it to you the rest of it I have to use to get some things with for myself we are mustered in for pay every two months and from the aperance of things this war will not last long as it is nearly over now we are takeing all of their strong position[s] which they have had here to fore and it is the opinion of every one that one more month will settle it and then we will be all free again from soldieran. if such is the case and that I am well and in good health I shall return once more to you and the childeran which may be about fall or sooner. We have recently gained some very grate victories which is of grat importance to us Thare has [been] since the first of Desember about twenty

of those victories which has placed in our hands over 4000 prisoner from the southeran army if this so called southeran Confederacy is recognized by the powers of Europe thay will be disappointed when thay come here thay will be no such thing as the southern confederacy thay are getting downhearted and say that their leaders has deceived them and they will not be fooled any more by such men. Dear wife let me know how your health and that of the childrens is and how you are situated and my advice to you is that you would keep Catherine at home and for you to live as comfortable as possible now coming over towards your old age and also I advise you to rent for your selfe a small farm and keepe one or the two boys at first as you think proper. for my part I think is is just as good for you to stay as to come as to come [to] this country on account of this war it will take some time to settle it. give my best respects to all enquiring friends I will now close this letter by sending my love and best respects to you and all the children form you[r] Dear husband
    Charles Devlin

Direct your letters as follows
Charles Devlin Company B 35 Regt
first Irish I. Vols in care of the Rev. Father Cooney Chaplain
now stationed in the state of Kentucky[88]

Charles appears to have been in agreement with his wife that it was a bad time for her to consider coming out. His optimism with respect to the war was borne from the early success of Union forces in the Western Theater, typified by the victories at Forts Henry and Donelson, Tennessee in February 1862. The final full letter on file was written only two days later, on 11 March 1862.[89]

March the 11th 1862
Munfordsville Ky

My Dear Wife

I have received your kind and affectionate letter but just one
day to[o] late for I had wrote a letter yesterday to let you
know that I sent $50 fifty dollars which amounts to 10 ten
pounds and is now allready on the way so that you may be on
the lookout for it I would have sent more but we only received
three months pay thear is two months pay yet due me which
I may probably get in perhaps in ten or fifteen days which I
will send you immediately as soon as I receive it you need not
be any ways uneasy about me as I am perfectly contended and
injoy good health at present and try to the best of my ability
to atend to my religious duties with the assistance of Almity
God and the kind instructions of our beloved pastor father
Coney who says a mass the first Friday of every month for the
benefit of the members of the temperance society of the regiment
he said an extray mass to day for thear benefit it is a good
society which I have the honor and pleasure to be a member of
receiving the benefits of the society and the masses said for it it
caused me a great deal of joy to hear that the children are well
and that you attended to them so well and that [sic] hope they
will allways continue to be good and obedient children and it
is my wish that Catheran shall stay at home and attend to
you in your old days and if it should be the will of god that
I should not return home I want Catheran to remember my
wishes to stay out and attend to you and for Catheran to not be
in a hurry to enter into marriage untill such time as I return
home or if it should be the will of god that I should not return
home for her to not marry at all events during her mothers life
but to live with her and attend to her in her old days and as

long as I live I shall never see any one of them to want for
any thing for remember my words that I have seen enough of
the world and got my eyes open at last

In my last letter I stated to you about you getting a piece of
land and having a home and living together in regard to that
I want you to use your own judgment which will be the easest
for you to live on a farm or on the money which you will put
to the best advantage you can all so I want you to mention
in your next letter the situation of the family and if they are
all together we are expecting to leave this place the day after
tomorrow for Nashville Tenn when you write direct you letter to
me in care of Rev Father Coney Company B 35 ind regiment /
Irish volenteers us army

    Charles Develin[90]

Despite having been away from home for some 17 years, Charles was
continuing to communicate with his wife and to offer advice on what
should happen with the children, particularly his desire for Catherine to
stay at home and mind Margaret in her advancing years. He may well
have been sincere regarding his intentions to be reunited with them one
day, but the degree to which he sought to insure that outcome remains
open to question, particularly given the events to come in 1862. That
summer saw the 35th Indiana engaged in the campaign in Kentucky,
which culminated in the Battle of Perryville on 8 October 1862. Following
the Confederate retreat, Charles and the regiment found themselves in
Nashville, Tennessee. It was there on 8 November that Charles Devlin
married Anne Donnelly in the Roman Catholic Cathedral, thereby
becoming a bigamist.[91]

It remains unknown if Charles Devlin had known Anne prior to his time
in Nashville, or if theirs was a whirlwind courtship. Anne would later swear
that she believed Charles to be unmarried when they wed in Tennessee,
and there is no reason to doubt that was the case. The couple only had

a few weeks together before Charles moved on with his regiment, but when he left Anne was carrying his child. Charles Devlin Junior was born in Nashville on 12 August 1863 and baptised the following month, on 12 September. Less than a week later the 35th Indiana was heavily engaged in the Battle of Chickamauga, Georgia, a fight in which large numbers of the regiment became prisoners. Charles fell into Rebel hands following heavy fighting near the Viniard Farm on 19 September and by the summer of 1864 was being held in Andersonville, Georgia.[92]

Whether Charles had ever communicated with his first family in Ireland following his second marriage is unknown, but the regiment's commander Major Dufficy wrote to Margaret in Tyrone to let her know of Charles' capture. Ten months after he became a prisoner, around July 1864, she had word directly from her husband. While in the camp he dictated a letter to Henry Dodridge, another Union prisoner and a member of the 81st Ohio Infantry. Likely sensing his end may be near, Charles recounted how he was 'labouring under a sore load of sickness' but maintained that if he recovered he would return to Ireland. He then provided explicit details as to his financial entitlements, namely his backpay and bounties, land entitlements and his pension for his Mexican War service. It was the last Margaret heard from him. Within days Charles was dead, succumbing on 26 July 1864 to pneumonia. He is today buried in Andersonville National Cemetery, in Grave 4021.[93]

On hearing news of his death, Charles' new wife Anne, presumably unaware of her husband's previous marriage, applied for a pension for her and her infant child. She was now living in New Orleans, where the soldier's backpay and bounty were sent to her. But eventually Margaret made a rival application from Ireland, via the US consul in Londonderry. Aided by her husband's letters and local affidavits, including one from her landlord Arthur Willoughby Cole-Hamilton, she demonstrated both the date of her marriage and that she had never been divorced. In consequence of this evidence, Anne's 1862 marriage to Charles was demonstrated to be invalid. She and her young son lost the pension, which was instead directed to Margaret in Ireland.[94]

Had Charles and Margaret Devlin's marriage been a loveless one? Perhaps Charles found it easier to live apart from his family in America, sending home the occasional support while making his own way in a new country. Or perhaps he had longed to bring his family out to join him, but either through ill fortune or ill choices was never able to raise sufficient funds to do so. Maybe it was Margaret who was reluctant to relocate. Whatever the truth, in 1862 he decided to start a new family, and by so doing indicated he thought it doubtful he would see his first wife and children in Ireland again. Despite the passage of almost twenty years he had maintained some sense of obligation towards them, something he once again reiterated, or reestablished, as he lay on his deathbed in Andersonville. Whether he did the same for his new family in New Orleans is unknown. A postscript to the story occurred in 1882, when William Devlin, Charles' son, wrote to the US Pension Bureau. The boy who all those years earlier had received a note from his father about all the cows in America was now in his forties, and still trying to make a living in the house Charles had left in 1845. Despite Charles' wishes, it appears to have been William, rather than Catherine, who looked after Margaret in her final years. William was apparently somewhat embittered, and wrote seeking to have his now deceased mother's pension transferred to him. Given he was not a minor child under the age of 16 years, his appeal would ultimately prove unsuccessful.

I William Devlin am the son of the late Charles Devlin who enlisted in the year 1861 in the 35 Regament Indiania volenters whose pay was 13 dollars a month and a hundred dollars of a bounty one hundred and sixty acres of land at the end of the war or 100 dollars in place of the land which we have not got … I am the only heir of it now and I claim it or the land my mother diyed on Sunday the fourth day of june in the year 1882 … so as the goverement has left me with out my father the[y] are entitled to comute the pension the[y] were giving to my mother by my father death and his bravery in the wars he was the same … to me that he was to her and if any differens more for I am his child and she was only his wife I have only the same way of living that she had and living in the same place in a small house and garden about half a rood of land attached to the little house and that is all I have that I can call my own I am the only one that stayed with her when the[y] all left her when all *her children left her and my father was fitting [fighting] in the American wars she had no one to look after her I stoped with her allalong so I believe that the goverement should look after me and let the same pension that the[y] were given to my mother continue to me for I will be true to the goverement as my father and mother was before me at anytime the[y] like to call upon me I would very well to go to that country as I have not a very good way of living on me in this country I would like to have the protection of the goverement ...*[95]

THE MANGANS: DUBLIN AND ILLINOIS

 '... stop at home for no matter how humble a home is, home is sweet.'[96]

As we have seen, the regular army still held an appeal for many Irish emigrants after the Civil War. A soldier's life brought with it a modicum of security and certainty that were attractive to men who were often reliant on employment opportunities that could be varied in both reliability and financial reward. For those who joined the army after 1865, a decision to enlist also raised the prospect of being placed on the front lines of the relentless march of 'manifest destiny'. Many Irish immigrants, often only recently arrived in the United States, were to the fore in the brutal suppression of the Native American peoples that took place during conflicts such as the Plains Indian Wars. One such immigrant was Sergeant Thomas Mangan, a 22-year-old who within a year of arriving in his new home found himself in the midst of the savage struggle for control of the Western Plains. From his isolated post in the Colorado Territory during 1866 and 1867, Thomas' letters travelled over 4,000 miles before arriving at their ultimate destination in inner-city Dublin. There they were read by his widowed mother, who was not spared the gory realities of violent death on the plains. Thomas also shared his thoughts on life on the frontier, his experiences since emigration, and his future plans for himself and his mother.[97]

Thomas Mangan Sr and Sarah Connolly were married in Castlekevin, County Wicklow on 3 February 1834. From there the couple moved to Dublin, where their son Thomas Jr was born in 1845; he was baptised in the church of St Andrew in Westland Row on 8 December that year. Thomas Sr died in 1857, leaving Sarah to raise their young son alone. Thomas Jr started his working life in Dublin at the age of 13, helping his mother to run the household. By the mid-1860s mother and son were living at 14 Wood Street in the heart of the city. Thomas appears to have been working on nearby York Street at this time, earning 5 shillings a week, while Sarah was employed in a nearby business. In the spring of 1865, Thomas decided to try his luck in the United States. He made his way to Chicago, where his maternal uncle Edward (Ned) Connolly lived. But things didn't work out for Thomas with his relative. The young man soon grew disillusioned with the support he got from his family in America, and after only eight months he enlisted in the United States Army. When he joined up on 2 January 1866 he was 21 years old. Thomas' papers described him as 5 feet 8 inches in height, with a fair complexion, grey eyes, brown hair and by occupation a clerk. Life on the frontier meant that months could pass between opportunities to write back to his mother in Ireland. When he did so, he was a soldier at Fort Sedgwick in Colorado Territory, an isolated post surrounded by large numbers of hostile Native Americans.[98]

Fort Sedgwick Colorado Territory
Sunday 2nd December 1866

Dear Mother after a long absence I take up my pen to write to you I would have wrote to you months before this only I was away on detached duty and I never could get the chance to do it then. This is not an easy place for a man to write that is knocked around and to let you know the reason we were knocked around is the Indians played hell here all summer and is expected to be worse they have killed over 100 men of our regiment alone besides men of other regts. and citizens they attack these trains passing over the plains here to California & Salt Lake and other places they attack those trains then take their stock and all, kills the men and scalps them. They likes to scalp well they carry those scalps they take on a cord or string round their body, thats an honour they think as much as a soldier thinks of medals on his breast and a great deal more. When they take a good lot of scalps any of them above others they make him a chief or warrior of them, a big brave they call him, so they like to scalp well then. I received that newspaper you had sent me and the other thing all right. I sent fifty dollars to Larry to send to you about 2 months ago and I don't know whether he sent it to you or not. He sent me a letter about 3 weeks ago, a blank sheet of paper in the envelope a powerful lot of news indeed, I told him to send me a couple of stamps to write to you and after a long absence he sent me one. Indeed I wrote t[w]o letters to him after I sent the money would be in the express office when he get[s] that letter and after 2 months absence he sends me a blank sheet of writing paper with one stamp, never letting me know one word about it one way or the other. I sent it back to him the same way. Dear Mother I must say he is very ungrateful. I even wrote to the man he is working for to know was he with him. The reason I followed it up so much is for you to get the money. All I say is I hope he has sent you the money or will against Christmas, it will be £6 or £7 pounds of English money.

Dear Mother I would like you to find out on the quay what is an American dollar worth there for I am sorry I didn't put the 50 dollars in a letter and sent it to you for a man in our Compy sent 100 dollars in a letter home to London, England and it went all wright and moreover I could send you money far oftener – they would change it on the quay for you I should think as well as London, now don't forget to let me know in your next letter. Dear Mother I remember by your last letter that you wanted to know is there any people out here or is there any winter. Well I will tell you there is a little town 4 miles from the post with about 40 people that is all, they call it a town it has about 4 or 5 log buildings and for the winter, I need not tell. [For] 3 or 4 hours one night last week it snowed it was more than [illegible] high the snow. The stage or mail coach drove into the river ... it was coming down so heavy the driver could not see [over the] horses heads and three people was nearly killed ... So you many guess the winter that is here by that.

Dear Mother if you have got the money I would like to send me the Dublin Nation newspaper every week to read by giving them my name and address. It would come to me, they would send it themselves from their office for to me for about 4s the price for six months. Dear Mother when I am paid I will send you some money also for some newspapers. A few dollars here is nothing to lay out and to send it home it would look something, it would give you as much reading for a year as you would wish besides having home news. When I get a letter from you I will send you some money for to give for papers. Its greenbacks I will send you when I hear from you about them in your letter by you seeing at the exchange office this side of the Custom House on Eden Quay.

Dear Mother I have in 11 months of my time to-day and against you get this I will have close on one year, so I intend to forward myself in reading, writing and so forth for the next

2 years. I am going on very well as you will see, the last letter I wrote to you I was only Corpl. but now I am a Sergeant so you must know that I am conducting myself well or a man won't be raising in the army.

I must conclude with wishing you a merry Christmas and a happy new year.

No more at present from your affection son Thomas Mangan.

Direct for Sergt. Thomas Mangan Co. E 3rd Batt. 18th US Inftry.

Fort Sedgwick Col. Ter.

Give my best respects to Mrs. Nolan, let me know how is her health, is her stock going on well. I hope both her and her business is for they could not go on better than I would wish, indeed I think I will see her yet in Ship Street and have a glass of cordial with her. Give my respects also to Mrs. Smyth & Eliza I hope they are going on well too as to Humphry I suppose he is in the country now if not he is any how in O'Briens with James and likewise to Mrs. Hart and husband and to all enquiring old friends let me know about James Routledge, James Daniel, Johnny Wichkam and all the boys. Tell Johnny Wickham to tell James Daniel I was asking for him I would like to hear from him, indeed enclosed is my directions for him to write to me. Tell Johnny Wickham to tell James Daniel to come to you for my directions if he gets them fro you let me know and if he is going to write and when to me.

I remember in your last letter of you saying that Mr. Sullivan was going to write to me I never heard from him any, tell him I was asking for him if he call'd and give him my respects.[99]

This remarkable letter combines descriptions of the savage fighting taking place during the Plains Indian Wars with thoughts of family, friends and business back in Dublin. It is difficult to imagine a sharper juxtaposition. Thomas does not spare his mother the details regarding what happened to those who fell at the hands of the Native Americans. The background to the confrontations had been the construction of a series of fortifications in the Powder River country of what is now Wyoming, along the route of the Bozeman Trail, which connected the goldfields of Montana with the Oregon Trail. The area was rich in resources, and was a particularly fruitful region in which to hunt. In the 1850s the territory had been part of the Crow homelands, but the Lakota, recognising its value, had conquered the Powder River country by 1859. When the white soldiers arrived, they found Lakota warriors who were in no mood to give up what they had so recently won. The violence that erupted would become known as 'Red Cloud's War' and would run from 1866 to 1868. Red Cloud was an Oglala Lakota war leader whose name became synonymous with the conflict.[100]

Less than three weeks after Thomas had written this letter to Dublin, the United States were rocked by a crushing defeat inflicted on their forces by a combined Lakota, Northern Cheyenne and Arapaho force near Fort Phil Kearney, the central fortification that had been constructed in the Powder River country. An entire detachment of eighty-one men was wiped out in what became known as the Fetterman Fight, the worst defeat government forces experienced until Custer's Last Stand at the Little Bighorn a decade later. Fully 25 per cent of the men who died with Fetterman were Irish-born. Thomas' next letter exhibits the shock that the defeat caused. In it he describes attempts to hunt down some of the Indians responsible, and mentions the risks of operating in freezing weather conditions. He also makes strong efforts to dissuade his mother from following him to America, encouraging her to stay at home and recounting his own poor experiences with their family already there. Instead Thomas hoped to himself return to Dublin one day, perhaps to set up a business.[101]

Fort Sedgwick Co. Ter.
Sunday Feb. 3rd 1867

Dear Mother I received your kind and welcome letter about 2 weeks ago. I would have wrote to you long before this only I was away on duty so I could not write till I got back. You told me you wish to come out to the States and you wish to know what I think of it and Laurance. I wrote to him twice about it and I got no answer from him, but my opinion is for you to stop at home for no matter how humble a home is home is sweet. Your sister may say a great lot of things in her letters to you, something like Ned and his family to me. When I was home I believed all they said then for I was foolish then. I have known it well since, I did not know the want of a home before I seen the way I was treated. I went off an enlisted, if you came out here and they treated you bad what would you do. In the first place how can you tell what kind of a man her husband is, it is very well to think he is a nice man by seeing him on your own floor in your own home, remember the old saying, if you want to know what I am come live with me. After I being 8 months or about with Ned I was only 3 days idle thats when I came there from home without working. I came to Neds on Sunday and went to work a Wednesday dear Mother and after 8 months when I left I paid her every cent I owed. Mrs. Kirwan turned and told somebody I owed her for three days when I landed board, you do not think on any account of coming out here at least while I am in the army. Stay at home and do not fret about Mrs. Nolan giving up for you shall never want a cent while I can get it. I am going to send you all my pay and live well and if you have anything over its all right. Every time I am paid I shall send you my money home. I intend to save £70 while I am in the army this 3 years. I shall send it all to you so if you have any over you can keep it against I am out of my time, I may go home and put up in a little bussiness for soldiering here is far worse than in England. A man never goes to church, I never seen a clergyman this last year and two months, if a man is discharged here and cannot get work what would he do in this part of the country about military posts. The few citizens when they are idle they have to pay £2 10s a week for board and only gets two meals a day for that, 1s for the washing of a shirt. If a man goes to the States he may not get work either. A soldier here is put down as a loafer, you may thing a soldier bad at home but here he is taught less than a dog if I may say it.

Dear Mother I am thinking when my time is up if I had a little money saved I could do well some place at home where I would not be known. I have a Cockney chap a comrade from London he is saving all his money and sending it home to his mother against he is done with the army here. Me and him enlisted the one day. I think he is doing a very good thing indeed. I suppose you read in the papers at home or heard of the fearful massacre of some of our soldiers here at Fort Phil Kearney. There was 90 men and 4 officers killed by the Indians. The[y] fought them 7 hours 5000 Indians there was. Our First Lieutenant were killed amongst the officers. When they were dead the[y] cut their breasts open took out there hearts and put them in their mouths, pulled out their eyes, cut off their ears, fingers, toes and noses and then scalped them, burned some of the wounded after doing all that. In fact I could not describe it to you. Just now as I write the Compy. of cavalry is coming into the Fort after being 15 days in the snow after them. They went out about 3 weeks ago the same and they had a little skirmish with them. They killed about 40 Indians and our Cavly. lost 1 man whom the Indians shot with their arrow knocking him off his horse and left to froze on the ground frozed to death, found dead in the snow next morning. When he was knocked off his horse the horse ran away and left the poor fellow to die. There was two more wounded not badly. There was 27 frozed of them, 3 of them since has lost both feet. The boy was frozed was Irish only 16 years of age. We are all armed here to the teeth. Every Cavlry. man had a 7 shooter carbine and 6 shooter revolver. There was never a man escaped of the 94, I forgot to tell you to tell the tale, not one, all butchered. I got a letter from my aunt McGurk yesterday I wrote to her to-day against you get this letter I will have money on the water to you.

I must conclude, give my best respected to Mrs. Nolan and Mrs. Smith.

No more at present from your affectionate,
Son Thomas Mangan.

Direct Sergt. Thomas Mangan Compy. E 36th US Inftry. Fort Sedwick [sic.] Colorado Territory.

I wish to tell you we are the 36th now under the new organisation in the US Army there is no more 2nd or 3rd Batts. every Batt. is a Regt. in itself now so leaves us the 36th Regt.

Thomas' reference to soldiering in England and finding a place in Ireland where he 'would not be known' raises the possibility that he might have served briefly in the British Army. His account of the mutilation of the soldiers' corpses is largely accurate. According to the Lakota White Bull, this was done both because the soldiers had killed so many Indians and to demonstrate their resolve to hold the Powder River country.

On 23 May 1867, a few weeks after writing this letter, Thomas was carrying his company's mail from Pole Creek Station to his unit on the Spring Creek in Dakota territory. Along the way he was set upon by a group of Cheyenne and killed. His body was found three days later near Lodge Pole Creek by his comrades.[102]

Thomas' death had knock-on consequences he would not have wanted, as it caused his mother to migrate to Omaha, Nebraska in order to pursue her pension claim. It would seem she lived out her final days in the United States. Ultimately the Dubliner had met the same fate he described in such detail in his letters home to Ireland. Like many other Irishmen, he fell in a pitiless campaign to suppress the Native Americans and take control of their lands that is now rightly regarded as one of the most shameful episodes in United States history. Men like Thomas Mangan are on the wrong side of that history. It is all too easy to view them simply as racist caricatures, but the reality, as Thomas' letters show, was far more complex.[103]

FOUR
A Death in Letters

The central event that ties all the widows and dependents files together – and led to their creation – is the death of a soldier. 'A Death in Letters' focuses on this event as it was experienced by eight different families. Contained within the stories are the last letters of soldiers written without an awareness of their imminent death, and the last words and wishes of those who were all too sensible of their demise. We explore how families discovered the details of their death, be it a hastily penned note found in one dead man's pocket, or the detailed description by a friend of the final moments of another as he faced the Civil War's most famous charge. The end was not always quick, and relationships could develop between caregivers and family at home as they corresponded back and forth, as was the case for one soon-to-be Irish widow. A soldier's death in battle often had a defining impact on those he left behind, in some cases causing a ripple effect that could last well into the twentieth century. We follow some families in the decades after their loss, in an effort to ascertain the full cost the events of 1861–65 had for some Irish emigrants.

THE COCHRANS: LONDONDERRY AND PENNSYLVANIA

 'Remember me to all the folks.'[1]

The course of Sarah Jane Cochran's life meant that she found herself effectively having to make two applications for a widow's pension. The documentation created as a result provides details on decades of this ordinary emigrant woman's experiences. It also reveals a story of hardship and hard choices, which included the necessity of surrendering a letter that was likely one of her most treasured possessions.

Sarah Jane Smith was born around the year 1829 near the town of Limavady, County Londonderry. We know little of her life before 1848, when the then 19-year-old boarded the ship *Barque Creole* in Londonderry. Her destination was Philadelphia, where Sarah arrived on 31 July that year. We next encounter her on 25 June 1856, when she married fellow Irish emigrant Richard (Richey) Cochran at the 9th Presbyterian church, on the corner of 16th and Samson Street in Philadelphia. Richey was a teamster. The couple initially made their home on Rhoads Street in the city, where they celebrated the birth of their first child, Jane, on 16 April 1857.[2]

After Jane's birth, the young family decided to try their fortunes elsewhere in Pennsylvania. When the federal census enumerator visited them on 5 June 1860 they had moved across the state to Allegheny City, where they made their home in the 2nd Ward. They were boarding with another Irish family, the Donaldsons, made up of Joseph and Mary and their children Margaret and Thomas. It is likely the Donaldsons were fellow Ulster Presbyterians, and like Richey, Joseph worked as a teamster. It wasn't long before the Cochrans were on the move again. They relocated across the Allegheny River to Pittsburgh, where they moved in to No. 42 Virgin Alley. Here they celebrated the birth of a second child, William Richard, on 22 March 1861.[3]

The Cochrans' young son was not yet 6 months old when Richey enlisted in Pittsburgh's 'McCullough Guards' on 6 August 1861, a unit that became Company H of the 63rd Pennsylvania Infantry. Thereafter Richey wrote home regularly to his wife. Though unable to write herself, Sarah Jane was either able to read or had her husband's letters read to her by a friend. When Richey and his comrades went to the Virginia Peninsula in the summer of 1862 as participants in the Union drive towards Richmond, he made sure to keep her regularly up to date with his experiences:

In Camp Near Richmond
June the 26th 1862

Sarah

I take the opportunity of sending you theas few lines to let you know that I am in good health and hope that this few lines may find you all enjoying the same I forgot to date the last letter I left it to the last and then forgot it we have had a fairly hard time of it since we have been fairly busy we moved our camp the day before yesterday and yesterday morning we left camp about 6 o clock and went out to the outside picket line and our regiment was detailed for skirmishing the woods in front and it was a very unpleasant job the brush was so thick some pleases that we could not see a man 5 yards from us and some pleases we could not go thrugh in line but we got thrugh the best way we could and drove in their pickets and their reserves to we came to their main lines and then we stopt to the rest came up and formed in line and drove in their whole line and took their rifil pitts [rifle pits] from them and a redout but our regiment was not engaged only with the pickets when we were in line of battle the [there] were no attack maid on our front the the [sic] regiments on our right and left had it very hard we lost no men only when we were skirmishing our company had 5 wounded I am not certain how many the other companys lost yet the [there] were some killed and last night the line behind us fired on us through mistake and killed 2 and wounded 3 or 4 but none in our company we were in line all night till 6 o clock this morning it was about 11 o clock that the mistake hapened the [there] were fairly sharp firing of musketry all night now and then but it has been fairly quiet all day in this part of the line but how long it may continue I canot say the [there] are some heavy fireing on the right this evening

June the 27th we were called out last night before I got finishing but we got in again soon the [there] were great cheering last night along all our lines and heavy fireing on our right the reports was here that the [they] were driving them on the right and some of our bands played till 12 o clock but the real cause I canot say we [were] all called out this morning ready to march and the fireing is still going on on our right but you will hear the results in the papers before this reaches you I have not time to write much more as our guns is stacked and we have to fall in at any time I was at the hospital a few days ago to see crampton he is geting better I seen the 2 Mc lelanns and the [they] are both geting better so I will have to finish this time till I get more time. Remember me to all the folks

So no more for now at present
but remains your
husband
Richey Cochrans[4]

The fighting Richey was describing was the start of the Seven Days' Battles around Richmond, which saw a series of engagements over the course of consecutive days. On 25 June the skirmishing he participated in formed part of the Battle of Oak Grove, while the firing he heard to the right on 26 June was the Battle of Beaver Dam Creek (or Mechanicsville). The cheering Richey recorded on the night of 26 June was due to an announcement made by the adjutant of the 63rd Pennsylvania regarding the fighting at Beaver Dam Creek. He told the men that 'General Porter attacked the enemy today at Beaver Dam, and has beaten them at every point. The rebels are in full retreat'. Although the engagement did result in a tactical victory for the Union, the Rebels had no intention of retreating, as evidenced by the firing that Richey was listening to as he wrote on 27 June, which marked the start of the Battle of Gaines' Mill. Although, as Richey anticipated, the 63rd were called to march towards the firing, they were halted when the fighting died down that evening.[5]

Almost exactly three days after Richey finished the letter to his wife, he found himself crouching behind a breastwork of fence-rails with the rest of his regiment, as the Seven Days' Battles dragged on. Looking out across an open field towards woods some 300 yards away, he and his comrades awaited a Confederate attack they knew was coming. In the meantime, they had to endure an artillery barrage, and watch helplessly as the Rebels unleashed a furious assault on the Pennsylvania Reserves to their left. They saw the Reserves driven back, all the while knowing that their turn to face the onslaught was fast approaching. As the artillery fire intensified on their position, Richey watched a group of terrified slaves flee from a slave cabin midway between the lines. Not long afterwards, they were followed across the field by a veritable tide of soldiers in grey. Richey, his regiment and his division saw the federal batteries to their front meet the Rebels with a hail of fire. The cannon poured shot into the advancing southerners, mowing them down by the dozen. But no matter how many gaps they tore in the advancing lines, more Confederates constantly seemed on hand to fill them. With the Union artillery seemingly doomed, the men of the 63rd Pennsylvania were ordered forward to their support. With a cry of 'Up! Up! Boys! Charge!' the men broke cover and entered the field, surging past their threatened guns and forcing the Confederates back. Fighting at one point broke out in relatively close quarters around the slave cabin, but eventually the horrific cost exacted on the attacking waves forced the Rebels to retire. The men of the 63rd pulled back to their guns, where they hugged the ground and continued to pour fire into the enemy. Throughout the course of the afternoon they would repulse a further three attacks. One general remarked that Richey and his comrades had 'won for Pennsylvania the laurels of fame'. What became known as the Battle of Nelson's Farm, or Glendale, was over. The Union army could resume its march and the

Seven Days' fighting would continue. Pittsburgh's Company H recorded the loss of five men wounded and two killed in the engagement. One of those left dead on the field was Richey Cochran, felled by a gunshot wound.[6]

Back at 42 Virgin Alley in Pittsburgh, it is impossible to comprehend Sarah Jane's reaction upon hearing the news. Aside from the emotional distress she must have experienced, she also faced the very real prospect of economic disaster, particularly with two young children to support. Less than four weeks after Richey's death she made application to retrieve Richey's backpay, and by 1863 she was seeking a widow's pension. Her efforts were successful, and she was granted a payment of $8 per month. Tragically for Sarah Jane, her hardships did not end with the death of Richey. On 31 March 1864 their son William died, just a few days short of his third birthday. He was buried in Grave 3, Lot 14 of Mount Union Cemetery in Pittsburgh. William's death seems to have been the final straw for Sarah Jane. The last time she drew her pension in Pittsburgh was on 5 September 1864. She had taken the decision to leave America behind and return to Ireland with her daughter.[7]

The year 1880 found a 51-year-old Sarah Jane once again resident in Limavady. That year she applied for the reinstatement of her pension and also sought additional entitlements that she had not previously claimed when her daughter had been under 16 years of age. Her Pennsylvania-born daughter Jane was now 24 years old and living in Foyle Hill, County Londonderry. She had been 5 when her father had died, but still remembered him, as she outlined in her statement to support her mother's claim. She affirmed that she was 'the daughter of Richard Cochrane a soldier killed in the late American War' and that 'she remembers her father Richard Cochrane living with her mother before his death'. Sarah Jane had moved back to Londonderry to be closer to her relatives, and two of her first cousins – grocer William McCloskey and Jane McCloskey of Drumagosker – swore affidavits on her behalf. Another who did so was Mathilda Lindsay of Coleraine, who interestingly gave evidence that she had lived close to the Cochrans in Philadelphia, another demonstration that not everyone who emigrated stayed in America.[8]

There can be little doubt that Sarah Jane's application for the reinstatement of her pension was the result of dire financial need. Aside from the affidavits of her relatives and friends, she also submitted the last letter she had ever received from Richey. This was an action she felt was necessary in order to conclusively prove their relationship. There can be little doubt it was a treasured possession, as she had kept it carefully for almost twenty years. Following its inclusion with her application, she would never see it again. It remains in the Cochran pension file in Washington DC, stamped with the date of its arrival at the pension office, 28 June 1880. Sarah Jane Cochran had her pension reinstated, and she collected it every month up until her death in March 1905. Almost forty-three years had passed since the death of her husband Richey upon whose service it was based.[9]

THE FINNERTYS: GALWAY, MERSEYSIDE AND ILLINOIS

 'I have left … thinking that I can better myself.'[10]

The Irish experience of the American Civil War was not restricted to those living in Ireland or the United States. Anywhere where large Irish communities had become established felt its touch. Though many Irish emigrants travelled to the United States via ports such as Liverpool, not all just passed through. Britain was a major emigrant destination in its own right, and many Irish chose to make their homes there. In the 1860s cities such as London and Liverpool boasted large Irish communities; when the American Civil War came, many of them looked with an anxious eye at events across the Atlantic as they sought to discern the fate of loved ones. One such family was the Finnertys.

Bridget Ridge and John Finnerty were married in the Parish of St Nicholas in Galway City on 14 January 1826. Their son James was baptised in the same place on 2 July 1835. It is unclear how many other children the couple had, but they had at least one daughter. At some point over the years that followed the family decided their future lay away from the City of the Tribes. John Finnerty took them to England, where they would eventually set up home in Birkenhead. There they were surrounded by many other Irish emigrants, including at least some of Bridget Ridge's family relations. Their son James spent long enough in England to develop friendships, but in the 1850s the young Galwegian decided to strike out for North America. He may be the 19-year-old 'James Feenerty' recorded as arriving in New York from Liverpool aboard the *De Witt Clinton* on 19 November 1853.[11]

Whatever his date of arrival, by late 1858 James was in Grove Mills, Canada West (modern-day Ontario). On 7 September that year he took the opportunity to write back to his parents and sister in Birkenhead, letting them know he was ok. Clearly not a regular writer, James admitted to his family that things were not going quite as he had hoped in his new home. He described how he had suffered from 'the rumetism' both that spring and the spring before, and that 'times is very hard', particularly due to the price of essentials. Still, if his health was spared he hoped to be able to go home for a visit, though he later wrote, 'I will send you my likeness in my next letter if I can, for I fear that I shall not see you'. James' family were obviously suffering from the sense of loss that remains familiar to many split by emigration, as he felt it necessary to tell those at home that he was 'sorry to see that you are greaving for me …' One wonders how many homes in Ireland and the United Kingdom had to make do with similar likenesses sent from America.[12]

It seems likely that James never managed a visit home. Nearly four years after writing from Canada he was across the border in Chicago, Illinois. On 15 August 1862 he took the decision to enlist in the Union army, becoming a private in Company B of the 72nd Illinois Infantry, often called the 'First Chicago Board of Trade Regiment'. At the time James was recorded as a 26-year-old painter (he was 27), some 5 feet 6 inches in height with dark hair, grey eyes and a light complexion. James had been in the employ of English-born painter Francis Rigby in Chicago's 2nd Ward, but had decided he had better prospects in the army. The day before he joined up he wrote a letter to his mother.[13]

Chicago August 14th 1862

Dear Mother,

I hope you will excuse me for not writing before now as I have been moveing about for I have left Mr. Rigby thinking that I can better myself. I was very sorry to hear of my fathers death on the 18 of March last. How is Bridget getting along and likewise yourself, please write back as soon as you can and I will try and save you a little money. I dont know how things are going on with you in England but they are pretty hard here. I am glad to say I am in good health as stout as ever let me know [how] James Ridge and his mother and sisters are. I suppose you are living in the old place yet. Now dear mother be sure and answer this as soon as you can and send your directions so that my letter can find you. Give my love to Bridget and James Ridges family and receive the same yourself,
    I remain your loving son,
    James Finerty.[14]

James seems to have continued his habit of erratic correspondence, having not written home since hearing of the death of his father in Birkenhead a few months previously. This may at least be partially due to the fact that James appears to have been illiterate – the 1858 letter from Canada and the 1862 one from Chicago are composed in different hands. Despite saying that he was seeking to 'better himself' (a common theme in letters from men explaining their decision to enlist) it appears that he may not have told his mother that he intended to do so by becoming a soldier.[15]

By early September James was on the march to Kentucky. His regiment participated in a number of expeditions that October, before being ordered to Tennessee in November. James was at Holly Springs, Mississippi when he next wrote to England, this time to a Mrs Bailey. In the letter James describes the fate of Cheshire native James Harrison, a 30-year-old who had also listed his pre-war profession as painter, and had enlisted on the same day as James. It seems probable the two had known each other (and perhaps worked together) prior to their service.[16]

Holly Springs Nov the 30) 1862

Mrs Bailey,

This letter finds me in good health hoping that yours is the same and im sorry to say that Harrison died on the 25 day of Oct he lay sick in the tent with Typhoid Fever 2 weeks till he got so sick that I could take care of him no longer and then he was sent to the hospital were he lay 3 days and I was with him when he died and stoped with him till we laid him out he was buryed next day. Me and Becker made up his accounts and sent the bill includeing the 50$ that he had in the Illinois Saving Bank that is all he had, it was all sent to Becker to be sent home to his father. While we were in Columbus our company was sent on an expedition down to Tennessee, your letter came when I was down there and I did not have time to answer it till now. We left Columbus a week ago Thursday for Lagrange, we left the latter place 3 days ago and we are now 8 or 10 miles south of Holly Spring Miss. Before we left Lagrange there were issued rations for 85000 men and that whole army is in motion, ready to meet the enemy and he is not far off, for they left Holly Springs the day before we got there. It would do you good to see the whole army in squad and companies before there camp fires at night for we have no tents with us, nothing but our blankets and the woods for shelter. It is a grand panorama to see and we enjoy ourselves first rate, a deal better than you would think we would I tell you. There is an awful sight of troops here in the west, the river is literally black with troops

Roseincrans [Rosecrans] has a very large army so has Grant and we are with the latter in Quimby [Quimby's] division. Our whole regiment is out on picket duty today and I think ther[e] is a battle going on about 10 miles from us judgeing from the cannonadeing that we hear and I do not know how soon we may [be] called into it also. I send my best respects to Eliza and the Duke and also to Dick and Dave also to Mr. Rigby and famly and also to sesesh Bill this is all I have to write at presant direct your letter to me,

    Co B 72 Reg in Quimby Division by Cairo Ill

    Yours truly,

    James Finerty.[17]

As things transpired, the 72nd Illinois were not engaged in battle that November and eventually returned to the vicinity of Memphis, Tennessee. However, they were to be involved in Grant's efforts to capture Vicksburg in the months that followed. It was as a part of that campaign that James' regiment fought their first major engagement at Champion Hill, Mississippi on 16 May 1863. But there were bloodier times ahead. On 22 May Ulysses S. Grant launched an assault all along the Rebel line at Vicksburg. The 72nd Illinois, as part of the Army of the Tennessee's 2nd Brigade, 6th Division of the 17th Corps, were in the front ranks. On that fateful morning, the regiment's brigadier, General Thomas E.G. Ransom, moved his men forward at about 10 a.m. Under the cover of sharpshooters, they had to scramble through ravines 'filled with fallen timber and canebrakes' as they struggled to make headway towards the Rebel entrenchments. Getting to within 60 yards of the works, Ransom massed the men for the final assault. But the Confederates were ready for them. The Yankee charge was met with a 'continuous blaze of musketry' poured into their ranks, while Rebel artillery, which enfiladed the line, 'threw … shot and shell … with deadly effect'. Although some of Ransom's men managed to cling desperately to the Confederate works for a few minutes, they were unable to gain a foothold. Grant's assault failed, and it proved costly to the Illinoisans. Ransom's brigade sustained 476 casualties, 100 of them from the 72nd. Among them was Galway's James Finnerty.[18]

It isn't recorded how Bridget Finnerty discovered her son was dead. Perhaps she was sent a letter by one of James' comrades or officers. Often such communications sought to soften the blow as to precisely how a loved one had died, attempting to downplay the horrors that modern war could inflict. Unfortunately, in Bridget's case, we know that she discovered exactly how her son lost his life. Although she may have been comforted by the fact his end had come instantly, his fate must nevertheless have shaken her to the core. That she learned graphic detail of his death is demonstrated in her pension file. Included within it is a newspaper clipping listing the casualties of the 72nd Illinois at Vicksburg. James' name has been marked with ink where he is mentioned, twice. The second entry was included because of how he died – the macabre specifics revealed that he had been 'literally blown in pieces by a shell'. Though she would never see her son again, 50-year-old Bridget did receive a pension based on his service. From her home in 13 Elden Place, Birkenhead, she relied heavily on the US consul in Liverpool to help her secure it. The consul wrote to Washington to relate that Mrs Finnerty was one of 'many poor persons here who have lost sons or husbands in the war', demonstrating just what a toll the American Civil War was having on British communities, and on Irish communities in Britain particularly. He described Bridget as a 'miserably poor widow' who was among those who were too illiterate to write to the pension bureau herself, and too poor to get anyone to do it for them. Thankfully, and largely as a result of the consul's efforts, Bridget Finnerty's dependent mother's claim was approved.[19]

THE HANDS: LOUTH AND PENNSYLVANIA

 '… please excuse this letter as I am confused.'[20]

At 1319 North 16th Street, Philadelphia on 3 July 1863, Irish mother Jane Hand would have been going about her daily routine. Her two daughters were likely proving a handful; as her eldest, Lucy Ann, was just 5 and her youngest, Mary Jane, 3, they were exactly the right age to get stuck under her feet. This wouldn't have been made easier by the fact that the 27-year-old was heavily pregnant – her third child was expected to arrive in a matter of weeks. Regardless of any tribulations at home, that afternoon Jane's thoughts were probably on events elsewhere in Pennsylvania. The day before, Philadelphia newspapers had carried scanty details of a major battle off to the west. On the morning of 3 July, she awoke to headlines telling of 'A Desperate Battle at Gettysburg' and 'Second Day's Fight! Victory Reported!' Such accounts must have made Jane anxious for her husband, James, then a sergeant in the 69th Pennsylvania Infantry. That very same afternoon, the titanic struggle at Gettysburg was raging on for a third day. At its vortex, 137 miles from Jane's front door, James Hand was fighting for his life in the face of the most famous charge of the American Civil War. When it was finally over, James' friend, Charles McAnally – a future Medal of Honor recipient – penned an emotional letter to the soon-to-be mother-of-three.[21]

James Hand was a native of County Louth, where he had been born around 1834. He and Jane Phelan married in the Roman Catholic church of St Malachy, Philadelphia on 17 August 1856. The 1860 Federal Census found the couple living with their two young daughters in the 1st Division of the 20th Ward, where James worked as a painter. When war came he mustered in as a sergeant on 31 October 1861, becoming a member of the 69th Pennsylvania's Company D. He soon became fast friends with another member of the company, First Sergeant Charles McAnally from County Derry. By the time of Gettysburg, Charles had risen to the rank of first lieutenant. On 3 July 1863, the Irish Pennsylvanians found themselves behind a small stone wall near Gettysburg, facing the full force of the

Pickett-Pettigrew-Trimble assault. Two days later, Charles described to Jane what had happened next.[22]

Camp of 69th Regt P.V.
Near Gettysburg Pa
July 5th 1863

Mrs Jane Hand,

It is a painfull task for me to communicate the sad fate of your husband (my own comrade). He was killed on the 3rd inst he received a ball through the breast & one through the heart & never spoke after. I was in command of the skirmishers about one mile to the front & every inch of the ground was well contested untill I reached our Regt. The Rebels made the attack in 3 lines of Battle, as soon as I reached our line I met James he ran & met me with a canteen of watter. I was near palayed [played] he said I was foolish [I] dident let them come at once that the 'ol 69th was waiting for them. I threw off my coat & in 2 minuets we were at it hand to hand. They charged on us twice & we repulsed them they then tryed the Regt on our right & drove them, which caused us to swing back our right, then we charged them on their left flank & in the charge James fell may the Lord have mercy on his soul. He never flinched from his post & was loved by all who knew him. He is intered along side of Sergt James McCabe, Sergt Jeremiah Gallagher of our Co & 5 others of our Co that you are not acquainted with. Our Co lost in killed wounded & missing twenty as follows: Killed 8, Wounded 10 & Missing 2. Although we fought the Rebels 10 to one on the 2nd & killed or captured a whol Corps our Co had only one man wounded that day. The loss in the battle of the 3rd was heavy but all did not discourage the boys, we were determined that as long as a man lived he would stand to be killed too rather than have it said that we left on the battle field in Pennsylvania the laurels that we so dearly won in strange states. The loss in the Regt killed, wounded & missing was one hundred & fifty eight & our Colnell & Lieut Colnell & 2 Capts Duffy & Thompson killed & Lieut Kelly & 6 officers wounded. We killed 6 Rebel Generals & nearly all the line officers & killed

or captured every man that attacked us & [on] both days fighting. There
[was] never a battle fought with more determination, in the first days fight
the Rebels had our battery on the first charge & we retook it again. Mrs
Hand please excuse this letter as I am confused & I hope you will take your
trouble with patience, you know that God is mercifull & good to his own.
No one living this day was more attached than Jas & my self, when I was
engaged in front he wanted to get out to my assistance. I lost a loyal comrade
in him. No more at present from your Sorrowing friend,

Chas McAnally
Lieut Co 'D' 69th
Regt P.V.

P.S. this letter will answer for Sergt McCabe he was shot through the head
he died in 2 minutes after. McCabe had 35 cents of money & $20 he lent to
Lieut Fay or our Co.

C. Mc. A.
We got no mail since the 19th ult the Rebs retreated last night.[23]

On 23 July 1863, twenty days after his death at the Battle of Gettysburg, Sergeant James Hand's third child was born. It was a boy – the couple's first son. Jane chose the name James Charles for the infant. The choice of James was presumably for his father; one wonders if the middle name Charles was selected to honour the friend who had so kindly broken the news of James' loss. Unfortunately, the newborn whose name may well have been a testament to a friendship forged by war would not long outlive his father. Philadelphia records show that James Charles Hand was buried in Old Cathedral Catholic Cemetery on 12 February 1864, at the age of just 7 months. Jane and her daughters would have to forge their lives without both father and son.[24]

Charles McAnally survived 1863 to take part in the savage battles of the Overland Campaign. At Spotsylvania on 12 May 1864 he captured a Confederate flag in hand-to-hand combat, an act for which he would receive the Medal of Honor in 1897. Ending the war as a captain in the 69th Pennsylvania, Charles died in 1905.[25]

THE McNAMARAS: IRELAND AND NEW YORK

 *'Goodbye for a while.'*[26]

On 8 June 1864 Captain Dexter Ludden and his men from the 8th New York Heavy Artillery were picking their way through corpses. They had been assigned the unpleasant task of burying some of the many, many dead who had fallen assaulting the Confederate works at Cold Harbor. By then the men they were interring – who were from their own brigade – had lain on the field for five days. As they went about their gruesome work, Ludden's soldiers checked each of the bodies for anything that might identify them. Turning over one of the lifeless forms, they hunted through the dead man's pockets. Finding two scraps of paper inside, the burial party alerted the officer to their discovery. Reading through them, Captain Ludden recognised the papers as a hastily penned letter, written by the dead man before the assault. Later, Ludden sat down to sketch a few brief words of his own to add to it, before sending what amounted to the fallen soldier's last words on their way to New York.[27]

This is what Dexter Ludden wrote on the back of one of the pieces of paper recovered from the body:

Battlefield 7 miles from Richmond Va
June 8 1864

Madam,
This was cut from the pocket of a man I had buried last eve –
he was killed – June 3d 1864 – & buried on the spot where he
fell.
    The place was marked by a cut on a tree where his head lies
by Sergt Ewell of my company.
Yours Truly

S. Dexter Ludden

Capt 8 NY Arty
Miss Mary McNamara
Buffalo NY²⁸

The body that Dexter Ludden and his men had buried was that of Irishman Hubert McNamara, a private in the 155th New York Infantry, Corcoran's Irish Legion. Hubert had enlisted in Buffalo on 28 August 1862, when he was 34 years old. Before becoming a soldier, he had supported his wife Mary and three children by working as a cartman. Described as 5 feet 6 inches in height, he had hazel eyes, brown hair and a light complexion. Hubert had married Mary Donovan on 2 January 1859, but that had not been his first marriage. His first wife Margaret (*née* McGrath) had passed away in Hudson, New York on 26 January 1855, leaving Hubert to support their 3-year-old daughter Maria alone until his remarriage. By 1864, Mary had borne Hubert two more children at their home on Exchange Street: Thomas, who arrived on 30 November 1859 and Margaret, born on 6 May 1862. Hubert's youngest daughter was only a month past her second birthday when her father met his death.²⁹

By 2 June 1864, the day Hubert wrote his last letter, Corcoran's Irish Legion had been with the Army of the Potomac for less than a month. By the standards of many other brigades, their first eighteen months of service had been relatively quiet. That had all changed in May 1864, when they joined up with the Army of the Potomac at Spotsylvania, Virginia. In the days following, the Irishmen had to become accustomed to almost constant combat – and ever-mounting casualties. It was in this context that Hubert penned the few words to his wife on 2 June. He was aware when he wrote them that he was going to be involved in an assault on the Rebel works the following day. Given the strength of the enemy's position, many of his unit would have been apprehensive about what lay ahead. On the fateful day of battle at Cold Harbor, the 155th was brought into action by Captain Michael Doran. As Doran dressed his men's lines for the advance, Hubert and his comrades were temporarily shielded from fire behind a slight ridge. When they moved forward beyond this cover they could see the main Confederate line, rising from the earth some 150 yards away. They would never reach it. Almost immediately a storm of fire erupted from the Rebel position. One member of the regiment recalled how the 'balls commenced literally to mow us down', while another said that the attack 'was murder, not war'. The Irishmen never stood a chance; by the time they got to within 50 yards of the enemy position the charge was halted, and soon forced back. The slaughter cost the 155th some 130 casualties, almost half their number. Unfortunately, Hubert was one of those to fall, with the newly written letter to his family still unsent in his pocket.[30]

Mary McNamara included the three pages of writing recovered from Hubert's body in her widow's pension application, in order to prove both Hubert's death and her relationship with him. They were written in faded pencil, which, together with their exposure on the battlefield with Hubert's body, makes transcription difficult. Additionally, Hubert's literacy level means that they are difficult to interpret – the versions below have been edited for ease of reading by modern readers.

Page 1
[Prior text missing] … almighty God that we will soon get through with them I [am] alright so far thanks be to the almighty God for his mercy … [illegible] … possible to, I am addressing you with a few lines. I hope to find you and the children in good health as the departure [of] these few lines leaves me in at present thanks be to the almighty God for his [mercy] to me. We are fighting with [the] Rebels for [the] last 10 days and we have drove them for as much [as] 30 miles, but there is [a] great many of our men killed and wounded but they [are] pretty well surrounded in the [?].

Page 2
June the 2nd 1864
Camp of the Army of the Potomac 7 miles from Richmond.
Dear wife and children, I take the favourable opportunity …
[illegible] … tell what moment I would get killed or wounded,

but I trust in God for his mercy to me. There is awful fighting
going on here, we are fighting night and fighting day. Dear wife
and children there is nothing more that I can let you know
now I have no time.

Page 3
It is very hard to get paper or ink [or] anything else
here. John Dempsey is well and also Michael Lawler is,
I wish that you would tell his wife. There is nothing more
my dear wife and children then I think, so goodbye for a
while. No more at present from your affectionate husband
Hubert McNamara, 2nd Corps, 2nd Division, 4th Brigade,
Company I, 155th New York, Army of the Potomac.
Goodbye write soon.[31]

The precise sequence in which Hubert's letter was intended to be read is
not clear from the separate pages. Their order as presented above is based
on content. It seems likely that the first page was part of a letter Hubert
may have been writing prior to his arrival at Cold Harbor. In it he refers
to fighting the Rebels for the 'last 10 days' which would place it around
28 May. It seems likely that Hubert had retained the letter as he had not
had an opportunity to finish and post it given the nature of the campaign.
Then, finding himself in front of the works at Cold Harbor in early June
and realising he was about to go into action, he abandoned his previous
letter to jot down a few words on the back in the event of his death,
labelled 'Page 2' above. If this is the case, then it makes the letter all the
more poignant. The section designated 'Page 3' may have also been written
at Cold Harbor, though that is not clear. Captain Ludden wrote his note
to Hubert's wife on the back of this page. Of those comrades mentioned
in Hubert's correspondence, Michael Lawler also died at Cold Harbor.
The former labourer was mortally wounded, and left behind a wife and
four children. John Dempsey seems to have also been wounded at Cold
Harbor, but ultimately recovered. Hubert's wife Mary lived a long life after

her husband's death, remaining a widow for more than half a century. The elderly Irishwoman passed away at the Holy Family Home in Williamsville, New York on 2 September 1916.[32]

THE CAIRNS: DUBLIN AND NEW HAMPSHIRE

 'Should this Book be ever found on my dead body.'[33]

On 27 January 1865 a Union prisoner of war was found dead in the yard of Salisbury Prison, North Carolina. The soldier, recently transferred from Libby Prison in Richmond, appeared to have died from a combination of exposure and disease. He apparently had no close friends to look out for him, so fellow prisoners searched his remains, hoping to find some clue as to his identity. On his body they found two photographs of a woman, some correspondence from Ireland, and a Bible. Inside the Bible they found a message:

> Miss Helen Mitchell, Care of Mrs. Greeley – 19 South High St. Baltimore, Maryland. Should this Book be ever found on my dead body let the party know of the above address, who will acquaint my wife & family with my fate. Colin Cairns.[34]

Some weeks later the men who had found Colin's body arranged for a visitor to call at Mrs Greeley's and fulfil the dead soldier's wishes. Helen Mitchell was the unfortunate man's sister-in-law. She now had the unpleasant task of relaying the news to her sister, Colin's wife, who was then in County Kerry.

To: Mrs. Anne Cairns, Tralee, Co. Kerry, Ireland.
St. Patrick's Day, 1865, 19 South High Street, Baltimore, Md.

My dear Sister,

It gives me great pain to have to communicate the sad news of Cairns's death. You have already heard that he was taken prisoner by the Rebels and confined in Libby Prison, Richmond. How long he is dead or how he died we have not yet learned. He was removed from there to Salisbury, North Carolina where he died. What he died of I don't know. The party who brought us word did not know anything merely that he was desired to call to say he was dead and brought some papers that were found on his person. After his death there were two likenesses of yours and a couple of certificates which you had sent. The gentleman told us he was found in the yard of the prison dead. We all think it was from the bad treatment he got in prison. They are treated worse than dogs. I am going to write to the party in N. Hampshire who sent the papers and learn more about him.

Dear Sister I know it is sad news for you but try and bear up with it patiently. I trust God has shown mercy to him. Oh if he had any one belonging to him in his dying hour to give him some consolation but far away from home and friends it is really awful. But dear Anne don't grieve for not coming you could not see him even if you were here nor hear from. I only had one note since he had been taken prisoner. I guess he was not allowed to write. Confinement in those Southern prisons is slow death. He [sic] think he had a hard time of it ever since he joined the army. As soon as I hear anything more I will send you word. Aunt Collins is no better. All the rest of us are well. How are all at home. I hope poor Cairns is in a better world than this for indeed it has been a dreary one with many of us. With fond love to all at home and accept the same from your fond Sister.
Ellen. Love to the children.[35]

Colin Cairns had been born in Perth, Scotland around 1828. In the 1850s he had been living in Dublin, where he worked as a draper and resided at 71 Summer Hill. It was while in Ireland that he met combmaker's daughter Anne Mitchell, who lived at 17 Bedford Street in the city. The two hit it off, and on 7 July 1856 were married in St George's church. The following year they celebrated the birth of their first child, Mary Ann, born on 31 October 1857 and baptised in St Michan's church on Dublin's North Anne Street. On 15 May 1859 their second daughter, Jane Isabella, arrived, and was baptised in St Paul's church on Arran Quay.[36]

Colin and Anne's youngest daughter was not even 6 months old when he decided to try his luck in America. It is not clear why he left, but it seems likely that it was for financial reasons. Returning to Scotland, he took passage from Glasgow aboard the *United Kingdom* and arrived in New York on 21 December 1859. Colin seems to have taken little interest in the Civil War during its early years and was instead focused on trying to earn a living, probably sending a portion of his wages back to Ireland for his wife and children. He is almost certainly the 'Colin Cairnes' who was working as a salesman and living at 9 Jay Street in New York in June 1863, when he was recorded as part of the draft registration. In the end, Colin decided not to wait to be drafted, instead choosing to enter the army as a substitute.[37]

On 11 August 1863 Colin Cairns enlisted in Company D of the 10th New Hampshire Infantry, presumably gaining a considerable financial windfall in the process. From there he was transferred to Company A of the 2nd New Hampshire Infantry and joined up with his unit in time for the Overland Campaign. It was during the Battle of Fair Oaks and Darbytown Road, Virginia, on 27 and 28 October 1864, that fate took a hand in Colin's future. His commander, Lieutenant-Colonel Joab N. Patterson, remembered that on 27 October the 2nd New Hampshire had orders to advance along the Williamsburg Road with its brigade, deploying to the right of the thoroughfare in the late afternoon. Colin and his comrades found themselves deep in the woods, where they began to take artillery fire. When night came on the brigade was ordered to retire, and fifty men of the 2nd New Hampshire were selected as part of a picket to hold the line while the rest of the army withdrew. It seems probable that Colin was part of this party; the confusion of darkness combined with the dense undergrowth was a perfect recipe for disorientation – the Scotsman became one of nine men from the regiment reported as captured or missing during the engagement.[38]

Colin Cairns' decision to travel to the United States ultimately proved to be a fatal mistake. The consequences it had for Anne and her children go unrecorded. She eventually received a US military pension in Dublin for herself and her young children. Anne may have regretted not travelling to America to try to see her husband, but ultimately her destiny did take her far from Ireland. She died on 18 April 1893 on the other side of the world, in Inverell, New South Wales, Australia. The last correspondence in Colin Cairns' widow's pension file relates to the girl who was only a baby when her father went to America, Jane Isabella. Now the couple's only surviving child, in 1893 she attempted to secure payment of the pension that had resulted from the service of a father she had never known. It would appear that her efforts ultimately proved unsuccessful.[39]

THE CARROLLS: IRELAND AND NEW YORK

 'He … desired me to take the proper steps to have his children put in your charge.'[40]

On the evening of 6 April 1862, at Pittsburgh Landing, Tennessee, the men of the 12th Illinois Infantry trudged back to their quarters after a hard day's fighting. They had just endured the first day of the Battle of Shiloh – the most brutal contest of the war thus far – and the stunned soldiers gathered around their tents to discuss what they had just experienced. The danger, though, had not passed. The enemy remained close, and indeed the furious contest would resume the following morning. As Corporal Con Carroll and Sergeant Henry Wager chatted by their tent, a Rebel shell suddenly exploded opposite them. The projectile killed another man in their regiment, before its lethal shrapnel spiralled towards the two friends and tore through Con's foot, mutilating it. Despite the shock of the moment, Wager and other comrades rushed to Con's side. Fearing the worst, the Irishman turned to Wager and asked him to take on two important tasks: the first was to write to his brother-in-law in Albany, informing him of what had happened. The second, and most important, was to make sure steps were taken to get his two young daughters to New York. It was understandable that the fate of his daughters loomed large in Con Carroll's mind as life slipped away from him on the Shiloh battlefield. Only three months previously, news had come to him that his wife had died back in Chicago. In his final hours, Con knew that his death would make the girls orphans.[41]

Irish couple Cornelius Carroll and Ellen O'Donnell had been very young – probably in their late teens – when they were married by the Revd Patrick McCloskey in St John's church, Albany, on 30 October 1849. Their first child, Johanna, was born on 4 September 1851, before the couple decided to strike out for new opportunities in Chicago. There a second daughter, Mary Ellen, followed on 10 September 1855. Although the exact timing of the incident is unknown, at some point in the 1850s or 1860s tragedy struck the family when Johanna suffered injuries that left her a lifetime cripple. The 1860 Census found the family in Chicago's 5th Ward, and indications are that they suffered from financial hardship. Con worked as a labourer, but when war came he quickly took the opportunity to enlist. He first signed up for three months on 24 April 1861 in Chicago, converting his term to three years at Cairo, Illinois on 1 August, and becoming a corporal in Company K of the 12th Illinois. Con was then 28 years old and was described as 5 feet 8 inches tall, with red-brown hair, blue eyes and a ruddy complexion.[42]

Con was a man with serious economic concerns in 1861 and 1862. The $100 bounty money for his enlistment must have been a major attraction for him, given his need to provide for his family. However, it seems likely that the notoriously sporadic nature of soldier's pay during the war had a major impact on his wife and children left at home. News arrived early in 1862 of Ellen's death in Chicago on 22 January, apparently as a result of 'destitution'. This immediately plunged Johanna and Mary

Ellen's future into uncertainty, and undoubtedly played heavily on Con's mind as he marched through the south in the ranks of the 12th Illinois. He never had an opportunity to resolve the situation. The Confederate shell fragment that struck him at around 7 p.m. on 6 April 1862 ended his life some twenty hours later. With more fighting to be done the following day, it would be 9 April before his friend Henry B. Wager could start honouring Con's dying wish and write to his brother-in-law John Kennedy.[43]

Pittsburg Landing Tennse.
April 9th 1862
John B. Kennedy Esq.
Albany, New York

Dear Sir,
It becomes my painful duty to inform you of the death of our mutual friend Cornelius Carroll. On Easter Sunday morning about 7 O Clk the enemy attacked us. Our regiment participated in the hardest part of the fight during the day. At sundown we were ordered to our Quarters, and were dismissed, were talking over the incidents of the day when an unfortunate shell dropped opposite our tent, killing one man instantly, and mangling the right foot of our poor friend in a shocking manner. We immediately carried him to our Hospital tent where every attention our limited means would allow, were shown him (the tent being at the river attending to the wounded there). We were forced to vacate our camp until late in the evening, when every exertion in the power of man was made to procure the aid of a surgeon, but without success until the following Monday morning, but his system had received such a shock, that it could not sustain the operation of amputation. He died Monday about 3 pm. I had no idea his death was so near, or I should most certainly have been with him during his last moments. The Company received the news of his death with much feeling, for poor fellow he was a great favorite not only amongst his immediate associates in the Company but throughout the Regiment. Poor fellow let us hope that he has gone to a better

place. *The whole Company sincerely sympathize with yourself and family in this bereavement. Con appeared to think from the first that he would not recover and requested me, in case the worst would happen to inform you of the circumstances concerning his death. He also desired me to take the proper steps to have his children put in your charge which I shall do, so soon as I have finished this. I shall write to Bishop Duggan of Chicago informing him of poor Cons wishes in regard to them, and enclose your letter to him in reference to your willingness to receive them and would advise your writing to him immediately on the subject. I think Con wrote you last Saturday, enclosed please find a letter he commenced writing to your wife, but did not have time to finish. I have some letters of his which I will send to you the earliest opportunity.*

I am Very Respectfully &c.

Henry B. Wager
Sergeant, Comp. K, 12th Regt. Ill. Vol.

Please drop me a line at your convenience. Direct to Paducah to follow the Regiment. HBW.

The Captain will have the necessary papers made out as soon as possible so that his children can receive his back pay and bounty. Yours Respectfully, Hy. B. Wager.[44]

Other members of the regiment also stepped in to help Con's children. The captain who had first enlisted him as a three-month soldier, James Hugunin, penned this letter to the Bishop of Chicago and Maynooth, County Kildare-native Revd James Duggan:

Pittsburgh, Tennessee
April 10. 1862.
Revd James Duggan,
Bishop of Chicago

Dear Sir,

I would respectfully inform you that Cornelius Carroll, a Corporal in my Company, was killed in the battle at this place on Sunday April 6th. He was the same man whose wife was said to have died of destitution in Chicago last January. He left two children, who, after the death of his wife, were sent to some one of the Catholic charitable institutions.

Carroll was not killed instantly, he lived about 20 hours after he was hit, during his last hours he requested that his two children should be sent to his sister, a Mrs. Kennedy, living in Albany, N.Y.
He left no effects. He has pay due him from Dec 31st 1861 – out of which there is to be deducted a small sum for clothing drawn – also, his heirs are entitled to his bounty of $100. Perhaps his children will be entitled to a pension but, as to that, I am not fully informed.

The reason of my writing to you is that I do not know his friends or relatives at Chicago. Neither do I know the name of priest or 'Father' whose parish he belonged in, but I believe it was Father Dunn. And I know no person who would be more able and willing to trace out these two lost children and help to carry out Carroll's last wishes more readily than yourself.

And I would, respectfully, request that you take such action in the case as may, to you, seem best and most likely to carry out the dying request of as brave a soldier as ever fought or fell in defense of his country's rights and his country's honor.
I am, Sir, Your Obdt Servt,

James R. Hugunin
Capt Co. K 12th Regt Ills. Vols[45]

It transpired that Con's daughters had been moved to the orphan asylum run by the Sisters of Mercy. Informed of this, Con's brother-in-law John Kennedy had to get to Chicago and bring them to their new home. John was an Albany-based grocer who had two daughters of his own with Con's sister Mary: Ellen, who was around 5 years old, and Mary who was 4. As news of the plight of the orphaned Carroll girls spread (Johanna was now

10 and Mary Ellen 6), the Governor of New York Edwin Morgan stepped in to help John in his mission. Governor Morgan contacted John V. L. Pruyn (himself a state senator) who was a major shareholder in the New York Central Railroad, and asked if he could be of assistance.[46]

THE NEW YORK CENTRAL RAIL ROAD COMPANY
PRESIDENTS OFFICE
Albany, June 2d 1862

To the Officers of the Rail Roads between Buffalo or Suspension Bridge & Chicago

At the instance of Governor Morgan who informs me he has inquired into the circumstances, I have given to the bearer, John B. Kennedy, a pass to Buffalo & return, to aid him in his effort to bring to this City, the two infant children of his brother in law Cornelius Carroll who was killed at the Battle of Pittsburgh Landing in April last. These children are now orphans, entirely destitute, and are to be cared for hereafter by their relatives here, who are in humble circumstances.

I therefore hope that Mr. Kennedy will be permitted to pass free to Chicago, & to return in like manner with the two children referred to.
John V.L. Pruyn.[47]

John succeeded in bringing the girls to his family in Albany. The 1870 Census records them all in Albany's 1st Ward, John (50) and Mary (36) with their now three daughters Ellen (13), Mary (11) and Emma (6) and the two Carroll girls Johanna (19) and Mary Ellen (14). The situation had not much changed by 1880, though by now John appears to have passed away. Mary Ellen was working in confectionery, but there was no work for Johanna. She was recorded on that census as 'at home, broken back'. Johanna's permanent disability had a devastating impact on her life. Her physician recorded how it had permanently arrested her physical development – with curvature of the spine and hip disease she was referred to as a 'hunchback'. Her left leg was 4 inches shorter than her right, and she never grew beyond 4 feet 3 inches. Johanna required a crutch or staff to walk, and every once in a while her hip would become inflamed, festering and discharging pus; during these bouts she couldn't move around at all. Efforts began to get her a pension based on her father's service, as it was noted that Johanna 'would have been provided for by her father if he had not lost his life'.[48]

In the 1890s, a special act of Congress provided Johanna Carroll with a pension of $12 per month. By 1900, her Kennedy cousins had all gone on to have lives of their own, but the two sisters stuck together. Johanna had refused to give in to her disability, and by this time was working as a music teacher. The orphaned girls would ultimately spend their entire lives in each other's company, until Johanna passed away in Albany on 9 June 1920. Mary Ellen wrote to the pension bureau to inform them of her sister's death:[49]

I am 65 years of age and have to work every day for a living. My pay will be deducted for my time taken off to-day in attending to this matter [communicating with the pension bureau]. Then while she [Johanna] was sick I lost about three weeks from my work while taking care of her.[50]

Despite her efforts, Mary Ellen did not receive any compensation for her sister's illness or funeral. She lived on for many more years on her own, appearing on both the 1930 and 1940 Census. She was still in full-time employment at the age of 72, working as a servant. Now the last of her family, Mary Ellen Carroll undoubtedly led a tough life. Having lost her parents at a young age, she then spent decades helping her older sister, particularly on those occasions when her disability became too much. How different might the Carroll family's fortunes have been had the American Civil War not erupted in 1861. The impact of that conflict on Johanna and Mary Ellen Carroll followed them throughout the course of their lives, and was still being felt in the middle of the twentieth century.[51]

THE WELSHS: IRELAND AND PENNSYLVANIA

'Your heart is prepared I trust for the confirmation of all your fears.'[52]

During the Civil War, families often relied on volunteers to keep them informed of a loved one's condition in hospital. Over time, bonds could develop between these caregivers and the soldiers' wives far away. The correspondence between Emma Smith of St Elizabeth Hospital, Washington DC and Sarah Welsh of Fayette County, Pennsylvania, is a case in point. This poignant collection of letters charts in some detail the final days of Sarah's husband Christy Welsh, a man who appears to have been unaware of his impending death. It also contains intriguing detail regarding a request from Sarah for an image of her husband – a request that precipitated an urgent effort to secure a 'Daguerreotype Artist' to expose the image of Christy while alive, and before all that could be sent was a *memento mori*.[53]

Irish emigrant Christy Welsh had married Sarah Boyle in Pennsylvania in 1843. The 1860 Census enumerated them in North Union, Fayette County, where they lived with Mary (15), Ann (12) Amanda (10) John (8), William (3) and Catharine (1). Another daughter, Sarah, aged 5 in 1860, does not appear with them on the census. Of the couple's stated six children in 1862, only John, Sarah and William were recorded as dependents under the age of 16. Christy was around 41 years old when he mustered in as a private in the 85th Pennsylvania Infantry on 12 November 1861. The regiment was soon sent to Washington DC, where, on 29 January 1862, Christy was engaged in nighttime sentinel duty at Fort Baker outside the city. In the pitch dark he stumbled, falling out of the fort and into the moat. The accident left him with a compound fracture of the thigh. It was that injury which would ultimately result in his death at St Elizabeth Hospital, Washington DC, a little over seven months later.[54]

The first letter from Emma to Sarah was dated 2 August 1862. By then it had become apparent that Christy would die, and that Sarah had asked Emma to get an image taken of her husband before the inevitable occurred:

St. Elizabeth Aug 2d 62

My Dear Mrs. Welsh,

Your letter received your husband is very gently sinking away – he does not suffer is very cheerful. His leg has not mortified but the heat of last month has worn on him and taken his appetite away. He takes egg nog & wine & brandy – anything he fancies we have in plenty – I have sent for a daguerrian artist I am expecting him every moment to take his picture – one of the men is now shaving & changing his shirt – he is much pleased with the idea of having it taken – may Our Father comfort you,

In heart sympathy,

yours,

Emma D. Smith.[55]

The daguerreotype had been invented by Louis Daguerre in 1839, and had become very popular in the United States in the 1850s. Daguerreotypes were exposed directly onto a polished copper plate and so each one was unique, and were favoured for portraits. Emma's next letter to Sarah was written two days later, after Christy's death. The efforts to have his image exposed before his end are again to the fore, as are the circumstances which prevented this from happening. A *memento mori*, a post-mortem image that was a common means of remembering a loved one during this period, was now all that could be produced. This was to be sent to Sarah along with some of the clothing he was wearing in the daguerreotype. Emma closes the letter with a detailed account of Christy's final hours, including a relation of how she read to him the 'Parable of the Sower' and the 'Parable of the Unjust Judge' from the Bible.[56]

St. Elizabeth Aug 4th
Monday

My Dear Mrs. Welsh,

Your heart is prepared I trust for the confirmation of all your fears. Last night, Sunday, Heaven's gate opened wider, angels sung a song of welcome & escorted by an angelic guard your best loved one entered in to receive (no doubt) a victor's crown – don't think of him as dead, but gone before to wait and welcome you & the little ones he loved so fondly. Saturday morning he was very much interested in preparing to have his picture taken it seemed to give him new life he was shaved & had on a pink striped shirt, which he fancied very much – I carried him a box of collars and cravats to choose from not new ones but the best we had – he had one of the men stand before him & try several on & chose one which I will send you.

The artist disappointed us he could not get a wagon to bring out his instruments. I sent to town, as soon as I received your letter, for he tells me he spent hours in trying to find a conveyance – engaged one and the harness broke – he feels very badly about it – he came early this morn & has spent all day nearby trying to get a good one. I will send you the best one he took tomorrow.

I think it looks so peaceful – may it comfort you. I put the cravat he selected on for it to be taken. Saturday he was unusually bright & cheerful eat his usual meals & lunch at 11 o'clock – took egg nog – in the evening he had a chill but passed a comfortable night – Sunday morn he wished to be per[k] ed[?] again to have his picture taken – eat two eggs & some toast for breakfast – egg-nog and sponge cake for lunch stewed tomatoes & light pudding with a glass of wine and cup of milk for dinner. At three o'clock I read him one or two of the dear saviours parables in poetry the parable of the sower & the unjust judge – he said they were very good seemed much pleased with them – told me he had been a methodist fifteen years – his wife was a presbyterian spoke of the breast pin I had on asked its cost for his girls were to love pins and ear-hops – at half past three said he would have some egg-nog – at four another chill came on – after it he slept & passed gradually away. May God sustain you. I will write again soon – can I do anything for you. I feel as though I had known you years. The doctor has his descriptive list.

Yours in sorrow
    E.D. Smith

I cut some of his hair off for you[57]

Emma sent a final letter to Sarah on 16 August 1862. In it the bond that had developed between the two women is apparent, as Sarah has clearly asked Emma details about her own family circumstances. Emma revealed that Christy had not been aware he was dying, and she could not bring herself to tell him that he was:

St. Elizabeth Aug 16th 62

My Dear Mrs. Welsh,
Yours of the 10th was gladly received I shall be always sincerely glad to hear from you & your little family and shall feel nothing a trouble I can do for you. As you requested I've had the few clothes your husband brought put in his knap-sacks – he had a dress coat & over coat & a few little articles – I'm very

sorry – he left his revolver in camp – he spoke of it several times and proposed giving it to a friend – I've forgotten whom. He thought to the last he would get well I do not think he was once pained by the thought of dying – it seemed only cruel to tell him – you know till almost the last we had hopes for him he always expressed strong christian hopes – he once spoke of the soldiers wickedness – said they could get along very well in health but when sick or wounded they would feel their need of something better – I think his hopes of Heaven were bright & strong. After I received your letter asking his feeling I tried in every way to draw them out but his mind wandered. I could not make him talk – the afternoon before he died a good army chaplain who had been preaching here to the soldiers came in to speak to him of Jesus.

Please don't blame me for not telling him his situation I felt it would only make his heart ache with sad thoughts of leaving you – forgive me if I was wrong. I received a kind letter from Judge Ewing expressing kindest regard for your husband & his family. I have another small lock of your husband's hair I saved one day when his hair was cut a few weeks since.

You kindly asked about my mother – she lives in Philadelphia – or rather she is boarding there, while I stay here – our native place is Providence, R.I.

Thank you for your kind interest in me – I wish there was something I could do to prove my earnest interest in your family – 'tis so pleasant to think that one day in Our Father's happy home we shall all meet where there are no partings. My kind love to our little Douglass

Yours lovingly,
Emma D. Smith.[58]

There is a misconception that all the soldiers who fought in the Civil War were young men. In fact, many of those who served, be they ideologically or economically motivated (or both), were men of middle age. This is certainly true of large numbers of Irish emigrants. Unfortunately, these older troops were far more susceptible to disease and the rigours of campaigning. Such proved to be the fate of Christy Welsh. He was fortunate that during his illness he could rely on the care of Emma Smith, a woman who clearly took her responsibilities seriously. Emma served as a vital conduit between Christy and Sarah Welsh during his final days. The emotionally charged correspondence that she and Sarah shared helped to form a bond between them that must have been a comfort to the Irish woman in what were extremely trying times.

THE SCANLANS: IRELAND AND NEW YORK

 '*After I am dead, write to my wife.*'[59]

The widows and dependents pension files record the stories of many Irish families who were devastated by the American Civil War. The information contained in each can reveal much about both the families behind Irish soldiers and the long-term impact of the conflict on generations of Irish-Americans. But the files can also provide a more immediate insight into the experience and communication of death during wartime. In the case of Ann Scanlan, whose husband Patrick lost his life in the service of the Irish Brigade, it also contains her husband's last words to his family.[60]

Ann Leskey married Patrick Scanlan when both were in their early twenties, on 29 April 1851. At the time they were living in Charleston, South Carolina. Patrick, a labourer, must have been a striking individual. He stood at an above-average 6 feet in height, had blue eyes, brown hair and a light complexion. Within a year the couple's first child arrived – John, born on 26 March 1852. A daughter, Catherine, followed on 23 February 1854, with a second son, James, on 7 November 1856. John and Catherine were baptised in St Mary's in Charleston while James was baptised at the Cathedral of St John and St Finbar in the city. Sometime after James' birth the family decided to move to New York. A third son, Cornelius, was born there on 30 June 1860, but tragedy left its mark on the family when the baby died just a few months later on 17 January 1861. Within the year Patrick had enlisted in what would become the 63rd New York Infantry, soon to be one of the famed regiments of the Irish Brigade. When he mustered in on 11 October 1861 Ann had recently become pregnant with their fifth child; Sarah Ann was born on 4 May 1862. Patrick would most likely not have seen his new daughter, as he was bound for the Peninsula Campaign in Virginia and the hard fighting that was to be the Brigade's lot throughout the summer of 1862. It appears he was wounded at Antietam that September, but recovered to be with his regiment for their next major battle, the ill-fated assault on Marye's Heights, Fredericksburg on 13 December 1862. The big Irishman went into the engagement holding the rank of corporal, a highly reliable and well-respected member of the regiment.[61]

As the 63rd New York and the Irish Brigade advanced on 13 December, Patrick Scanlan's luck ran out. A bullet struck him in the right knee, lodging in the joint. It appears that efforts may initially have been made to save his leg, but infection set in. Removed to Lincoln Hospital in Washington DC, he underwent surgery on 26 December where his right leg was removed at the thigh. The shock of the amputation must have been colossal. On 1 January 1863 Patrick's wound haemorrhaged, weakening the already dangerously ill soldier. When his wound again haemorrhaged on 6 January he was operated on once more, in an attempt to try to stem the bleeding in his inner thigh, an area known as Scarpa's triangle. The surgeon's efforts ultimately proved in vain. Patrick Scanlan died in Ward 10 of Lincoln Hospital on the evening of 14 January 1863, a month after receiving what proved to be his fatal wound at Fredericksburg. Minutes after his death, a man called William Duffie sat down to write a letter to the newly widowed Ann. He informed her of her husband's death, offered words of comfort, and communicated Patrick's final words to his family. Ann later had to surrender the letter as proof of her relationship with Patrick; the fact that her marriage had taken place in what was now the Confederacy meant she did not have access to the records that would allow her to demonstrate the relationship with the Irish Brigade soldier.[62]

Ward 10
Lincoln Hospital Washington DC
Jan. 14th 1863

Mrs. Ann Scanlan,

Dear Madam— its become my very painful duty to inform you that your husband has just breathed his last. He died at 25 minutes to seven o'clock this evening without pain. As quietly as the infant sinks to rest from the bosom of its mother so peacefully did he breathe out his last sigh and resign his spirit into the hands of the God who gave it. I know how great will be your grief upon reception of this sad news but it is the will of God that it should be so and you must try and bear the bereavement with resignation, knowing that is not for you to question His right to do with His own as He sees fit: 'The Lord gave and the Lord taketh away: blessed be the name of the Lord!' Every heart knoweth its own sorrow; and there is a grief which cannot be expressed in word, God alone has power to comfort you and to bind up your wounded and bleeding heart, in this your season of great distress; turn then to Heaven and may He who is the refuge of the weary – the hope of the sorrowing of earth, be with you and sustain you in this hour of trial and throw the arms of His everlasting salvation around you! Mr. Scanlan received the last rights of his religion this morning – the Sister, who has charge of this ward, has been constant in her attendance upon your husband and has done all in her power to alleviate his sufferings. I am not myself a Catholic and do not therefore understand the peculiarities of that faith, but Sister told me that the Priest had administered all the last rites necessary in such cases provided. The Priest has seen him several times and was present last Sunday morning and the Sacrament was I believe administered. It will be a great satisfaction to you to know that it is, as it is in this respect I have thought of the difference between the case of your husband and of another poor fellow who died recently and belonging to a different faith. He passed away without so much as having a Minister of Religion near him to breathe a prayer for the peace of his departing soul – such is the difference between the two religions. It has set me to thinking and I shall do so seriously I assure you after this. Your last letter was received, and I offered to write an answer knowing that you would naturally feel anxious to hear from him, but he said he'd wait a day or two first to see if there would be any change for the better. He felt sensible, I think, that his end was approaching for he requested me to make a note of his feelings at that time – this was yesterday forenoon, I think. He did not talk a great deal as it hurt him to do so much. 'After I am dead, write to my wife and tell her that I died a natural death in bed, having received the full benefits of my church'. 'Say that I felt resigned to the will of God and that I am sorry I could not see her and the children once more. That I would have felt better in such a case before I died. It is the will of God that it should not be so, and I must be content to do without'. This was about the substance of what he said. I read it to him and he said it was all that would be necessary to write. His pay amounts to some 6 ½ months not having received any since the 1st of July. This of course you are entitled to draw and you can do so by getting some friend to assist you, [who] understands about it. The few things in this letter are all his personal effects. The rest of his things letters & c. he said to burn – which will be done. I will close for the present.

I remain very truly your well wishes, William Duffie. If you wish to answer this, please direct to me Lincoln Hospital, Washington, DC, Ward 10.[63]

Ann would receive a pension for the service of her husband, and was also given aid for each of her surviving children until they reached the age of 16. Neither did Patrick's comrades in the 63rd New York forget her. In a remarkable gesture, the surviving men of the regiment held a collection to assist the widow and children of a man they had clearly been close to. Unusually, the charitable effort was recorded in the *New York Irish-American*, along with the names of the men who gathered together a total of $100 for Ann and her children. Unfortunately, though, her tribulations were not over. As so often seems to be the case, the spectre of death once again visited her family in 1863. On 6 August 1863 her youngest child Sarah Ann died, barely over a year old. It is unclear if the little girl had ever seen her father. One can only imagine the renewed anguish that this loss brought to Ann and her family.[64]

The charitable collection for Patrick Scanlan as recorded in the *Irish-American* is reproduced below, as is the ultimate fate of each of the men who contributed (recorded in parentheses after their donation):

GENEROSITY OF THE IRISH BRIGADE
New York, May 5th, 1863

To the Editors of the Irish-American: Your journal has often chronicled the deeds of the Irish Brigade on the battlefield. The fame of their daring and valor was spread and resounded over the whole extent of this continent, and even their very enemies have wafted it across the Atlantic and reechoed it throughout Europe. And what wonder? They have rendered every battle-field, where they have fought, memorable for some bold, unexpected, astonishing deed, won renown amidst disaster, and left the enemy, where they at least, happened to be, little cause for triumph or exultation. These things have often thrilled us through, and made us involuntarily speak a blessing and a prayer for the proud little cohort which shed such lustre on our race and land, and proved that the story of the prowess was no fiction. Such things as these excite our admiration and our pride. But the men of the Brigade do other things, which affect us to tears; they can prove themselves as kind-hearted and generous as they are brave. Standing again in the front, diminished in numbers, but not dismayed, and ready to interpose their bodies again between their country (for they have no other now) and the deadly thrusts of its destroyers, they rise above the tumult, the passion and horrors of war, and give way to the better impulses of their nature, the higher and nobler feelings of the heart. When at last, they receive their long looked for and much needed pay, their own wants alone are not uppermost in their minds; the memory of a dead comrade, and of his heroic deeds, comes back upon them, and they think of his widowed wife and orphan children. For them to conceive the generous deed, is to perform it, and as a proof of this, I enclose a note and a list of the names of the brave officers and men of the company of the deceased soldier, who contributed, it having accompanied the money remitted by Captain Condon, now commanding the 63d Regiment in front of the enemy. I know not whether I am doing exactly right in sending you the note and list of contributors for publication; but the amount sent (one hundred dollars) is so liberal, so generous, for so small a number of men, most of whom receive but a very small pittance in the way of pay, that I cannot help thinking that giving a place in your paper to so signal an act of generosity is as much due to the brave soldiers of the Brigade themselves, as it will be pleasing to your many readers to know about it. Patrick Barry [transferred to 24th Veteran Reserve Corps in 1864], another brave and generous soldier of Company A, 63d N.Y.V., sends to the 'Limerick Fund' a contribution of two dollars, which I enclose, hoping you will be pleased to apply it, as you may deem fit, in accordance with the wish of the kind contributor.

Very respectfully yours, P.J.O. [Patrick J. O'Connor, First Lieutenant, Company E, discharged 28th May 1863]

ON PICKET NEAR SCOTT'S FORD, VA., April 2d, 1863

My Dear O.

You will please hand over the enclosed one hundred dollars to Mrs. Scanlan, widow of the late Patrick Scanlan, of my Company, who died from the effects of wounds received at the late battle of Fredericksburg. The generosity here displayed by the few remaining comrades of the gallant corporal towards his widow and orphans shows the estimation in which he was held by them, as also their own goodness of heart. He was beloved by all for his manliness and bravery. The officers whose names are attached were so well pleased with the action of the men in the affair that they have subscribed the sums set opposite to their names. In handing to Mrs. Scanlan the enclosed, please mention the honest and heartfelt expression of sympathy by the comrades of her husband in her bereavement.

I am, my dear O, very truly yours, P.J. Condon, Capt. [Captain Patrick J. Condon, Company G, mustered out 12 June 1863]

Sergeant Ed. Lynch, $5.00 [Mustered out with regiment, 30 June 1865]

Sergeant P.H. Vandewier $1.00 [Mustered out 12 June 1863]

Sergeant Wm. Hayden $5.00 [Mustered out 12 June 1863, later service Company I, 2nd Artillery]

Corporal James Cline $1.00 [Mustered out with regiment, 30 June 1865]

Corporal John Tinsley $1.00 [POW Chancellorsville, mustered out 17 September 1864]

Corporal Hugh Hamilton $1.00 [Deserted on expiration of veteran furlough, January 1864]

Corporal Sam. Walsh $1.00 [Deserted on expiration of veteran furlough, January 1864]

Private Peter O'Neil $1.00 [Wounded at Spotsylvania, 18 May 1864, absent wounded at muster out in 1865]

Private James Smith $1.00 [Deserted 29 June 1863, Frederick, Maryland]

Private Charles Hogan $5.00 [Killed in action, 2 July 1863, Gettysburg, Pennsylvania]

Private Michael Byrns $1.00 [Died of disease, 20 February 1864, Douglas Hospital, Washington DC]

Private Patrick Power $1.00 [Deserted on expiration of veteran furlough, January 1864]

Private James Riely $5.00 [Wounded Antietam, Maryland; killed in action 5 May 1864, Wilderness, Virginia]

Private Patrick Collins $5.00 [Mustered out with regiment, 30 June 1865]

Private James Crowe $2.00 [Wounded Antietam, Maryland; transferred to Veteran Reserve Corps, 23 February 1864]

Private Richd. Hourigan $1.00 [Wounded Antietam, Maryland; mustered out 16 September 1864, Petersburg, Virginia]

Private P. Pendergast $1.00 [No record after 10 April 1863]

Private John McCarthy $1.00 [Mustered out with regiment, 30 June 1865]

Private Patrick Harkin $1.00 [Mustered out 22 September 1864, New York City]

Private Patrick Lucy $1.00 [Mustered out with regiment 30 June 1865]

Private Anthony Campbell $1.00 [Deserted on expiration of veteran furlough, January 1864]

Private P.J. Lynch $2.00 [Discharged for disability 9 February 1863?]

Hospital Steward John J. Corridon $1.00 [Mustered out with regiment, 30 June 1865]

Private James Guiney Company F $1.00

Dr. Lawrence Reynolds 63rd N.Y.V. $5.00 [Mustered out with regiment, 30 June 1865]

Dr. Smart $5.00 [Discharged 29 March 1864 to become assistant surgeon in US Army]

Major Geo. A. Fairlamb 148th P.V. $5.00 [Wounded Chancellorsville, Virginia; wounded and captured, Spotsylvania, Virginia; discharged for disability 24 February 1865]

Mr. Coleman, Sutler 63rd N.Y.V. $5.00

Captain Dwyer $5.00 [Wounded Antietam, Maryland; mustered out 12 June 1863]

Captain Quirk $5.00 [Wounded Fredericksburg, Virginia; mustered out 12 June 1863]

Lieutenant Ryan $1.00 [Mustered out 12 June 1863]

Lieutenant Gallagher $3.00 [Mustered out 12 June 1863]

Lieutenant Maher $2.00 [Mustered out as captain, Company D, 30 June 1865]

Lieutenant Murray $5.00 [Mustered out 12 June 1863]

Captain Condon $12.00 [Mustered out 12 June 1863]

Total $100.00.[65]

Epilogue:
The Forgotten Irish

In July 1926 an employee of the US Pension Bureau searched out one of the old files for which he was responsible. Although surrounded by thousands of others like it, this was one of an ever-dwindling number that remained active. The addition he was about to make would change that status. Opening the bundle of ageing documents, he held in his hands detail on a family story that spanned more than seventy years. Carefully placing the new, freshly stamped document with the others, he sealed it up and replaced it on the shelf. His final addition had been a death certificate, just arrived from Northern Ireland. It recorded the death of Jane Kelley at Cloughfin, County Antrim on 4 June 1926. The certificate described her as a 'widow of soldier', and noted that the 95-year-old had passed away as a result of 'senile decay'. The sealing of her file brought to a close a pension entitlement that had been in place since the end of the American Civil War. Contained within its pages was some of the story of Jane's life, from her marriage to Ballyvaddy labourer Daniel Kelley at Glenarm's Anglican church in 1854, to the birth of her two sons in the years that followed. It also charted her husband's military service, which ended with his death at a Murfreesboro, Tennessee Hospital in 1864; news which Jane received in her home at Black Head, Islandmagee, back in County Antrim. Her file did not relate whether Daniel had left his family in Ireland out of necessity, agreement or abandonment, but none of that mattered in 1926, as the book was closed on the final chapter in their story. With the file replaced on the shelf, the Kelleys joined the growing ranks of the Forgotten Irish.[1]

The experiences of Irish immigrants during the American Civil War era are well-remembered and well-studied in the United States, but such is not the case in Ireland. There remains a lack of appreciation for the scale of Irish involvement in this conflict, which in turn has led to neglect in terms of both historical analysis and public interest. This is partly due to an historical insularity in the coverage of emigration that, in the words of one leading historian of the diaspora, sees much analysis end 'with tearful farewells at Irish ports'. It is a pattern that has been maintained in Ireland over recent years. A huge rise in the popularity of commemorative events has seen anniversaries become a major focus of academic, popular and State-run programmes, as well as drawing significant media focus. Between 2014 and 2016 the 100th anniversaries of the First World War and the 1916 Rising, the 150th anniversary of the birth of William Butler Yeats, and the 200th anniversary of the Battle of Waterloo have all garnered significant attention. Comparatively speaking, the 150th anniversary of the American Civil War passed with relatively little fanfare, despite the historical reality of its impact on hundreds of thousands of Irish people. Such a myopic and insular view of Irish history comes at a price. For example, it is not possible to understand the true ramifications of tragedies such as the Great Famine without examining the later lives of those who felt they had to emigrate as a result of it, a decision that would ultimately lead many to fight – and some to die – in the American Civil War. By extension, a failure to examine in detail the lives of Irish emigrants after their departure deprives Irish scholars of opportunities to identify and utilise resources such as those contained within the widows and dependents pension files. It is my hope that some of what is contained within this book will highlight the potential of this material, and inspire others to examine what is surely one of the greatest untapped resources on the social history of nineteenth-century Irish emigrants in the world. They are certainly stories that deserve to be told.[2]

Bibliography

PENSION FILES

The files are held at the National Archives and Records Administration, Washington DC.

Case Files of Approved Pension Applications of Widows and Other Dependents of the Army and Navy Who Served Mainly in the Civil War and the War with Spain, Record Group 15, Records of the Department of Veterans Affairs.

Widow's Certificate No. 523, Approved Pension File for Mary Ellen and Johanna Carroll, children of Cornelius Carroll, Company K, 12th Illinois Volunteer Infantry.

Widow's Certificate No. 2415, Approved Pension File for Catharine Conway, widow of John Conway, Company K, 69th New York Volunteer Infantry.

Widow's Certificate No. 4869, Approved Pension File for Bridget Tiernan, mother of Martin Tiernan, Company B, 61st New York Volunteer Infantry.

Widow's Certificate No. 6033, Approved Pension File for Sarah Welsh, widow of Christy Welsh, Company E, 85th Pennsylvania Volunteer Infantry.

Widow's Certificate No. 12280, Approved Pension File for Jane Hand, widow of James Hand, Company D, 69th Pennsylvania Volunteer Infantry.

Widow's Certificate No. 14220, Approved Pension File for Sarah Jane Cochran, widow of Richard Cochran, Company H, 63rd Pennsylvania Volunteer Infantry.

Widow's Certificate No. 22113, Approved Pension File for Barbah [*sic*] Murray, widow of John D. Murray, Company A, 99th New York Volunteer Infantry.

Widow's Certificate No. 22521, Approved Pension File for Mary Kelley, mother of Patrick Kelley, Company G, 28th Massachusetts Volunteer Infantry.

Widow's Certificate No. 28175, Approved Pension File for Margaret Sharkey, mother of James Sharkey, Company C, 21st New York Volunteer Cavalry.

Widow's Certificate No. 31621, Approved Pension File for Bridget Finnerty, mother of James Finnerty, Company B, 72nd Illinois Volunteer Infantry.

Widow's Certificate No. 45770, Approved Pension File for Elizabeth McIntyre, mother of William McIntyre, Company H, 95th Pennsylvania Volunteer Infantry.

Widow's Certificate No. 51795, Approved Pension File for Catharine McCabe, widow of Michael McCabe, Company H, 170th New York Volunteer Infantry.

Widow's Certificate No. 57226, Approved Pension File for Maria Ridgway, widow of George Ridgway, Company L, 1st United States Cavalry.

Widow's Certificate No. 60522, Approved Pension File for Ellen Martin, widow of Patrick Martin, Company F, 182nd New York Volunteer Infantry.

Widow's Certificate No. 76801, Approved Pension File for Mary McNamara, widow of Hubert McNamara, Company I, 155th New York Volunteer Infantry.

Widow's Certificate No. 78263, Approved Pension File for Catharine Garvin, mother of Cornelius Garvin (alias Charles Becker), Company I, 52nd New York Volunteer Infantry.

Widow's Certificate No. 83473, Approved Pension File for Ann Scanlan, widow of Patrick Scanlan, Company G, 63rd New York Volunteer Infantry.

Widow's Certificate No. 94648, Approved Pension File for Mary Keegan, widow of Joseph Keegan, Company A, 183rd Pennsylvania Volunteer Infantry.

Widow's Certificate No. 95845, Approved Pension File for Isabella Nugent, widow of Michael Nugent, Company H, 72nd Illinois Volunteer Infantry.

Widow's Certificate No. 100612, Approved Pension File for Nancy Carr, mother of Barnard Carr, Company C, 79th Illinois Volunteer Infantry.

Widow's Certificate No. 109831, Approved Pension File for Timothy Durick, father of Jeremiah Durick, Company C, 88th New York Volunteer Infantry.

Widow's Certificate No. 112001, Approved Pension File for Ann Cairns, widow of Colin Cairns, Company A, 2nd New Hampshire Volunteer Infantry.

Widow's Certificate No. 115828, Approved Pension File for Ellen Bowler, widow of Thomas Bowler (alias Thomas Murphy), Company A, 69th New York Volunteer Infantry.

Widow's Certificate No. 116097, Approved Pension File for Thomas Delaney, father of Thomas Delaney, Company I, 19th Pennsylvania Volunteer Cavalry.

Widow's Certificate No. 116873, Approved Pension File for Mary Kennedy, mother of Thomas Madigan, Company I, 69th New York State Militia.

Widow's Certificate No. 117744, Approved Pension File for Catharine Kennedy, mother of John Kennedy, Company E, 10th Ohio Volunteer Infantry.

Widow's Certificate No. 120393, Approved Pension File for Jane Kelley, widow of Daniel Kelley, Company H, 141st New York Volunteer Infantry.

Widow's Certificate No. 121014, Approved Pension File for Catharine Galvin, mother of William Galvin, Company C, 11th United States Infantry.

Widow's Certificate No. 123532, Approved Pension File for Mary Horan, mother of Dennis Horan, unassigned recruit, 8th United States Cavalry.

Widow's Certificate No. 126148, Approved Pension File for Mary Daly, widow of John Daly (alias John Ryan), Company A, 51st New York Volunteer Infantry.

Widow's Certificate No. 128634, Approved Pension File for Ellen Walsh, widow of Patrick Walsh, Company K, 22nd Illinois Volunteer Infantry.

Widow's Certificate No. 134991, Approved Pension File for Eunice Coyle, mother of Hugh Coyle, Company F, 8th Pennsylvania Volunteer Cavalry.

Widow's Certificate No. 141783, Approved Pension File for Mary Welch, mother of Thomas Welch, Company H, 20th Maine Volunteer Infantry.

Widow's Certificate No. 144447, Approved Pension File for Sarah Mangan, mother of Thomas Mangan, Company E, 36th United States Infantry.

Widow's Certificate No. 153520, Approved Pension File for Jane Murphy, mother of Michael Murphy, Company G, 90th Illinois Volunteer Infantry.

Widow's Certificate No. 161452, Approved Pension File for Margaret Devlin, widow of Charles Devlin, Company B, 35th Indiana Volunteer Infantry.

Widow's Certificate No. 169686, Approved Pension File for Bridget Donohoe, mother of John Donohoe, Company H, 1st United States Artillery.

Case Files of Approved Pension Applications of Widows and Other Dependents of Navy Veterans, 1861–1910, Record Group 15, Records of the Department of Veterans Affairs.

Navy Widow's Certificate No. 2479, Approved Pension File for John O'Donnell, father of Charles O'Donnell, United States Marines.

Navy Widow's Certificate No. 2867, Approved Pension File for John Finan, father of Patrick Finan, USS *Wabash*.

OTHER MANUSCRIPT COLLECTIONS AND PUBLIC DOCUMENTS

Research for this book relied on a large range of military and census documents, largely accessed through websites such as www.ancestry.com, www.Fold3.com and www.findmypast.com. In all instances, only scans of original documents were consulted. These primary sources and their repositories of origin are detailed here.

Historical Society of Pennsylvania, Philadelphia
Pennsylvania, Church and Town Records, 1708–1985

Library and Archives Canada, Ottawa
Census of Canada 1871

Lincoln Financial Foundation Collection, Allen County Public Library, Fort Wayne, Indiana
The Catharine Garvin Collection

National Archives and Records Administration, College Park, Maryland
Record Group 92
Interment Control Forms, 1928–1962

National Archives and Records Administration, Washington DC

Record Group 24
Weekly Returns of Enlistments at Naval Enlistment Rendezvous, 1855–1891

Record Group 29
Eighth Census of the United States, 1860
Ninth Census of the United States, 1870
Tenth Census of the United States, 1880
Twelfth Census of the United States, 1900
Fifteenth Census of the United States, 1930
Sixteenth Census of the United States, 1940
Minnesota Census Schedules for 1870

Record Group 36
Passenger List of Vessels Arriving at New York, New York, 1820–1897
Passenger Lists of Vessels Arriving at Philadelphia, Pennsylvania, 1800–1882

Record Group 45
Subject Files for the Confederate States Navy, 1861–1865

Record Group 94
Final Statements 1862–1899
Register of Enlistments in the US Army, 1798–1914
Registers of Deaths of Volunteers, Compiled 1861–1865

Record Group 109
Compiled Service Records of Confederate Soldiers Who Served in Organizations from the State of South Carolina

Record Group 110
Consolidated Lists of Civil War Draft Registrations, 1863–1865

Record Group 249
Selected Records of the War Department Commissary General of Prisoners

Relating to Federal Prisoners of War Confined at Andersonville, GA, 1864–1865

National Archives, Dublin
Census of Ireland, 1911
Petty Sessions Court Order Books, 1822–1925

National Library of Ireland, Dublin
Catholic Parish Registers

New England Historic Genealogical Society, Boston
1855 Massachusetts State Census

New York Public Library, New York
Emigrant Savings Bank Records

New York State Archives, Albany
Civil War Muster Roll Abstracts of New York State Volunteers, United States
    Sharpshooters, and United States Colored Troops
Census of Inmates in Almhouses and Poorhouses 1875–1921

Pennsylvania Historical and Museum Commission, Harrisburg
Civil War Muster Rolls and Related Records, 1861–1866

Philadelphia City Archives, Philadelphia
Philadelphia City Death Certificates, 1803–1915

PUBLISHED FEDERAL AND STATE DOCUMENTS

Bates, Samuel Penniman, *History of Pennsylvania Volunteers, 1861–5; Prepared in
    Compliance with Acts of the Legislature*, Volume 3 (Harrisburg: B. Singerly, 1869)
Bates, Samuel Penniman, *History of the Pennsylvania Volunteers, 1861–5: Prepared in
    Compliance with Acts of Legislature*, Volume 5 (Harrisburg: B. Singerly, 1871)
Gould, Benjamin Apthorp, *Investigations in the Military and Anthropological Statistics
    of American Soldiers* (Cambridge: Hurd and Houghton for the United States
    Sanitary Commission, 1869)
Massachusetts Adjutant General, *Massachusetts Soldiers, Sailors, and Marines in the
    Civil War*, Volume 3 (Norwood, Massachusetts: The Norwood Press, 1932)
New Hampshire Legislature, *Revised Register of the Soldiers and Sailors of New
    Hampshire in the War of the Rebellion 1861–1866* (Concord: Ira C. Evans, 1895)
New York State Adjutant General's Office, *Annual Report of the Adjutant-General
    of the State of New York for the Year 1894. Registers of the 20th, 21st, 22d, 23d,
    24th, 25th and 26th Regiments of Cavalry, New York Volunteers in War of the
    Rebellion* (Albany: James B. Lyon, 1895)
——*Annual Report of the Adjutant-General of the State of New York for the Year 1900.*

Registers of the Fifty-First, Fifty-Second, Fifty-Third, Fifty-Fourth, Fifty-Fifth and Fifty-Sixth Regiments of Infantry (Albany: James B. Lyon, 1901)

——*Annual Report of the Adjutant-General of the State of New York for the Year 1900. Registers of the Fifty-Seventh, Fifty-Eighth, Fifty-Ninth, Sixtieth, Sixty-First and Sixty-Second Regiment of Infantry* (Albany: James B. Lyon, 1901)

——*Annual Report of the Adjutant-General of the State of New York for the Year 1901: Registers of the Sixty-Third, Sixty-Fourth, Sixty-Fifth, Sixty-Sixth, Sixty-Seventh, and Sixty-Eighth Regiments of Infantry* (Albany: James B. Lyon, 1902)

——*Annual Report of the Adjutant-General of the State of New York for the Year 1901. Registers of the Eighty-Eighth, Eighty-Ninth, Ninetieth, Ninety-First, Ninety-Second and Ninety-Third Regiments of Infantry* (Albany: James B. Lyon, 1902)

——*Annual Report of the Adjutant-General of the State of New York for the Year 1901. Registers of the Sixty-Ninth, Seventieth, Seventy-First, Seventy-Second, Seventy-Third and Seventy-Fourth Regiments of Infantry* (Albany: James B. Lyon, 1902)

——*Annual Report of the Adjutant-General of the State of New York for the Year 1902. Registers of the Ninety-Fourth, Ninety-Fifth, Ninety-Sixth, Ninety-Seventh, Ninety-Eighth, and Ninety-Ninth Regiments of Infantry* (Albany: The Argus Company, Printers, 1903)

——*Annual Report of the Adjutant-General of the State of New York for the Year 1904. Registers of the One Hundred and Forty-Seventh, One Hundred and Forty-Eighth, One Hundred and Forty-Ninth, One Hundred and Fiftieth, One Hundred and Fifty-First, One Hundred and Fifty-Second, One Hundred and Fifty-Third, One Hundred and Fifty-Fourth and One Hundred and Fifty-Fifth Regiments of Infantry* (Albany: Brandow Printing Company, 1905)

——*Annual Report of the Adjutant General of the State of New York for the Year 1904. Registers of the One Hundred and Fifty-Sixth, One Hundred and Fifty-Seventh, One Hundred and Fifty-Eighth, One Hundred and Fifty-Ninth, One Hundred and Sixtieth, One Hundred and Sixty-First, One Hundred and Sixty-Second, One Hundred and Sixty-Third, One Hundred and Sixty-Fourth, One Hundred and Sixty-Fifth, One Hundred and Sixty-Sixth and One Hundred and Sixty-Seventh Regiments of Infantry* (Albany: Brandow Printing Company, 1905)

——*Annual Report of the Adjutant-General of the State of New York for the Year 1905. Registers of the One Hundred and Seventy-Eighth, One Hundred and Eightieth, One Hundred and Eighty-First, One Hundred and Eighty-Second, One Hundred and Eighty-Third, One Hundred and Eighty-Fourth, One Hundred and Eighty-Fifth, One Hundred and Eighty-Sixth and One Hundred and Eighty-Seventh Infantry* (Albany: Brandow Printing Company, 1906)

New York Monuments Commission for the Battlefields of Gettysburg and Chattanooga, William Freeman Fox, and Daniel Edgar Sickles, *Final Report on the Battlefield of Gettysburg* (Albany: James B. Lyon Company, 1900)

Ohio Roster commission, *Official Roster of the Soldiers of the State of Ohio in the War of the Rebellion, 1861–1866, Volume 2* (Akron: Werner Co., 1886)

Otis, George A., and D.L. Huntington, *The Medical and Surgical History of the War of the Rebellion. Part 3, Volume 2. Surgical History* (Washington DC: Government Printing Office, 1883)

Phisterer, Frederick, *New York in the War of Rebellion, 1861–1865, Volume 4* (Albany: James B. Lyon, 1912)

Reid, Whitelaw, *Ohio in the War: Her Statesmen, Generals, and Soldiers, Volume 2* (New York: Moore, Wilstach & Baldwin, 1868)

Terrell, W.H., *Report of the Adjutant General of the State of Indiana, 1861–1865, Volume 5* (Indianapolis: Samuel M. Douglass, 1866)

United States Congress, *Report on the Treatment of Prisoners of War, By the Rebel Authorities, during the War of the Rebellion: To Which Are Appended the Testimony Taken by the Committee, and Official Documents and Statistics Etc* (Washington DC: Government Printing Office, 1869)

United States Pension Bureau, *List of Pensioners on the Roll January 1, 1883: Giving the Name of Each Pensioner, the Cause for Which Pensioned, the Post-Office Address, the Rate of Pension Per Month, and the Date of Original Allowance, as Called for by Senate Resolution of December 8, 1882* (Washington DC: US Government Printing Office, 1883)

United States Surgeon General's Office, *Report on Epidemic Cholera in the Army of the United States, during the Year 1866* (Washington DC: US Government Printing Office, 1867)

United States War Department, *The War of the Rebellion: A Compilation of the Official Records of the Union and Confederate Armies* 128 volumes (Washington DC: US Government Printing Office, 1880–1902)

Books

Anbinder, Tyler, *Five Points: The 19th-Century New York City Neighborhood That Invented Tap Dance, Stole Elections, and Became the World's Most Notorious Slum* (New York: Simon and Schuster, 2001)

Baker, La Fayette Curry, *History of the United States Secret Service* (Philadelphia: L.C. Baker, 1867)

Benn, Carl, *Historic Fort York, 1793–1993* (Toronto: Dundurn Press, 1993)

Burton, Brian K., *Extraordinary Circumstances: The Seven Days Battles* (Bloomington: Indiana University Press, 2010)

Burton, William L., *Melting Pot Soldiers: The Union Ethnic Regiments* 2nd edition (New York: Fordham University Press, 1998)

Clark, Dennis, *The Irish in Philadelphia: Ten Generations of Urban Experience* (Philadelphia: Temple University Press, 1982)

Core, John, *Historical Record of the 2nd (Now 80th), or Royal Tyrone Fusilier Regiment of Militia, From the Embodiment in 1793 to the Present Time* (Omagh: Alexander Scarlett, 1872)

Cozzens, Peter, *This Terrible Sound: The Battle of Chickamauga* (Urbana: University of Illinois Press, 1996)

Crenson, Matthew A., *Building the Invisible Orphanage: A Prehistory of the American Welfare System* (Cambridge, Massachusetts: Harvard University Press, 2001)

Desjardin, Thomas A., *Stand Firm Ye Boys from Maine: The 20th Maine and the Gettysburg Campaign* Fifteenth Anniversary Edition (New York: Oxford University Press, 2009)

Elliott, Bruce S. *Irish Migrants in the Canadas: A New Approach* (Montreal: McGill-Queen's Press, 2004)

Ernsberger, Don, *At the Wall: The 69th Pennsylvania 'Irish Volunteers' at Gettysburg* (Bloomington: Xlibris, 2006)

Gallman, J., Matthew, *Receiving Erin's Children: Philadelphia, Liverpool, and the Irish Famine Migration, 1845–1855*, 1st New Edition (Chapel Hill: The University of North Carolina Press, 2000)

Gerrish, Theodore, *Army Life: A Private's Reminiscences of the Civil War* (Portland: Hoyt, Fogg & Donham, 1882)

Gleeson, David T., *The Green and the Gray: The Irish in the Confederate States of America* (Chapel Hill: The University of North Carolina Press, 2013)

Hays, Gilbert Adams, *Under the Red Patch: Story of the Sixty Third Regiment, Pennsylvania Volunteers, 1861–1864* (Pittsburgh: Sixty-third Pennsylvania Volunteers Regimental Association, 1908)

Henry & Coughlan, *Henry and Coughlan's General Directory of Cork* (Cork: Henry & Coughlan, 1867)

Hunt, Roger D., and Jack Brown, *Brevet Brigadier Generals in Blue*, 1st Edition (Gaithersburg, Maryland: Stan Clark Military Books, 2014)

Jacobson, Eric A., *For Cause & for Country: A Study of the Affair at Spring Hill & the Battle of Franklin*, 2nd Edition (Franklin, Tennessee: O'More Publishing, 2007)

Janney, Caroline E., *Remembering the Civil War: Reunion and the Limits of Reconciliation* (Chapel Hill: The University of North Carolina Press, 2013)

Kennedy, Liam, Paul S. Ell, E.M. Crawford and L.A. Clarkson (eds), *Mapping the Great Irish Famine: An Atlas of the Famine Years* (Dublin: Four Courts Press, 2000)

Kennedy, Liam, and Philip Ollerenshaw, *Ulster Since 1600: Politics, Economy, and Society* (Oxford: Oxford University Press, 2013)

Kenny, Kevin, *Making Sense of the Molly Maguires* (New York: Oxford University Press, 1998)

Lewis, Samuel, *A Topographical Dictionary of Ireland*, 3 volumes (London: S. Lewis & Co., 1837)

Lytle, William Haines, *For Honor, Glory, and Union: The Mexican and Civil War*

Letters of Brig. Gen. William Haines Lytle edited by Ruth C. Carter (The Lexington: University Press of Kentucky, 2009)

Livermore, Thomas Leonard, *Days and Events, 1860–1866* (Boston; New York: Houghton Mifflin Company, 1920)

McElroy, John, *Andersonville: A Story of Rebel Military Prisons, Fifteen Months a Guest of the So-Called Southern Confederacy: A Private Soldier's Experience in Richmond, Andersonville, Savannah, Millen, Blackshear, and Florence* (Toledo: D. R. Locke, 1879)

McPherson, James M., *The Abolitionist Legacy: From Reconstruction to the NAACP* (Princeton, New Jersey: Princeton University Press, 1976)

——*Battle Cry of Freedom: The Civil War Era* Trade Paperback Edition (New York: Oxford University Press, 2003)

Miller, Kerby A., *Emigrants and Exiles: Ireland and the Irish Exodus to North America* Reprint edition (New York; Oxford: Oxford University Press, 1988)

Monnett, John H., *Where a Hundred Soldiers Were Killed: The Struggle for the Powder River Country in 1866 and the Making of the Fetterman Myth* (Albuquerque: University of New Mexico Press, 2010)

Muffly, J. W., *The Story of Our Regiment. A History of the 148th Pennsylvania Vols* (Des Moines, Iowa: Kenyon Printing & Mfg. Co., 1904)

Murdock, Eugene Converse, *One Million Men: The Civil War Draft in the North* (Madison: State Historical Society of Wisconsin, 1971)

Regosin, Elizabeth A. and Donald R. Shaffer, *Voices of Emancipation: Understanding Slavery, the Civil War, and Reconstruction through the U.S. Pension Bureau Files* (New York: New York University Press, 2008)

Rhea, Gordon C., *Cold Harbor: Grant and Lee, May 26–June 3, 1864*, 1st edition (Baton Rouge: Louisiana State University Press, 2007)

Rosenwaike, Ira, *Population History of New York City*, 1st Edition (Syracuse, New York: Syracuse University Press, 2015)

Ruth Ann M. Harris, Donald M. Jacobs, and B. Emer O'Keeffe, *The Search for Missing Friends: Irish Immigrant Advertisements Placed in the Boston Pilot, 1831 –1920* (Boston: New England Historic Genealogical Society, 1989)

Sawislak, Karen, *Smoldering City: Chicagoans and the Great Fire, 1871–1874* (Chicago: University of Chicago Press, 1995)

Schmidt, James M., *Notre Dame and the Civil War: Marching Onward to Victory* (Charleston: The History Press, 2010)

Sears, Stephen W., *Chancellorsville*, Reprint edition (Boston: Mariner Books, 1998)

——*Landscape Turned Red: The Battle of Antietam*, 1st Edition (Mariner Books, 2003)

Shiels, Damian, *The Irish in the American Civil War* (Dublin: The History Press, 2014)

Swan, James B., *Chicago's Irish Legion: The 90th Illinois Volunteers in the Civil War*

(Carbondale: Southern Illinois University Press, 2009)

Twain, Mark, *Mark Twain's Notebook* (New York: Harper and Brothers, 1935)

Ural, Susannah J., *The Harp and the Eagle: Irish-American Volunteers and the Union Army, 1861–1865* (New York: New York University Press, 2006)

Walford, Edward, *The County Families of the United Kingdom; Or, Royal Manual of the Titled & Untitled Aristocracy of Great Britain & Ireland* (London: Robert Hardwicke, 1860)

Warner, Ezra J., *Generals in Blue* (Baton Rouge: Louisiana State University Press, 2006)

Whelan, Bernadette, *American Government in Ireland, 1790–1913: A History of the US Consular Service* (Manchester: Manchester University Press, 2010)

Williams, Chris, *A Companion to 19th-Century Britain* (Oxford: Blackwell Publishing, 2004)

Williams, William H., *'Twas Only an Irishman's Dream: The Image of Ireland and the Irish in American Popular Song Lyrics, 1800–1920* (Urbana: University of Illinois Press, 1996)

Winslow, Stephen N., *Biographies of Successful Philadelphia Merchants* (Philadelphia: J.K. Simon, 1864)

ARTICLES AND ESSAYS

Casey, Marion R., 'Refractive History: Memory and the Founders of the Emigrant Savings Bank' in *Making the Irish American: History and Heritage of the Irish in the United States*, edited by J. J. Lee and Marion R. Casey (New York: New York University Press, 2006), pp. 302–31

Clark, Dennis, 'Kellyville: An Immigrant Enterprise', *Pennsylvania History* 39, No. 1 (1972), pp. 40–49

Delaney, Enda, 'Directions in Historiography: Our Island Story? Towards a Transnational History of Late Modern Ireland', *Irish Historical Studies* 37, No. 148 (November 2011), pp. 83–105

Holmes, Amy E., '"Such Is the Price We Pay": American Widows and the Civil War Pension System' in *Toward a Social History of the American Civil War: Exploratory Essays*, edited by Vinovskis, Maris A. (Cambridge: Cambridge University Press, 1990), pp. 171–95

McClintock, Megan J., 'Civil War Pensions and the Reconstruction of Union Families' in *The Journal of American History* 83, no. 2 (1 September 1996), pp. 456–80

Shiels, Damian, 'The Long Arm of War: Exploring the 19th-Century Ulster Emigrant Experience through American Civil War Pension Files' in *Irish Hunger and Migration: Myth, Memory and Memorialization* (Connecticut: Quinnipiac University Press, 2015), pp. 145–54

Vinovskis, Maris A., 'Have Social Historians Lost the Civil War? Some Preliminary Demographic Speculations' in *Toward a Social History of the American Civil War: Exploratory Essays*, edited by Vinovskis, Maris A., (Cambridge: Cambridge University Press, 1990), pp. 1–30

NEWSPAPERS

Boston Herald
Cleveland Morning Leader
Dublin Evening Mail
Dublin Freeman's Journal
New York Herald
New York Irish American Weekly
New York Irish World
New York Weekly News
New York Times
Ohio Plain Dealer
Omaha World Herald
Philadelphia Inquirer
Philadelphia North American
Troy Daily Times
Troy Record
Washington DC Evening Union
Washington DC National Republican

WEBSITES

Census of Ireland, 1911, online database. Available at http://www.census.nationalarchives.ie/pages/1911/. Accessed 2 January 2015.

'CMOHS.org – Official Website of the Congressional Medal of Honor Society'. Available at http://www.cmohs.org/. Accessed 31 January 2016.

'Find A Grave - Millions of Cemetery Records'. Memorial to John Sharkey. Available at http://www.findagrave.com/cgi-bin/fg.cgi?page=gr&GSln=sharkey&GSiman=1&GScid=1330177&GRid=105283385&. Accessed 31 March 2016.

Gibson, Campbell, and Lennon, Emily, 'Tech Paper 29: Table 4. Region and Country or Area of Birth of the Foreign-Born Population, With Geographic Detail Shown in Decennial Census Publications of 1930 or Earlier: 1850 to 1930 and 1960 to 1990', 2011. Available at http://www.census.gov/population/www/documentation/twps0029/tab04.html. Accessed 14 June 2014.

Griffith's Valuation, online database. Available at http://www.askaboutireland.ie/griffith-valuation/. Accessed 29 December 2014.

Hannigan, Ken. 'Wicklow and the Famine'. *Roundwood and District Historical and Folklore Journal*, 20 (2009). Available at http://www.rte.ie/radio1/the-history-show/programmes/2013/0127/364769-the-history-show-sunday-27-january-2013/. Accessed 16 January 2015.

'History – America's First Look into the Camera: Daguerreotype Portraits and Views, 1839–1862 – Collection Connections | Teacher Resources – Library of Congress'. Available at http://www.loc.gov/teachers/classroommaterials/connections/daguerreotype/history.html. Accessed 31 January 2016.

'History of the Andersonville Prison – Andersonville National Historic Site (US National Park Service)'. Available at http://www.nps.gov/ande/learn/historyculture/camp_sumter_history.htm. Accessed 20 January 2016.

'Illinois Civil War Muster and Descriptive Rolls Database'. Available at http://www.ilsos.gov/isaveterans/civilmustersrch.jsp. Accessed 28 December 2014.

'Ireland Genealogy | Ireland Birth Death & Marriage Records'. Available at http://ifhf.rootsireland.ie/?gclid=Cj0KEQiA8f6kBRCGhMPFtev8p58BEiQAaMLmqeLjrfz0m6WhVXZ5PEN_8hBNFJfh2D00vjuusyG_3jsaAvbC8P8HAQ. Accessed 28 December 2014.

'Irish Family History Foundation: Irish Birth Death Marriage Records for Ireland'. Available at http://rootsireland.ie/. Accessed 21 January 2015.

'NUI Galway Landed Estate Database. Estate Record: Digby (Aran)'. Available at http://landedestates.nuigalway.ie/LandedEstates/jsp/estate-show.jsp?id=798. Accessed 29 December 2014.

'NUI Galway Landed Estate Database Estate Record: Fleming (Gorthlyon)'. Available at http://www.landedestates.ie/LandedEstates/jsp/estate-show.jsp?id=1525. Accessed 2 March 2016.

Shiels, Damian. 'How Many Irish Fought in the American Civil War?' *Irish in the American Civil War*. Available at http://irishamericancivilwar.com/2015/01/18/how-many-irish-fought-in-the-american-civil-war/. Accessed 18 January 2015.

—— 'The Fetterman Fight – Irish Casualties', *Irish in the American Civil War*. Available at http://irishamericancivilwar.com/resources/fetterman-fight/. Accessed 7 November 2012.

——'Visualising the Impact of the American Civil War in Ireland with Palladio', *Irish in the American Civil War*. Available at http://irishamericancivilwar.com/2014/05/31/visualising-the-impact-of-the-american-civil-war-in-ireland-with-palladio/. Accessed 31 May 2014.

'The Battle of Williamsburg Summary & Facts | Civilwar.org'. Available at http://www.civilwar.org/battlefields/williamsburg.html. Accessed 29 December 2014.

Notes

Abbreviations

HSP	Historical Society of Pennsylvania, Philadelphia
LAC	Library and Archives Canada, Ottawa
LFFC	Lincoln Financial Foundation Collection, Allen County Public Library, Fort Wayne, Indiana
NAI	National Archives of Ireland, Dublin
NARA	National Archives and Records Administration, Washington DC
NARACP	National Archives and Records Administration, College Park, Maryland
NEHGS	New England Historic Genealogical Society, Boston
NLI	National Library of Ireland, Dublin
NYPL	New York Public Library, New York
NYSA	New York State Archives, Albany
OR	The War of the Rebellion: A Compilation of the Official Records of the Union and Confederate Armies
PCA	Philadelphia City Archives, Philadelphia
PHMC	Pennsylvania Historical and Museum Commission, Harrisburg

PREFACE

1   Widow's Certificate No. 51795, Approved Pension File for Catharine
     McCabe, widow of Michael McCabe, Company H, 170th New York
     Volunteer Infantry.

2   *Ibid.* The 1.28 million files form part of the *Case Files of Approved Pension
     Applications of Widows and Other Dependents of the Army and Navy Who Served
     Mainly in the Civil War and the War with Spain* at the National Archives and
     Records Administration in Washington, DC. They are part of the Records of
     the Department of Veteran Affairs, Record Group 15. Each file is referred
     to by a unique Widow's Certificate (WC) number and is referenced as such
     throughout. In addition to the widows' files that are the subject of this book,
     the National Archives also house millions of other pension records relating
     to service between 1861 and 1917, the majority relating to the American
     Civil War. They include around 2,000,000 applications made by US army
     veterans, around 26,000 applications by US naval veterans and around
     20,000 applications by US naval widows and other dependents (two of the
     latter are also featured in this book).

3   Gibson, Campbell and Lennon, Emily, 'Tech Paper 29: Table 4. Region and
     Country or Area of Birth of the Foreign-Born Population, With Geographic
     Detail Shown in Decennial Census Publications of 1930 or Earlier: 1850
     to 1930 and 1960 to 1990' https://www.census.gov/population/www/
     documentation/twps0029/tab04.html (Accessed 14 June 2014); Rosenwaike,
     Population History of New York City, p.42; Shiels, 'How Many Irish Fought in
     the American Civil War?' http://irishamericancivilwar.com/2015/01/18/
     how-many-irish-fought-in-the-american-civil-war/ (Accessed 18 January
     2015) The figure of 150,000 Irishmen serving in the Union forces is the most
     frequently cited, e.g. see Susannah J. Ural, *The Harp and the Eagle: Irish-American
     Volunteers and the Union Army, 1861–1865*, 2. However, these figures almost
     certainly require upward revision. The 150,000 figure owes its origin to the
     1869 analysis of Benjamin Apthorp Gould in his *Investigations in the Military
     and Anthropological Statistics of American Soldiers*, in which he places the number
     of Irish volunteers in the service during the war at 144,221 (Apthorp Gould
     1869, 27). However, Gould's figure, aside from reflecting only federal service,
     also excludes Irish who served in branches such as the navy and regular army
     as well as those in the territories and California. A comprehensive new analysis
     of the figures for Irish service is therefore required. Though large numbers of
     Irish fought in the conflict, there were also many among the Irish-American
     population who had little interest in supporting the war effort. For example,
     the Irish were to the fore in incidents such as the New York Draft Riots. For
     a discussion of the motivations behind Irish service in the Union Army, see
     Susannah J. Ural, *The Harp and the Eagle: Irish-American Volunteers and the Union*

Army, 1861–1865 and William L. Burton, *Melting Pot Soldiers: The Union Ethnic Regiments*. For the most comprehensive study of the Irish in the Confederacy, including the statistical analysis behind the figure of 20,000 for Irish service in the South, see David T. Gleeson, *The Green and the Gray: The Irish in the Confederate States of America*.

4   Vinovskis, Maris A., 'Have Social Historians Lost the Civil War? Some Preliminary Demographic Speculations,' pp.22, 26–7; McClintock, 'Civil War Pensions and the Reconstruction of Union Families,' p.458. It should be noted that this and subsequent acts applied only to those in Union service. Former Confederates and their families would not become entitled to federal pensions until 1958, although many received pensions through the state in which they lived.

5   Holmes, Amy E., '"Such Is the Price We Pay": American Widows and the Civil War Pension System,' pp.172 –4; McClintock, 'Civil War Pensions and the Reconstruction of Union Families,' pp.463, 468.

6   Shiels, 'The Long Arm of War: Exploring the 19th-Century Ulster Emigrant Experience through American Civil War Pension Files,' p.146; United States Pension Bureau, *List of Pensioners on the Roll January 1, 1883*; Shiels, 'Visualising the Impact of the American Civil War in Ireland with Palladio' https://irishamericancivilwar.com/2014/05/31/visualising-the-impact-of-the-american-civil-war-in-ireland-with-palladio/ (Accessed 31 May 2014); Whelan, *American Government in Ireland*, pp.149–153. Although this book is the first to concentrate on the pension files in order to explore the Irish experience, their importance has been highlighted with respect to other groups. Perhaps most notable is their application in shedding light on the lives of former African-American slaves. See Elizabeth A. Regosin and Donal R. Shaffer, Voices of Emancipation: Understanding Slavery, the Civil War, and Reconstruction through the US Pension Bureau Files

CHAPTER ONE

1   Baker, *History of the United States Secret Service*, p.448.

2   Widow's Certificate No. 78263, Approved Pension File for Catharine Garvin, mother of Cornelius Garvin (alias Charles Becker), Company I, 52nd New York Volunteer Infantry. The Garvin spelling of the surname was also sometimes interchanged with Gavin; 'Irish Family History Foundation: Irish Birth Death Marriage Records for Ireland' http://www.rootsireland.ie/ (Accessed 21 January 2015) – although Catherine recorded her marriage as 1838 in Grange, a Church Marriage Record recorded on this website lists a wedding in Knocklong and Glenbrohane for 30 July 1843 between Matthew Garvin and Catherine Madden, which may also relate to the couple; 'Narrative of Cornelius

Garvin's Life,' The Catharine Garvin Collection, LFFC; Passenger Lists of Vessels Arriving at New York, New York, 1820–1897, NARA Record Group 36, Microfilm Publication M237, 675 Rolls.

3   'A Lunatic Abducted from the County Home and Sold as a Substitute,' Broadside in The Catharine Garvin Collection, LFFC.

4   Widow's Certificate No. 78263; 'Letter from J. Harrison to all whom it may concern,' The Catharine Garvin Collection, LFFC.

5   A Lunatic Abducted from the County Home and Sold as a Substitute," Broadside in The Catharine Garvin Collection, LFFC; Widow's Certificate No. 78263

6   *Ibid.*

7   *Washington DC National Republican*, 19 November 1863.

8   Widow's Certificate No. 78263; *Cleveland Morning Leader*, 16 March 1864.

9   Widow's Certificate No. 78263; *Cleveland Morning Leader*, 16 March 1864; McPherson, *Battle Cry of Freedom*, pp.600 –1; Baker, *History of the United States Secret Service*, p.448; *Washington DC Evening Union*, 18 April 1864.

10   'Letter from James Thorn to Horatio Seymour', The Catharine Garvin Collection, LFFC.

11   Widow's Certificate No. 78263; New York State Adjutant General's Office, *Registers of the Fifty-First, Fifty-Second, Fifty-Third, Fifty-Fourth, Fifty-Fifth and Fifty-Sixth Regiments of Infantry*, p.284.

12   'Letter from Fernando Wood to Abraham Lincoln', The Catharine Garvin Collection, LFFC.

13   'Note from Abraham Lincoln to Edwin Stanton', The Catharine Garvin Collection, LFFC.

14   Widow's Certificate No. 78263; *New York Times*, 29 April 1894.

15   'Letter from J. Rutherford Worster to Provost Marshal at Fredericksburg', The Catharine Garvin Collection, LFFC.

16   *Troy Daily Times*, 12 July 1865; Widow's Certificate No. 78263.

17   *Troy Daily Times*, 20 June 1864.

18   *Ohio Plain Dealer*, 30 June 1864; *Troy Daily Times*, 20 June 1864.

19   *Troy Daily Times*, 1 July 1864; *The Dublin Evening Mail*, 16 July 1864; *Troy Daily Times*, 12 July 1865; *New York Irish-American Weekly*, 29 July 1865.

20   'Letter from H. Hays to Surgeon Commanding USA Genl. Hospital', The Catharine Garvin Collection, LFFC.

21   Widow's Certificate No. 78263.

22   New York State Adjutant General's Office, Registers of the Fifty-First, Fifty-Second, Fifty-Third, Fifty-Fourth, Fifty-Fifth and Fifty-Sixth Regiments of Infantry, 284, 259; Widow's Certificate No. 78263.

23   Livermore, *Days and Events, 1860–1866*, pp.400 –1.

24   Baker, *History of the United States Secret Service*, pp.447–51.

25   Widow's Certificate No. 78263; *Troy Record*, 18 December 1965. Special

thanks are due to Jane E. Gastineau, the Lincoln Librarian at the Lincoln Financial Foundation Collection in Fort Wayne. She answered an appeal on www.irishamericancivilwar.com seeking information about the whereabouts of the papers, identifying their connection with the Garvin case. The material was digitised and made available online by the Foundation in 2015 and greatly added to this chapter.

26 Widow's Certificate No. 153520, Approved Pension File for Jane Murphy, mother of Michael Murphy, Company G, 90th Illinois Volunteer Infantry.

27 *Ibid.*

28 For a history of the regiment see James B. Swan, *Chicago's Irish Legion: The 90th Illinois Volunteers in the Civil War*; 'Illinois Civil War Muster and Descriptive Rolls Database' http://www.ilsos.gov/isaveterans/ civilMusterSearch.do?key=183273 (Accessed 28 December 2014).

29 Widow's Certificate No. 153520. The 'likeness' Michael is referring to is his photograph. Charles Hudson was likely a family in-law. The muster rolls for the regiment record that First Lieutenant David Duffy was from County Meath and First Sergeant Lawrence McNamara was from County Roscommon. Like Michael, Private Patrick Smith was a native of County Monaghan. Camp Sherman was located in Mississippi – See Swan, *Chicago's Irish Legion: The 90th Illinois Volunteers in the Civil War*, p.80.

30 Widow's Certificate No. 153520; Swan, *Chicago's Irish Legion: The 90th Illinois Volunteers in the Civil War*, p.114.

31 Widow's Certificate No. 153520. Prolapsus Uteri, or uterine prolapse, has a number of potential causes, which include trauma resulting from childbirth.

32 Widow's Certificate No. 153520.

33 *Ibid.*

34 *Ibid.*

35 'Ireland Genealogy | Ireland Birth Death & Marriage Records' ifhf. rootsireland.ie/?gclid=Cj0KEQiA8f6kBRCGhMPFtev8p58BEiQAaM LmqeLjrfz0m6WhVXZ5PEN_8hBNFJfh2D00vjuusyG_3jsaAvbC8P8 HAQ. (Accessed 28 December 2014) although it should be noted that this marriage is recorded for 29 January 1830; Widow's Certificate No. 153520.

36 Widow's Certificate No. 169686, Approved Pension File for Bridget Donohoe, mother of John Donohoe, Company H, 1st United States Artillery.

37 *Ibid.*

38 'Griffith's Valuation of Ireland' online database: County of Galway, Barony of Aran, Union of Galway, Parish of Inisheer http://www.askaboutireland. ie/griffith-valuation/index.xml?action=doNameSearch&Submit. x=38&Submit.y=8&familyname=Donohoe&firstname=First+Name&ba ronyname=ARAN&countyname=GALWAY&unionname=&parishname =INISHEER (Accessed 29 December 2014); 'NUI Galway Landed Estate Database' Estate Record: Digby (Aran) http://landedestates.nuigalway.

ie:8080/LandedEstates/jsp/estate-show.jsp?id=798 (Accessed 29 December 2014; Widow's Certificate No. 169686.

39   Widow's Certificate No. 169686; Register of Enlistments in the US Army, 1798–1914, NARA (Microfilm Publication M233, 81 Rolls).

40   'The Battle of Williamsburg Summary & Facts | Civilwar.org' http://www. civilwar.org/battlefields/williamsburg.html (Accessed 29 December 2014).

41   OR Series 1, Volume 11, Part 1, Report of Maj. Charles S. Wainright, Chief of Artillery, 470–472; OR Series 1, Volume 11, Part 1, Return of Casualties in the Union Forces at the Battle of Williamsburg, p.450.

42   Widow's Certificate No. 169686.

43   *Ibid.*

44   *Ibid.*

45   Widow's Certificate No. 134991, Approved Pension for Eunice Coyle, mother of Hugh Coyle, Company F, 8th Pennsylvania Volunteer Cavalry.

46   Lewis, *A Topographical Dictionary of Ireland*, Volume 1, p.355; Widow's Certificate No. 134991.

47   Widow's Certificate No. 134991; Miller, *Emigrants and Exiles*, p.387.

48   Widow's Certificate No. 134991; Bates, *History of Pennsylvania Volunteers, 1861–5,* Volume 3, pp.115, 133.

49   Widow's Certificate No. 134991.

50   *Ibid.*

51   *Ibid.*

52   Kennedy and Ollerenshaw, *Ulster Since 1600*, p.97.

53   Widow's Certificate No. 117744, Approved Pension File for Catharine Kennedy, mother of John Kennedy, Company E, 10th Ohio Volunteer Infantry.

54   *Ibid.*; Eighth Census of the United States, 1860, Cincinnati Ward 13, Hamilton, Ohio, NARA (Microfilm Publication M653, 1,438 Rolls); the modern county of Offaly was known as King's County in the nineteenth century.

55   Widow's Certificate No. 117744.

56   Ohio Roster Commission, *Official Roster of the Soldiers of the State of Ohio in the War of the Rebellion*, Volume 2, p.304; Burton, *Melting Pot Soldiers*, pp.145–6; Widow's Certificate No. 117744; Reid, *Ohio in The War*, Volume 2, p.78; Hunt and Brown, *Brevet Brigadier Generals in Blue*, p.401.

57   Widow's Certificate No. 117744.

58   William Haines Lytle and Ruth C. Carter (ed.), *For Honor, Glory, and Union*, p.23; Widow's Certificate No. 117744.

59   Widow's Certificate No. 117744.

60   Widow''s Certificate No. 57226, Approved Pension File for Maria Ridgway, widow of George Ridgway, Company L, 1st United States Cavalry.

61   *Ibid.*

62 *Ibid.*; Benn, *Historic Fort York, 1793–1993*, p.85. I am grateful to the Ridgway's present-day descendants in Dublin, notably Carol Mitchell, for details as to George's British army service.

63 Register of Enlistments in the US Army, 1798–1914, NARA (Microfilm Publication M233, 81 Rolls).

64 Widow's Certificate No. 57226.

65 Widow's Certificate No. 57226; Widow's Certificate No. 128634, Approved Pension File for Ellen Walsh, widow of Patrick Walsh, Company K, 22nd Illinois Volunteer Infantry.

66 Widow's Certificate No. 57226.

67 *Ibid.*

68 *Ibid.* This may not have been the only half-truth Maria told. Her descendant Carol Mitchell, who has conducted research into Maria's life, has found evidence to suggest she may have remarried in 1882. If true, this would have voided her entitlement to a pension. If such was the case she would have been one of a large number of women who concealed their remarriage in order to keep hold of the valuable payments.

69 Census of Ireland 1911, Henrietta Street, Inns Quay, Dublin, NAI (Microfilm) http://www.census.nationalarchives.ie/pages/1911/Dublin/Rotunda/ Britain_Street__Great/30051/ (Accessed 2 January 2015); Widow's Certificate No. 57226. Maria had seventeen grandchildren according to the 1911 census, thanks to Carol Mitchell for details as to her total number.

70 Widow's Certificate No. 57226.

71 Widow's Certificate No. 109831, Approved Pension File for Timothy Durick, father of Jeremiah Durick, Company C, 88th New York Volunteer Infantry.

72 Widow's Certificate No. 109831; United States Pension Bureau, *List of Pensioners on the Roll January 1, 1883*, 640; 'Griffith's Valuation of Ireland' online database, County of Tipperary, North Riding, Barony of Owney and Arra, Union of Nenagh, Parish of Castletownarra.

73 Widow's Certificate No. 109831; Court Order Book, Nenagh Petty Sessions Court, County Tipperary, December 1852–December 1853, NAI (CS/ PS/7736).

74 Elliott, *Irish Migrants in the Canadas*, 251; Widow's Certificate No. 109831.

75 New York State Adjutant General's Office, *Registers of the Eighty-Eighth, Eighty-Ninth, Ninetieth, Ninety-First, Ninety-Second and Ninety-Third Regiments of Infantry*, p.42; Widow's Certificate No. 109831.

76 New York Monuments Commission for the Battlefields of Gettysburg and Chattanooga, *Final Report on the Battlefield of Gettysburg*, pp.512–3; Widow's Certificate No. 109831.

77 Phisterer, *New York in the War of Rebellion, 1861–1865*, Volume 4, p.2978; OR Series 1, Volume 19, Part 1, *Report of Lieut. Col. Patrick Kelly, Eighty-Eighth New York Infantry, of the Battle of Antietam*, p.298; Sears, *Landscape Turned Red*, p.xi.

78   Widow's Certificate No. 109831.

79   *Ibid.*

80   *Ibid.*

81   Widow's Certificate No. 123532, Approved Pension File for Mary Horan, mother of Dennis Horan, unassigned recruit, 8th United States Cavalry.

82   Ural, *The Harp and the Eagle*, p.33.

83   Widow's Certificate No. 123532.

84   Widow's Certificate No. 121014, Approved Pension File for Catharine Galvin, mother of William Galvin, Company C, 11th United States Infantry. All of the main town of Athlone is today in County Westmeath, but in the nineteenth century those parts of the town on the west bank of the River Shannon were part of County Roscommon. The Galvins appear to have lived on the western side of the river throughout their time in the town.

85   Widow's Certificate No. 123532; Widow's Certificate No. 121014.

86   Widow's Certificate No. 121014.

87   Widow's Certificate No. 121014; United States Surgeon General's Office, *Report on Epidemic Cholera in the Army of the United States*, vi, ix, p.6.

88   Widow's Certificate No. 123532; United States Surgeon General's Office, *Report on Epidemic Cholera in the Army of the United States*, xiii; Twain, *Mark Twain's Notebook*, pp.48–49. Another to succumb to Cholera in Nicaragua that December was William Gamble. A native of County Tyrone, he served as a federal brigadier-general in the Civil War, which made him one of the highest-ranking Irishmen to serve in that conflict. He is buried in Nicaragua's Virgin Grove Cemetery (See Ezra J. Warner, *Generals in Blue,* 166).

89   Widow's Certificate No. 121014; Widow's Certificate No. 123532; United States Surgeon General's Office, *Report on Epidemic Cholera in the Army of the United States*, 19.

90   Widow's Certificate No. 123532.

91   Widow's Certificate No. 121014.

92   *Ibid.*

93   Widow's Certificate No. 123532.

Chapter Two

1   Navy Widow's Certificate No. 2479, Approved Pension File for John O'Donnell, father of Charles O'Donnell, United States Marines.

2   *Ibid.*

3   *Ibid.*; Clark, 'Kellyville: An Immigrant Enterprise,' pp.42–49; Winslow, *Biographies of Successful Philadelphia Merchants*, pp.158–163; Clark, *The Irish in Philadelphia*, p.108.

4   Clark, 'Kellyville: An Immigrant Enterprise'.

5   Navy Widow's Certificate No. 2479; Eighth Census of the United States,

1860, Philadelphia Ward 24 Precinct 3, Philadelphia, Pennsylvania, NARA (Microfilm Publication M653, 1,438 Rolls)

6   *Ibid.*; Navy Widow's Certificate No. 2479.

7   Navy Widow's Certificate No. 2479.

8   *Ibid.*

9   *Ibid.*

10 *Ibid.*

11 Widow's Certificate No. 94648, Approved Pension File for Mary Keegan, widow of Joseph Keegan, Company A, 183rd Pennsylvania Volunteer Infantry.

12 Ibid.; Hannigan, 'Wicklow and the Famine' http://www.rte.ie/radio1/the-history-show/programmes/2013/0127/364769-the-history-show-sunday-27-january-2013/ (Accessed 16 January 2015).

13 Widow's Certificate No. 94648; Passenger Lists of Vessels Arriving at Philadelphia, Pennsylvania, 1800–1882, NARA (Microfilm Publication M425, 108 Rolls); Gallman, *Receiving Erin's Children*, p.32; Eighth Census of the United States, 1860, Philadelphia Ward 9, Philadelphia, Pennsylvania, NARA (Microfilm Publication M653, 1,438 Rolls).

14 Widow's Certificate No. 94648; Pennsylvania Civil War Muster Rolls and Related Records, PHMC (Series 19.11, 153 cartons); Bates, *History of the Pennsylvania Volunteers, 1861–5*, Volume 5, p.128.

15 Bates, *History of the Pennsylvania Volunteers,* Volume 5, p.128; OR Series 1, Volume 36, Part 1, *Report of Brig. Gen. Nelson A. Miles, US Army, commanding First Brigade*, p.370; OR Series 1, Volume 36, Part 1, *Report of Lieut. Col. George T. Egbert, One hundred and eighty-third Pennsylvania Infantry*, p.385.

16 'History of the Andersonville Prison - Andersonville National Historic Site' https://www.nps.gov/ande/learn/historyculture/camp_sumter_history.htm (Accessed 20 January 2016); Widow's Certificate No. 94648.

17 United States Congress, *Report on the Treatment of Prisoners of War*, 1026. I am grateful to National Park Service Ranger Chris Barr for pointing me to this source, and for his advice on Andersonville.

18 Bates, *History of the Pennsylvania Volunteers, 1861–5*, Volume 5, p.132; McElroy, *Andersonville*, p.547.

19 Widow's Certificate No. 94648; Bates, *History of the Pennsylvania Volunteers, 1861–5*, Volume 5, p.132.

20 Philadelphia City Death Certificates, 1803–1915, PCA; Widow's Certificate No. 94648.

21 Widow's Certificate No. 116097, Approved Pension File for Thomas Delaney, father of Thomas Delaney, Company I, 19th Pennsylvania Volunteer Cavalry.

22 *Ibid.* In the nineteenth century County Laois was known as Queen's County.

23 *Ibid.*; Lewis, *A Topographical Dictionary of Ireland*, Volume 2, p.487.

24 Widow's Certificate No. 116097.

25 Kenny, *Making Sense of the Molly Maguires*, p.69.

26   Widow's Certificate No. 116097.

27   Eighth Census of the United States, 1860, Cass, Schuylkill, Pennsylvania, NARA (Microfilm Publication M653, 1,438 Rolls). The family name was recorded by the enumerator as 'Deleany'; Kenny, *Making Sense of the Molly Maguires*, p.86.

28   Lewis, *A Topographical Dictionary of Ireland*, Volume 2, p.487; Kenny, *Making Sense of the Molly Maguires*, pp.86–7, 89, 91, 93; Murdock, *One Million Men*, p.44.

29   Widow's Certificate No. 116097; Schmidt, *Notre Dame and the Civil War*, pp.45–47.

30   Widow's Certificate No. 116097.

31   Widow's Certificate No. 115828, Approved Pension File for Ellen Bowler, widow of Thomas Bowler (alias Thomas Murphy), Company A, 69th New York Volunteer Infantry.

32   *Ibid.*

33   Casey, 'Refractive History: Memory and the Founders of the Emigrant Savings Bank', pp.306–8.

34   Emigrant Savings Bank Records, NYPL (Microfilm Reels 1–20, ★R–USLHG ★ZI-815); New York State Adjutant General's Office, *Registers of the Sixty-Third, Sixty-Fourth, Sixty-Fifth, Sixty-Sixth, Sixty-Seventh, and Sixty-Eighth Regiments of Infantry*, p.186; New York Adjutant General's Office, *Registers of the Sixty-Ninth, Seventieth, Seventy-First, Seventy-Second, Seventy-Third and Seventy-Fourth Regiments of Infantry*, p.210; New York Adjutant General's Office, *Registers of the Eighty-Eighth, Eighty-Ninth, Ninetieth, Ninety-First, Ninety-Second and Ninety-Third Regiments of Infantry*, p.7.

35   Widow's Certificate No. 115828; *Henry and Coughlan's General Directory of Cork*, p.340.

36   Widow's Certificate No. 115828; OR Series 1, Volume 36, Part 1, *Reports of Maj. Gen. Winfield S. Hancock, US Army, commanding Second Army Corps, with statement of guns captured and lost from May 3 to November 1, and list of colors captured and lost from May 4 to November 1*, p.320.

37   Widow's Certificate No. 115828.

38   *Ibid.*; Census of Ireland 1911, Cork Lane, Youghal Urban, Cork, NAI (Microfilm) http://www.census.nationalarchives.ie/pages/1911/Cork/Youghal_Urban/Cork_Lane/446620/ (Accessed 2 January 2015).

39   Widow's Certificate No. 116873, Approved Pension File for Mary Kennedy, mother of Thomas Madigan, Company I, 69th New York State Militia.

40   Widow's Certificate No. 116873.

41   *Ibid.*; Kennedy et al., *Mapping the Great Irish Famine*, p.104.

42   Widow's Certificate No. 116873.

43   *Ibid.*

44   *Ibid.*

45   *Ibid.*; *New York Irish American Weekly*, 24 August 1861.

46   Widow's Certificate No. 116873; New York State Adjutant General's Office,

Registers of the One Hundred and Fifty-Sixth, One Hundred and Fifty-Seventh, One Hundred and Fifty-Eighth, One Hundred and Fifty-Ninth, One Hundred and Sixtieth, One Hundred and Sixty-First, One Hundred and Sixty-Second, One Hundred and Sixty-Third, One Hundred and Sixty-Fourth, One Hundred and Sixty-Fifth, One Hundred and Sixty-Sixth and One Hundred and Sixty Seventh Regiments of Infantry, p.415.

47 Widow's Certificate No. 116873; Anbinder, *Five Points*, pp.48, 98.

48 Widow's Certificate No. 116873.

49 *New York Irish American Weekly*, 18 October 1862; Widow's Certificate No. 2415, Approved Pension File for Catharine Conway, widow of John Conway, Company K, 69th New York Volunteer Infantry.

50 *New York Irish American Weekly*, 18 October 1862.

51 *Ibid.*

52 Widow's Certificate No. 2415.

53 *Ibid.*; McPherson, *The Abolitionist Legacy*, pp.25.

54 Eighth Census of the United States, 1860, Skaneateles, Onondaga, New York, NARA (Microfilm Publication M653, 1,438 Rolls); Widow's Certificate No. 2415.

55 Widow's Certificate No. 2415.

56 *New York Irish World*, 17 February 1894.

57 Widow's Certificate No. 126148, Approved Pension File for Mary Daly, widow of John Daly (alias John Ryan), Company A, 51st New York Volunteer Infantry; Celbridge – Catholic Parish Registers: Parish of Celbridge, Register of Baptisms, January 4 1857–December 19 1880, NLI (Microfilm 06613/09).

58 Widow's Certificate No. 126148.

59 *Ibid.*; New York State Adjutant General's Office, *Registers of the Fifty-First, Fifty-Second, Fifty-Third, Fifty-Fourth, Fifty-Fifth and Fifty-Sixth Regiments of Infantry*, p.192.

60 Widow's Certificate No. 126148.

61 OR Series 1, Volume 42, Part 1, *Report of Capt. Thomas B. Marsh, Fifty-First New York Infantry, of Operations September 30*, 585; *New York Times* 24 January 1865; Widow's Certificate No. 126148. Among the members of the regiment captured at Poplar Grove was Captain George Washington Whitman, brother of the famous American poet Walt Whitman.

62 Widow's Certificate No. 126148.

63 *Ibid.*

64 *Ibid.*

65 Widow's Certificate No. 126148.

66 Widow's Certificate No. 95845, Approved Pension File for Isabella Nugent, widow of Michael Nugent, Company H, 72nd Illinois Volunteer Infantry.

67 *Ibid.*

68 Holmes, '"Such Is the Price We Pay": American Widows and the Civil

War Pension System,' p.172; McClintock, 'Civil War Pensions and the Reconstruction of Union Families,' pp.477–8; Widow's Certificate No. 95845.

69   Widow's Certificate No. 95845; 'Illinois Civil War Muster and Descriptive Rolls Database' http://www.ilsos.gov/isaveterans/civilMusterSearch.do?key=188755 (Accessed 28 December 2014; Jacobson, *For Cause & for Country*, p.335.

70   Widow's Certificate No. 95845.

71   Sawislak, *Smoldering City*, pp.2–3; Widow's Certificate No. 95845.

72   Widow's Certificate No. 95845.

73   *Ibid.*

74   *Ibid.*; 'Illinois Civil War Muster and Descriptive Rolls Database' http://www.ilsos.gov/isaveterans/civilMusterSearch.do?key=89993 (Accessed 28 December 2014).

75   Widow's Certificate No. 95845.

76   *Ibid.*

77   *Ibid.*

78   *Ibid.*

79   *Ibid.*

80   *Ibid.*; McClintock, 'Civil War Pensions and the Reconstruction of Union Families', p.477.

81   Widow's Certificate No. 22113, Approved Pension File for Barbah Murray, widow of John D. Murray, Company A, 99th New York Volunteer Infantry.

82   *Ibid.*; Janney, *Remembering the Civil War*, p.109. The organisation is still going strong today and is now known as the Sons of Union Veterans of the Civil War.

83   Widow's Certificate No. 22113.

84   New York State Adjutant General's Office, *Registers of the Ninety-Fourth, Ninety-Fifth, Ninety-Sixth, Ninety-Seventh, Ninety-Eighth, and Ninety-Ninth Regiments of Infantry*, p.1328; Phisterer, *New York in the War of Rebellion, 1861–1865*, Volume 4, p.3143; Widow's Certificate No. 22113.

85   Widow's Certificate No. 22113.

86   *Ibid.*

87   *Ibid.*

88   *Ibid.*

89   Williams, *A Companion to 19th-Century Britain*, p.261; Widow's Certificate No. 22113. Although Barbara Murray spent some time in New York she appears to have lived the majority of her life in Dublin, with addresses such as 7 Nelson Street and 107 James Street in the city.

90   Widow's Certificate No. 60522, Approved Pension File for Ellen Martin, widow of Patrick Martin, Company F, 182nd New York Volunteer Infantry.

91   *New York Irish American Weekly*, 17 September 1864; Widow's Certificate No. 60522.

92   Widow's Certificate No. 60522; New York State Adjutant General's Office, *Registers of the One Hundred and Seventy-Eighth, One Hundred and Eightieth,*

One Hundred and Eighty-First, One Hundred and Eighty-Second, One Hundred and Eighty-Third, One Hundred and Eighty-Fourth, One Hundred and Eighty-Fifth, One Hundred and Eighty-Sixth and One Hundred and Eighty-Seventh Infantry, p.371.

93 Widow's Certificate No. 60522.

94 *Ibid.*

95 *Ibid.*; Crenson, *Building the Invisible Orphanage*, pp.71–2.

96 Widow's Certificate No. 60522.

97 *Ibid.*

98 *Ibid.*

99 *Ibid.*; United States Pension Bureau, *List of Pensioners on the Roll January 1, 1883*, p.638.

100 Census of Inmates in Almshouses and Poorhouses, 1875–1921, NYSA, (Series A1978, Reel A1978:100, Record Number: 11/1213 & Reel A1978:93 Record Number: 6/659).

CHAPTER THREE

1   Widow's Certificate No. 22521, Approved Pension File for Mary Kelley, mother of Patrick Kelley, Company G, 28th Massachusetts Volunteer Infantry.

2   *Ibid.*

3   *Ibid.* Massachusetts State Census 1855, Boston Ward 7, Suffolk, Massachusetts, NEHGS (Microfilm Reel 25, Volume 35).

4   Widow's Certificate No. 22521; Massachusetts Adjutant General, *Massachusetts Soldiers, Sailors, and Marines in the Civil War*, Volume 3, p.242.

5   Widow's Certificate No. 22521.

6   Massachusetts Adjutant General, *Massachusetts Soldiers, Sailors, and Marines in the Civil War*, Volume 3, p.243; Williams, *'Twas Only an Irishman's Dream*, p.73.

7   Widow's Certificate No. 22521.

8   *Ibid.*; Massachusetts Adjutant General, *Massachusetts Soldiers, Sailors, and Marines in the Civil War*, Volume 3, pp.241–243. Pat Hoben had enlisted on 7 December 1861 at age 24; Patrick O'Brien enlisted on 1 October 1861 at age 24; Patrick Killian enlisted on 30 December 1861 at age 30.

9   Widow's Certificate No. 22521.

10 *Ibid.*

11 Massachusetts Adjutant General, *Massachusetts Soldiers, Sailors, and Marines in the Civil War*, Volume 3, p.243. Mike Ney was 30 years old when he enlisted on 4 November 1861. He was captured again at Bristoe Station on 14 October 1863, exchanged, and mustered out on 19 December 1864.

12 Widow's Certificate No. 22521.

13 *New York Herald*, 29 April 1863, *New York Irish American Weekly*, 2 May 1863, *New York Irish American Weekly*, 9 May 1863, *Boston Herald*, 5 August 1863, *Freeman's Journal*, 15 May 1863, *New York Irish American Weekly*, 29 August 1863.

14 Widow's Certificate No. 22521.

15 Navy Widow's Certificate No. 2867, Approved Pension File for John Finan, father of Patrick Finan, USS *Wabash*.

16 Weekly Returns of Enlistments at Naval Enlistment Rendezvous, 1855–1891, NARA (Microfilm Publication M1953).

17 Navy Widow's Certificate No. 2867. Patrick's original letter follows the normal style of listing friends and neighbours at home to give his regards to – given the length of the list, these have been omitted from this transcription for ease of reading.

18 New York State Adjutant General's Office, *Registers of the Eighty-Eighth, Eighty-Ninth, Ninetieth, Ninety-First, Ninety-Second and Ninety-Third Regiments of Infantry*, p.51. Patrick Flannigan enlisted in the 88th New York Infantry at the age of 27 on 3 March 1862. He was captured in action at Chancellorsville on 3 May 1863 and paroled. Later transferred to the 114th Company of the 1st Battalion, Veteran Reserve Corps, he was transferred back to the 88th New York on 19 February 1864. He re-enlisted as a veteran volunteer on 22 March 1864 but deserted on 30 May 1864 on the expiration of his veteran furlough; Compiled Service Record of Michael Coggins, 3rd Palmetto Battalion, South Carolina Light Artillery, NARA (Microfilm Publication M267); Subject File of the Confederate States Navy, 1861–1865: Confederate Muster Rolls of Ships and Stations, NARA (Microfilm Publication M1091); Navy Widow's Certificate No. 2867. The Mulrooneys referenced in the letter were also relations, this was Patrick's mother's maiden name.

19 Navy Widow's Certificate No. 2867. The final portion of this letter contains a large number of individuals who Patrick wished to send his respects to, given their length they are omitted from this transcription for ease of reading.

20 Navy Widow's Certificate No. 2867.

21 *Ibid.*

22 *Ibid.*

23 *Ibid.*

24 *Ibid.*

25 *Ibid.*

26 Widow's Certificate No. 141783, Approved Pension File for Mary Welch, mother of Thomas Welch, Company H, 20th Maine Volunteer Infantry.

27 *Ibid.*

28 *Ibid.*

29 *Ibid.*

30 Gerrish, *Army Life*, pp.43–44.

31 Widow's Certificate No. 141783.

32 *Ibid.*; Desjardin, *Stand Firm Ye Boys from Maine*, p.180; Census of Canada, 1871, Fredericton Carleton Ward, York, New Brunswick, LAC (Microfilm C-10381).

33 Widow's Certificate No. 45770, Approved Pension File for Elizabeth

McIntyre, mother of William McIntyre, Company H, 95th Pennsylvania Volunteer Infantry.

34   *Ibid.*

35   *Ibid.*; Eighth Census of the United States, 1860, Philadelphia Ward 9, Philadelphia, Pennsylvania, NARA (Microfilm Publication M653, 1,p.438 Rolls); Bates, *History of Pennsylvania Volunteers, 1861–5*,Volume 3, p.371.

36   Widow's Certificate No. 45770.

37   *Ibid.*

38   *Ibid.*

39   Sears, *Chancellorsville*, p.154; Widow's Certificate No. 45770.

40   Widow's Certificate No. 45770.

41   OR Series 1,Volume 25, Part 1, Report of Brig. Gen. William T.H. Brooks, commanding First Division, p.568

42   Widow's Certificate No. 45770.

43   Widow's Certificate No. 28175, Approved Pension File for Margaret Sharkey, mother of James Sharkey, Company C, 21st New York Volunteer Cavalry.

44   Widow's Certificate No. 28175; Civil War Muster Roll Abstracts of New York State Volunteers, United States Sharpshooters, and United States Colored Troops, *c.* 1861–1900 NYSA (Microfilm, 1,185 Rolls).

45   Widow's Certificate No. 28175; Civil War Muster Roll Abstracts of New York State Volunteers, United States Sharpshooters, and United States Colored Troops, c. 1861-1900 NYSA (Microfilm, 1,185 Rolls); Widow's Certificate No. 28175.

46   Widow's Certificate No. 28175.

47   Widow's Certificate No. 28175; Eighth Census of the United States, 1860, Rochester Ward 6, Monroe, New York, NARA (Microfilm Publication M653, 1,438 Rolls); New York Adjutant General's Office, *Registers of the 20th, 21st, 22d, 23d, 24th, 25th and 26th Regiments of Cavalry*, pp. 339, 356; Civil War Muster Roll Abstracts of New York State Volunteers, United States Sharpshooters, and United States Colored Troops, *c.* 1861–1900 NYSA (Microfilm, 1,185 Rolls).

48   Widow's Certificate No. 28175.

49   *Ibid.* As was common in letters of this period, James listed a large number of friends and relations who he wished to have respects paid to. Given the length of the list, only a portion have been included in this transcription for ease of reading.

50   *Ibid.*

51   Widow's Certificate No. 28175; New York Adjutant General's Office, *Registers of the 20th, 21st, 22d, 23d, 24th, 25th and 26th Regiments of Cavalry*, p.339.

52   Widow's Certificate No. 28175.

53   *Ibid.*

54   For John Sharkey, Fairview Park Cemetery, St John, Kansas http://www.

findagrave.com/cgi-bin/fg.cgi?page=gr&GSln=sharkey&GSiman=1&GSci
d=1330177&GRid=105283385& (Accesed 31 March 2016).

55 Widow's Certificate No. 4869, Approved Pension File for Bridget Tiernan,
    mother of Martin Tiernan, Company B, 61st New York Volunteer Infantry.

56 *Ibid.*

57 *Ibid.*; Eighth Census of the United States, 1860, New York Ward 6 District 2,
    New York, New York, NARA (Microfilm Publication M653, 1,438 Rolls);
    Anbinder, *Five Points*, p.90. Though Bridget's file lists their address as 14
    Baxter Street on one occasion, this is likely a consequence of the events
    of 1863, and the subsequent affidavits of the Sands' and newspaper reports
    confirm it as 15 Baxter.

58 Widow's Certificate No. 4869; New York Adjutant General's Office, *Registers
    of the Fifty-Seventh, Fifty-Eighth, Fifty-Ninth, Sixtieth, Sixty-First and Sixty-
    Second Regiment of Infantry*, p.1080.

59 Widow's Certificate No. 4869.

60 *Ibid.*

61 *Ibid.*

62 *Ibid.*

63 *Ibid.*

64 OR Series 1, Volume 11, Part 1, Report of Col. Francis C. Barlow, Sixty-
    First New York Infantry, 772–773; OR Series 1, Volume 11, Part 1, Return
    of Casualties in the Army of the Potomac at the Battle of Fair Oaks,
    or Seven Pines, Va., May 31-June 1, 1862, 757; Registers of Deaths of
    Volunteers, Compiled 1861–1865, NARA (ARC ID: 656639).

65 Widow's Certificate No. 4869; 'NUI Galway Landed Estate Database' Estate
    Record: Fleming (Gorthlyon) http://landedestates.nuigalway.ie:8080/
    LandedEstates/jsp/family-show.jsp?id=1457 (Accessed 2 March 2016);
    Eighth Census of the United States, 1860, New York Ward 6 District 2, New
    York, New York, NARA (Microfilm Publication M653, 1,438 Rolls).

66 Anbinder, *Five Points*, pp.90–91; *New York Herald*, 10 June 1863; *New York
    Weekly News*, 13 June 1863; *New York Herald*, 11 June 1863.

67 Widow's Certificate No. 4869.

68 Widow's Certificate No. 100612, Approved Pension File for Nancy Carr, 68
    of Barnard Carr, Company C, 79th Illinois Volunteer Infantry.

69 Harris, Jacobs and O'Keeffe, *The Search for Missing Friends: Irish Immigrant
    Advertisements Placed in the Boston Pilot, 1831–1920*, p.564.

70 Widow's Certificate No. 100612; Ballinascreen – Catholic Parish Registers:
    Diocese of Derry, Parish of Ballinascreen (Draperstown), Baptisms June 1 1863–
    December 28 1880 (Microfilm 06613/09). I am particularly grateful to Barbara
    Harvey Freeburn for identifying the potential marriage record of the Carrs.

71 OR Series 1, Volume 38, Part 1, Report of Lieut. Col. Terrence Clark,
    Seventy-Ninth Illinois Infantry, 364.

72 Widow's Certificate No. 100612.

73 *Ibid.*

74 *Ibid.*

75 *Ibid.*

76 *Ibid.*

77 OR Series 1, Volume 38, Part 1, *Report of Lieut. Col. Terrence Clark, Seventy-Ninth Illinois Infantry*, p.364.

78 Widow's Certificate No. 100612.

79 *Ibid.*; *Omaha World-Herald*, 17 March 1898.

80 Widow's Certificate No. 161452, Approved Pension File for Margaret Devlin, widow of Charles Devlin, Company B, 35th Indiana Volunteer Infantry.

81 Widow's Certificate No. 161452; Walford, *The County Families of the United Kingdom*, p.737.

82 Widow's Certificate No. 161452.

83 Widow's Certificate No. 161452; Register of Enlistments in the US Army, 1798–1914, NARA (Microfilm Publication M233). Charles made specific reference to his Mexican-American War pension while he was a prisoner in Andersonville. This soldier is the only one to match Charles Devlin in the enlistment records, though it should be noted he is listed as 25 years old. In reality Charles Devlin was likely older than this, but may well have provided an inaccurate age during his Mexican War service.

84 Widow's Certificate No. 161452.

85 *Ibid.*

86 *Ibid.*; Terrell, *Report of the Adjutant General of the State of Indiana*, Volume 5, p.135; Schmidt, *Notre Dame and the Civil War*, pp.37–38.

87 Widow's Certificate No. 161452.

88 *Ibid.*

89 *Ibid.*

90 *Ibid.*

91 *Ibid.*

92 *Ibid.*; Cozzens, *This Terrible Sound*, pp.206, 209; OR Series 1, Volume 30, Part 1, *Report of Maj. John P. Dufficy, Thirty-Fifth Indiana Infantry*, pp.843–844.

93 Widow's Certificate No. 161452; Selected Records of the War Department Commissary General of Prisoners Relating to Federal Prisoners of War Confined at Andersonville, GA, 1864-65, NARA (Microfilm Publication M1303, 6 Rolls); Interment Control Forms, 1928–1962, NARACP (A1 2110-B).

94 Widow's Certificate No. 161452.

95 *Ibid.*

96 Widow's Certificate No. 144447, Approved Pension File for Sarah Mangan, mother of Thomas Mangan, Company E, 36th United States Infantry.

97   *Ibid.*

98   *Ibid.*;Thomas Mangan Final Statement, NARA (Microfilm Publication M233).

99   Widow's Certificate No. 144447.

100 *Ibid.*; Monnett, *Where a Hundred Soldiers Were Killed*, pp.14, 106–118.

101 *Ibid.*; Monnett, *Where a Hundred Soldiers Were Killed*; for full details on the twenty Irish-born soldiers killed during the battle, see Shiels, 'The Fetterman Fight – Irish Casualties' https://irishamericancivilwar.com/resources/fetterman-fight/ (Accessed 7 November 2012).

102 Widow's Certificate No. 144447; Monnett, *Where a Hundred Soldiers Were Killed*, p.143.

103 Widow's Certificate No. 144447.

Chapter Four

1   Widow's Certificate No. 14220, Approved Pension File for Sarah Jane Cochran, widow of Richard Cochran, Company H, 63rd Pennsylvania Volunteer Infantry.

2   Passenger Lists of Vessels Arriving at Philadelphia, Pennsylvania, 1800–1882, NARA (Microfilm Publication M425 Rolls # 1–108); Widow's Certificate No. 14220.

3   Widow's Certificate No. 14220.

4   Hays, *Under the Red Patch*, p.22; Widow's Certificate No. 14220.

5   For more on the Seven Days' see Burton, *Extraordinary Circumstances*; Hays, *Under the Red Patch*, p.114.

6   Hays, *Under the Red Patch*, pp.123–9, 133–4.

7   Widow's Certificate No. 14220.

8   *Ibid.*

9   *Ibid.*

10   Widow's Certificate No. 31621, Approved Pension File for Bridget Finnerty, Company B, 72nd Illinois Volunteer Infantry.

11   *Ibid.*; Passenger Lists of Vessels Arriving at New York, New York, 1820–1897, NARA (Microfilm Publication M237, 675 Rolls).

12   Widow's Certificate No. 31621.

13   'Illinois Civil War Muster and Descriptive Rolls Database' http://www.ilsos.gov/isaveterans/civilMusterSearch.do?key=82193 (Accessed 28 December 2014); Widow's Certificate No. 31621.

14   Widow's Certificate No. 31621.

15   *Ibid.*

16   *Ibid.*

17   *Ibid.*

18   OR Series 1, Volume 19, Part 1, *Report of Lieut. Col. Patrick Kelly, Eighty-*

Eighth New York Infantry, of the Battle of Antietam, pp.297–99; Widow's Certificate No. 31621.

19 Widow's Certificate No. 31621.

20 Widow's Certificate No. 12280, Approved Pension File for Jane Hand, widow of James Hand, Company D, 69th Pennsylvania Volunteer Infantry.

21 *Ibid.*; *Philadelphia North American* 3 July 1863; *Philadelphia Inquirer*, 3 July 1863.

22 Widow's Certificate No. 12280; Ernsberger, *At the Wall: The 69th Pennsylvania 'Irish Volunteers' at Gettysburg*, p.66; Eighth Census of the United States, 1860, Philadelphia Ward 20 Division 1, Philadelphia, Pennsylvania, NARA (Microfilm Publication M653, 1,438 Rolls); Bates, *History of Pennsylvania Volunteers*, Volume 2, p.719.

23 Widow's Certificate No. 12280.

24 *Ibid.*; Historic Pennsylvania Church and Town Records, HSP.

25 'CMOHS.org - Official Website of the Congressional Medal of Honor Society' http://www.cmohs.org/recipient-detail/869/mcanally-charles.php (Accessed 31 january 2016).

26 Widow's Certificate No. 76801, Approved Pension File for Mary McNamara, widow of Hubert McNamara, Company I, 155th New York Volunteer Infantry.

27 *Ibid.*

28 *Ibid.*

29 *Ibid.*; Eighth Census of the United States, 1860, Buffalo Ward 1, Erie, New York, NARA (Microfilm Publication M653, 1,438 Rolls); New York State Adjutant General's Office, *Registers of the One Hundred and Forty-Seventh, One Hundred and Forty-Eighth, One Hundred and Forty-Ninth, One Hundred and Fiftieth, One Hundred and Fifty-First, One Hundred and Fifty-Second, One Hundred and Fifty-Third, One Hundred and Fifty-Fourth and One Hundred and Fifty-Fifth Regiments of Infantry*, p.1323.

30 Rhea, *Cold Harbor*, p.335; Widow's Certificate No. 76801.

31 Widow's Certificate No. 76801. For those interested in the original spelling and grammar of Hubert's writing, they are as follows: … almigty god that we will soon get tru with them I all right soe far thank be tow the almighty god for his merci [illegible] possible [?] to I am [ad]dressing you with a few lines hope tow find you and the children in good helth as the departure thes few lines leves mee me in at present thank be to the almighty god for his to me we are fighting with rebble for last 10 days and we have drove them for as much 30 miles but there is grete many of our men kild and wonded but the purty well sourrounded in the [?].

Page 2: Jun the 2 1864 Camp of the armi of the portommack 7 miles from Richmond mi Dear wife and children I take the favorable opportunitie [?] [illegible] tell what moment I wold get kild or wonded but I trus in god for his mercis tow me there is afful fight ing going on her we ar fight ing knight and fight ing day my Dear wife an children there is no thing more that I can let you know now it I have now time.

Page 3: it is verry hard tow get paper or ink any thing els her John Dempsey is well and alsoe michael lawler is I wish that you wold tell his wife there is no thing more my Dear wife and children that I think soe good bie for afile now more at present from youre afectionate husband Hubert Mc Namara 2 Corps 2 Division 4 brigade Co I 155armi of the portom mac good bie write soon.

32   *Ibid.*

33   Widow's Certificate No. 112001, Approved Pension File for Ann Cairns, widow of Colin Cairns, Company A, 2nd New Hampshire Volunteer Infantry.

34   *Ibid.*

35   *Ibid.*

36   *Ibid.*

37   Passenger Lists of Vessels Arriving at New York, New York, 1820–1897, NARA (Microfilm Publication M237, 675 Rolls); Consolidated Lists of Civil War Draft Registrations, 1863–1865, NARA (NM-65, Entry 172, 620 Volumes).

38   Ayling, *Revised Register of the Soldiers and Sailors of New Hampshire in the War of the Rebellion 1861–1866*, p.521; OR Series 1, Volume 42, Part 1, *Return of the Casualties in the Union Forces, Fair Oaks and Darbytown Road, Va., October 27–28*, p.806; OR Series 1, Volume 42, Part 1, *Report of Lieut. Col. Joab N. Patterson, Second New Hampshire Infantry, commanding Third Brigade, of operations October 26–28*, p.151.

39   Widow's Certificate No. 112001.

40   Widow's Certificate No. 523, Approved Pension File for Mary Ellen and Johanna Carroll, children of Cornelius Carroll, Company K, 12th Illinois Volunteer Infantry.

41   *Ibid.*

42   *Ibid.*; Eighth Census of the United States, 1860, Chicago Ward 5, Cook, Illinois, NARA (Microfilm Publication M653, 1,438 Rolls); 'Illinois Civil War Muster and Descriptive Rolls Database' http://www.ilsos.gov/isaveterans/civilMusterSearch.do?key=40673 (Accessed 28 December 2014).

43   Widow's Certificate No. 523.

44   *Ibid.*

45   *Ibid.*

46   *Ibid.*; Ninth Census of the United States, 1870, Albany Ward 1, Albany, New York, NARA (Microfilm Publication M593, 1,761 Rolls).

47   Widow's Certificate No. 523.

48   Ibid.; Ninth Census of the United States, 1870, Albany Ward 1, Albany, New York, NARA (Microfilm Publication M593, 1,761 Rolls).; Tenth Census of the United States, 1880, Albany, Albany, New York, NARA (Microfilm Publication T9, 1,454 Rolls).

49   Widow's Certificate No. 523; Twelfth Census of the United States, 1900,

Albany Ward 2, Albany, New York, NARA (Microfilm Publication T623, 1,854 Rolls).

50   Widow's Certificate No. 523.

51   *Ibid.*; Fifteenth Census of the United States, 1930, Albany, Albany, New York, NARA (Microfilm Publication T626, 2,667 Rolls); Sixteenth Census of the United States, 1940, Albany, Albany, New York, NARA (Microfilm Publication T627, 4,643 Rolls).

52   Widow's Certificate No. 6033, Approved Pension File for Sarah Welsh, widow of Christy Welsh, Company E, 85th Pennsylvania Volunteer Infantry.

53   *Ibid.*

54   *Ibid.*; Eighth Census of the United States, 1860, North Union, Fayette, Pennsylvania, NARA (Microfilm Publication M653, 1,438 Rolls); Bates, *History of Pennsylvania Volunteers, 1861–5,* Volume 3, p.17.

55   Widow's Certificate No. 6033.

56   Ibid.; 'History – America's First Look into the Camera' http://www.loc.gov/teachers/classroommaterials/connections/daguerreotype/history.html (Accessed 31 January 2016).

57   Widow's Certificate No. 6033.

58   *Ibid.*

59   Widow's Certificate No. 83473, Approved Pension File for Ann Scanlan, widow of Patrick Scanlan, Company G, 63rd New York Volunteer Infantry.

60   Widow's Certificate No. 83473.

61   Widow's Certificate No. 83473; New York State Adjutant General's Office, *Registers of the Sixty-Third, Sixty-Fourth, Sixty-Fifth, Sixty-Sixth, Sixty-Seventh, and Sixty-Eighth Regiments of Infantry,* p.167.

62   Otis and Huntington, *The Medical and Surgical History of the War of the Rebellion. Part 3, Volume 2, Surgical History,* p.797; Widow's Certificate No. 83473.

63   Widow's Certificate No. 83473.

64   Widow's Certificate No. 83473; New York Irish-American Weekly 23 May 1863.

65   *New York Irish-American Weekly,* 23 May 1863; New York State Adjutant General's Office, *Registers of the Sixty-Third, Sixty-Fourth, Sixty-Fifth, Sixty-Sixth, Sixty- Seventh, and Sixty-Eighth Regiments of Infantry;* Civil War Muster Roll Abstracts of New York State Volunteers, United States Sharpshooters, and United States Colored Troops c. 1861–1900, NYSA (Microfilm, 1185 Rolls); Muffly, *The Story of Our Regiment, A History of the 148th Pennsylvania Vols,* pp.1052, 1067.

EPILOGUE

1   Widow's Certificate No. 120393, Approved Pension File for Jane Kelley, widow of Daniel Kelley, Company H, 141st New York Volunteer Infantry.

2   Delaney, 'Directions in Historiography Our Island Story? Towards a
    Transnational History of Late Modern Ireland,' p.84. There are many
    notable exceptions to this insular view of Irish historical study, but given
    the scale of the Irish diaspora, those specialising in the history of the
    transnational Irish experience remain chronically underrepresented. The
    absence of significant events in Ireland to mark the 150th anniversary of
    the American Civil War was notable. The single major state occasion was
    an Iveagh House Lecture hosted by the Department of Foreign Affairs on
    the topic of Irish involvement in the conflict. There were also a range of
    local and regionally driven initiatives, from the unveiling of an American
    Civil War commemorative statue in Ballymote, County Sligo, to a day
    of lectures on Irish involvement held as part of the Hay Festival in Kells,
    County Meath and a series of talks on Cavan and the American Civil
    War run by Cavan Library Service. The latter two events were the only
    dedicated series of talks related to the Irish involvement in the American
    Civil War held anywhere on the island between 2011 and 2015, and
    there was no comparable academic conference. A number of efforts to
    raise public awareness of the impact of the conflict on Irish people were
    proposed but did not succeed. These included seeking commemorative
    funding for an academic conference, the temporary display of the 69th New
    York flag in a publicly accessible location, and proposing the issuing of a
    commemorative stamp as part of the An Post Stamp Programme. To read
    some commentary on these efforts and thoughts behind the reasons they
    failed see www.irishamericancivilwar.com, particularly 'Has Ireland Missed
    the Last Opportunity to Remember Her American Civil War Dead', 'Selling
    "Ireland" and Forgetting the "Irish"? Some Thoughts on the Taoiseach's
    St. Patrick's Day Speech', 'Ireland Takes First Steps Towards Remembering
    Irish of the American Civil War', 'Diaspora Disregarded? How Ireland is
    Failing Her Emigrants Memory', 'The Time Has Come for "A History of
    the Irish in 100 Objects"', 'Memory, Memorials and The Gathering,' 'Irish
    Views on the American Civil War – Does Ireland Need a Memorial?' and
    'Ireland's Forgotten Famine Generation'. Full links to each of these articles
    can be found in the bibliography.

Index